JOURNAL FOR THE STUDY OF THE OLD TESTAMENT
SUPPLEMENT SERIES
108

Editors
David J.A. Clines
Philip R. Davies

THE SOCIAL WORLD OF
BIBLICAL ANTIQUITY SERIES
8

General Editor
James W. Flanagan

Almond Press
Sheffield

THE FORGING OF ISRAEL

Iron Technology, Symbolism,
and Tradition in Ancient Society

PAULA M. McNUTT

The Almond Press · 1990

The Social World of
Biblical Antiquity Series, 8

General Editor
James W. Flanagan (Missoula, MT)

Consultant Editor
David M. Gunn (Columbia Theological Seminary, Decatur, GA)

Editorial Associates
Frank S. Frick (Albion, MI), Norman K. Gottwald (New York, NY)
Howard Harrod (Nashville, TN), Bernhard Lang (Paderborn, F.R.G.)
Carol L. Meyers (Durham, NC), Eric M. Meyers (Durham, NC)
Pamela J. Milne (Windsor, Ont.), John W. Rogerson (Sheffield, U.K.)
Thomas W. Overholt (Stevens Point, WI), Robert R. Wilson (New Haven, CT)
Keith W. Whitelam (Stirling, U.K.)

Copyright © 1990 Sheffield Academic Press

Published by Almond Press
Editorial Direction: David M. Gunn
Columbia Theological Seminary
P.O. Box 520, Decatur
GA 30031, U.S.A.
Almond Press is an imprint of
Sheffield Academic Press Ltd
The University of Sheffield
343 Fulwood Road
Sheffield S10 3BP
England

Typeset by Sheffield Academic Press
and
Printed on acid-free paper in Great Britain
by Billing & Sons Ltd
Worcester

British Library Cataloguing in Publication Data

McNutt, Paula
 The forging of Israel—(The social world of biblical
 antiquity; 0265-1408, 8)—(Journal for the study of the
 Old Testament supplement; 0309-0787, 108).
 1. Palestine. Antiquities. Archaeological investigation
 I. Title   II. Series
 933

ISBN 1-85075-263-X

This book is dedicated to
the memory of my mother
Margaret Harrington McNutt
and to my father
DeWitt D. McNutt, Jr

CONTENTS

List of Tables	9
List of Maps	10
Acknowledgments	11

Chapter 1
INTRODUCTION 13
    Technology and Culture 13
    Background 19
    The Problem and Its Significance 20
    Method and Procedure 21
    Organization 36

Chapter 2
IRON TECHNOLOGY AND SYMBOLISM
IN AFRICAN CULTURES 39
    Introduction 39
    Africa: The Introduction of Iron Technology 43
    General Surveys on Iron and Symbols 44
    Survey of Traditional African Societies 46
    Analysis and Interpretation 82

Chapter 3
BACKGROUND TO THE DEVELOPMENT OF IRON
TECHNOLOGY IN THE ANCIENT NEAR EAST 97
    Introduction 97
    Bronze, the Precursor to Iron 102
    The Discovery of Iron 108
    Wrought Iron and the Early Processes
        of Smelting and Forging 112
    Sources of Iron Ore 114
    The Artifactual Information 116
    The Textual Information 129
    The Search for the Origins of Iron Technology 138

Chapter 4
THE EARLY IRON AGE   143
   Introduction   143
   The Transition from the Bronze Age to the Iron Age   145
   The Production of Steeled Iron   148
   The Adoption of Iron Technology   151
   The Artifactual Information   160
   Distributional Analysis: 'Philistine'
      vs 'Non-Philistine'   192
   Metallurgy and Symbols   206
   Implications for Reconstructing Israel's Early
      History   209

Chapter 5
BIBLICAL SYMBOLS   213
   Introduction   213
   Iron Technology   215
   The Symbolic Value of Iron   216
   The Symbolic Role of Artisan Gods in
      Ancient Near Eastern Mythology   228
   The Smith in Ancient Israel   235
   Egypt as an 'Iron Furnace'   249

Chapter 6
CONCLUSIONS   261

Bibliography   269
Index of Biblical References   291
Index of Authors   295
Index of Subjects   299

LIST OF TABLES

1. Iron Artifacts: Fifth and Fourth Millennia BCE — 118
2. Iron Artifacts: Third Millennium BCE — 119
3. Iron Artifacts: Middle Bronze Age (c. 2000–1600 BCE) — 122
4. Iron Artifacts: Late Bronze Age (c. 1600–1200 BCE) — 124
5. Iron Artifacts Predating the Iron Age — 129
6. Twelfth Century: 'Philistine' — 198
7. Twelfth Century: 'Non-Philistine' — 199
8. Eleventh Century: 'Philistine' — 200
9. Eleventh Century: 'Non-Philistine' — 201
10. Tenth Century: 'Philistine' — 202
11. Tenth Century: 'Non-Philistine' — 202
12. Average Number of Artifacts Per Site — 204
13. Total Numbers and Percentages of Iron Artifacts in 'Philistine' and 'Non-Philistine' Sites — 204
14. 'Philistine': Types of Iron Artifacts — 204
15. 'Non-Philistine': Types of Iron Artifacts — 204
16. Tool Subtypes — 204
17. Weapon Subtypes — 204
18. 'Philistine': Context of Iron Artifacts — 205
19. 'Non-Philistine': Context of Iron Artifacts — 205
20. Egypt as an 'Iron Furnace' — 252

LIST OF MAPS

1.	Africa	48
2.	Ancient Near East	117
3.	Iron Age I Palestine	159

ACKNOWLEDGMENTS

This project has been long in the making so there are many people to whom I owe thanks. My gratitude extends first and foremost to my parents—to my mother who never ceased believing in me and who died as my work on this manuscript drew to a close, and to my father who continues to stimulate my thirst for knowledge. My sisters and my brother have also been an important source of support over the years. I owe a special debt of gratitude to James W. Flanagan who first introduced me to the social world of ancient Israel and who first sparked my interest in iron technology while I was a student at the University of Montana. Conversations with Jim since my time in Montana have continued to shape my thinking and, especially, my approach to interpreting ancient texts and tells. He has been an unfailing source of both challenge and encouragement.

   The influence and support of my doctoral committee at Vanderbilt University have also contributed in significant ways to the production of this manuscript which is a revised version of the dissertation I wrote under their direction. Without their flexibility and openness to accepting the potentialities of multidisciplinary research, this study may not have been produced. Ronald Spores and Howard Harrod contributed in many ways to broadening my understanding of anthropology, archaeology, and sociology. Douglas A. Knight, Walter Harrelson, and James L. Crenshaw influenced and enriched my understanding of the ancient Israelite world and its literature and symbols. I owe special thanks to Doug Knight, my dissertation advisor, for reading the initial drafts of this manuscript so carefully and for his helpful comments and direction.

   Many others were invaluable in helping me to bring this study to fruition. Among them are my colleagues at Canisius College, especially Daniel P. Jamros, S.J., who was ever patient with assisting me in my endless struggle with the computer in the process of producing this manuscript. The participants in the Constructs of Ancient History and Religion Group, sponsored by the Society of Biblical Literature and the American Schools of Oriental Research, provided helpful comments and criticisms of my work along the way. Finally, I extend my thanks to those who were instrumental in helping to bring the manuscript through the various stages of production: to David M. Gunn of Almond Press who read the manuscript and continues to be an important source of sound advice; and to the editors and staff at Sheffield Academic Press, especially the publishers—David J. A. Clines for his careful reading of the proofs and Philip R. Davies for his assistance as the manuscript was being prepared at the press. To these persons and others not named, I am grateful.

This study was facilitated in part by research grants from Canisius College and Vanderbilt University. I am grateful to the staff of the Melville J. Herskovits Library of African Studies at Northwestern University who were so kind in helping me sort through the ethnographies and studies on ironworking in traditional African societies which informed my interpretation of ancient Israelite traditions.

Paula M. McNutt
Buffalo,
New York
February 1990

Chapter 1

INTRODUCTION

Technology and Culture

Technology and technological innovations have long been recognized as major contributors to the development of social and cultural systems and have tended to be closely related to crucial turning points in human history. For example, the development of food-producing technology during the 'Neolithic Revolution' in the ancient Near East has been called 'the most fundamental of all human technological breakthroughs' (e.g., Bernard and Pelto, 1972:317). After this technology was embraced, a chain-reaction of other technological developments followed in rapid succession—the invention of the wheel, the development of metallurgy and systems of writing, and succeeding innovations that contributed to the evolution of human culture. Accompanying these developments were increase in populations, the establishment of city-states, and eventually the founding of empires. Also interacting with technological changes in these processes were shifts in ideology and political and economic systems. New institutions were established, and customs, traditions, and ways of thinking and perceiving the world were altered.[1] During the twentieth century, the impact of new technologies on social and culture change has been so great that it has prompted a number of studies that express fear that technological advances are out of control (e.g., Ellul, 1964; Dubos, 1965; 1968; Mumford, 1967).

---

1 For a more comprehensive discussion of the interrelationship between technology and culture change see, e.g., Bernard and Pelto, 1972.

Technology also affects human symbol systems, which in turn contribute further to culture change. Since technologies are a major factor in the way people think and feel about themselves and others and about the world around them, the particular technologies used in a given culture determine in part the ways in which people relate to one another and to their social and natural environments. Essentially, technology mediates between human beings and their world. This interrelationship among human beings, technology, and environment affects the way we think and thus the way we communicate meaning. In fact, many of the dominant or key symbols in cultures throughout the world are technological symbols. In an important study on key symbols, Sherry Ortner has noted:

> In mechanized society... one root metaphor for the social process is the machine, and in recent times the computer represents a crucial modification upon this root metaphor. But the social is not the only aspect of experience which root-metaphor type symbols are used to illuminate; for example, much of greater Indo-Tibetan cosmology... is developed on analogy with the quite simple image of the wheel. (Ortner, 1973:1341)

In a recent study on the relationship of the computer to Western culture, J. David Bolter (1984:8-12) refers to technologies with cultural symbolic value as 'defining technologies'. Of defining technologies, Bolter says:

> ... the technology of any age provides an attractive window through which thinkers can view both their physical and metaphysical worlds... Very often a device will take on a metaphoric significance and be compared in art and philosophy to some part of the animate or inanimate world... a defining technology develops links, metaphorical or otherwise, with a culture's science, philosophy, or literature; it is always available to serve as a metaphor, example, model, or symbol. A defining technology resembles a magnifying glass, which collects and focuses seemingly disparate ideas in a culture into one bright, sometimes piercing ray. Technology does not call forth major cultural changes by itself, but it does bring ideas into a new focus by explaining or exemplifying them in new ways to larger audiences. (1984:10-11)

1. Introduction

That technology has had an impact on the way we order our perceptions of the world around us is evident in the symbolic labels we attach to historical periods. Designations such as 'Stone Age', 'Bronze Age', and 'Iron Age' are symbols that point beyond the technologies that were dominant during particular periods. Encapsulated in them are beliefs about the nature of social worlds, economic systems, political systems, level of social complexity, and so forth. Similar labels were applied to civilizations by ancient authors. The biblical book of Daniel outlines a scheme of historical periods using metals to designate successive periods (Dan. 2.31-45), as do other ancient authors such as Hesiod (*Works and Days* 109-201) and Ovid (*Metamorphoses* 1.89-150). Such labels are not given only to ages long past. We often characterize our own age as the 'Nuclear Age' or the 'Computer Age'. The use of technology as cultural and social metaphors occurs in cultures both ancient and modern, in cultures both simple and complex.

The symbolic value of these labels goes beyond conceptual organization and structuring of the world, however. For example, for the author of the book of Daniel and for others such as Hesiod and Ovid, each metaphor also points to particular qualitative associations. The 'Golden Age' typically represents an age of ideal happiness and prosperity, whereas the 'Iron Age,' the age in which these authors lived, represents a period of hardship, oppression, and cultural decline. Such labels arouse in people for whom they have meaning feelings, emotions, and attitudes toward the particular age in question. In contemporary American society, for example, 'Nuclear Age' conveys more than a simple meaning associated with degree of scientific and technological advancement. It also conjures up images and fears of potential catastrophe on a world-wide scale, a potential reversal from relative order to chaos. 'Computer Age' also conveys more than the meaning of advanced technology. Also implied are the ever-increasing complexity of our culture and society, a fast pace that is difficult to keep abreast of, and a rushing flow of new information—not only satisfaction with accomplishments, but anxiety associated with keeping up with a rapidly changing world.[1]

Recent studies on technology and symbolism incorporate a number of different emphases and derive from different disciplines. But the conclusions in these studies tend to support those drawn in the analysis of the symbolic representation of iron technology in ancient Israel in the following pages—that is, that technological symbols often serve as dominant cultural symbols.[2] Some analyses stress the interrelationship of technology, science, and art as general symbol-making activities (e.g., Smith, 1968; 1970; 1977). Others focus on specific technologies and/or particular historical periods. Several examples will be sufficient to indicate the substance of these studies.

James B. Harrod's study of the bow in ancient Greece (1981) uses a history of religions approach for analyzing the symbolic significance of this technology. Harrod examines the essential *techné* of the bow (i.e., its invention, structure, dynamics, and utility), summarizes its role in Greek religion, proposes a hermeneutic of the bow as expressed in mythology, and assesses the significance of this hermeneutic for ancient Greek self-understanding as a whole. He concludes that bow technology provides ontological *metaphors* (metaphors for self-understanding) and ontological *paradigms* (models for self-relating) which together comprise 'self-becoming'.[3]

Using a similar history of religions approach, Mircea Eliade (1968) examines the symbolism of the arrow as represented in a broad spectrum of ancient and contemporary 'primitive' societies. Eliade argues along similar lines that symbols associated with the arrow have an ontological or existential emphasis. For Eliade:

> Contrary to what may be called 'cosmic symbols'—stars, waters, the seasons, vegetation, etc.—which reveal both the structures of the Universe and the human mode of being in

---

[1] On the computer as a cultural symbol, see, e.g., Bolter, 1984.
[2] On cultural symbols see, e.g., Fernandez, 1965; Geertz, 1973. Geertz has argued that the entire cultural system is best understood through the analysis of symbols and their power in structuring and motivating that system.
[3] Compare Clifford Geertz's 'models of' and 'models for' (1973:93-94).

1. *Introduction*

the world, the symbolism of tools and weapons discloses specific existential situations. (1968:463)

In addition to examining the types of existential symbols evoked by the arrow, Eliade points to the ambivalence with which this technology is typically regarded (1968:465) and to the significance of the arrow as a mediating symbol, particularly as representing mediation between the divine and earthly realms (1968:468-75).

Similar studies of the impact of technology on symbol systems have been applied to more recent historical situations by scholars in the field of the history of technology. The use of technological metaphors in Early Modern European societies has recently been examined by Otto Mayr (1986). Mayr elucidates a pattern of technological metaphors applied to political systems in England and continental Europe during this period. He argues that technology, as a human activity, is an integral part of human culture that interacts with *all* other manifestations of human life and culture (1986:xv). With this principle in mind, Mayr asserts that in eighteenth-century continental Europe clocks were used as dominant metaphors in literature, science, and especially Cartesian philosophy. They functioned in these realms as metaphors for authoritarian systems of government in which, for example, monarchs were able to 'wind up' the state mechanism and keep its parts in motion. In Mayr's estimation, clock metaphors were saying several things:

> They idealized the qualities of regularity, order, and harmony.
>
> They insisted on the clock as the prototype for the world, with regard to both its creation and its normal functioning.
>
> By pleading the mechanical character of the physical world, they sought to discredit magic; they sought to advance rationality both in the selection of evidence and in the analysis of causal connections.
>
> They promoted the mechanical clock as a physical illustration of the hitherto amorphous notion of system, that is, of an integrated assembly of numerous, dynamically interacting parts.

> They advertised the advantages of authoritarian, centralist command structures, be they in the body, in society, or in the universe.
>
> They illustrated and thus reinforced the general world view of determinism. (Mayr, 1986:119)

In England, on the other hand, where the concern was more with 'self-regulating' political systems, metaphors based on technologies such as the self-regulating steam engine were used (Mayr, 1986:181-89; cf. Bolter, 1984:24-32).

As a final example, I point to a study by Leo Marx (1965; cf. 1964) in which the symbolism of the railroad in nineteenth-century America is considered. One of Marx's primary concerns is how technology affects the dominant structures of meaning and values in culture. He argues that the image of the railroad in nineteenth-century America functioned as a cultural symbol. Marx emphasizes the multiple levels of meaning encapsulated in this cultural symbol and the ambivalent attitudes that are conveyed in its various levels of meaning. As a positive cultural symbol, the railroad represented a newly acquired power of human beings over nature and the progress that was believed to accompany this acquisition. This level of meaning is represented in the image of 'the triumphant machine'. According to Marx, this was the most popular meaning of the symbol and reflected the dominant attitude that the railroad annihilates time and space and thereby opens the door to progress. A second level of meaning in this symbol Marx calls 'the ambiguous machine'. This image is one of a frightening monster that consumes natural resources and causes doubt and anxiety. It operates alongside the positive image associated with progress. The third level of meaning is identified as 'the menacing machine', which represents the potentially catastrophic impact of industrialization on society and associates the railroad with hostile and inhuman forces that alienate humans from nature and humans from humans.

The present study of the symbolic representation of iron technology in the Hebrew Bible poses questions similar to those asked in the studies on technology and symbolism reviewed briefly above. The basic question posed in the study is this:

1. *Introduction* 19

What kind of impact did the introduction of iron technology have on ancient Israelite culture, and how is this impact reflected in the use of iron technology as a cultural symbol?

Background

A number of studies over the last two decades have addressed the question of iron technology's introduction into the ancient Mediterranean world (e.g., Waldbaum, 1978; Wertime and Muhly, 1980; Stech-Wheeler et al., 1981). These studies have focused primarily on determining the dates and modes of iron's introduction and on the technological innovations that were necessary for it to overtake bronze as the preferred utilitarian metal. Some attention has also been given in these studies to the interrelationships among iron technology and the economic, political, social, and religious spheres of life in the ancient world. The impact of iron technology has also been emphasized in recent historical, archaeological, and social scientific studies of ancient Syro-Palestine (e.g., Dothan, 1982; Gottwald, 1979; Hopkins, 1985; Frick, 1985; Flanagan, 1988).

Because the development of iron technology was coincidental with or subsequent to the general social upheavals that occurred throughout the Near East toward the end of the Bronze Age, scholars have also attempted to determine how it was related to these disturbances. In Palestine, both the emergence of 'Israel' as a distinctive people and the arrival of the Philistines into the coastal regions are thought to fit into this general historical situation. Biblical scholars have often asserted that the Philistines were responsible for introducing the technology of ironworking into Palestine. However, the Philistine hypothesis and assertions that the Philistines had a 'monopoly' on iron are based on a passage in 1 Sam. 13.19 that does not even mention iron. At present, the archaeological record does not support this claim with any certainty.

The symbolic significance of the material iron has been touched upon briefly in many of the studies mentioned above. However, only two studies (Singer, 1980; Sawyer, 1983) have focused specifically on iron's symbolic representation in the texts of the Hebrew Bible. K. H. Singer's study on the symbolism of metals in the Hebrew Bible looks primarily at the efficiency of iron as a utilitarian metal. John F. A. Sawyer's study asserts that both the Hebrew term *barzel* and iron technology itself were of foreign origin. In Sawyer's estimation, *barzel* is used in the Hebrew Bible as an emotive term with unmistakeably hostile and aggressive overtones. This use of the term, he argues, derives from a combination of iron's foreign origin, the poor quality of most iron implements throughout most of the period covered by the texts of the Hebrew Bible, and the hostility and scorn with which the smith was regarded. Both studies offer insights into how iron technology was regarded by the ancient Israelites, but fail to take into account the 'multivocality' of symbols, the complexities of the interrelationship of technology with other spheres of culture, and the effect that technologies have on a people's self-understanding.

The Problem and its Significance

The impact that the introduction of iron technology had on ancient Israelite culture and society is still imperfectly understood. The textual references to iron and the technological processes of ironworking are sparse and scattered and make no direct reference to the time of their introduction, how the technological process of producing iron was understood and regarded, or how it affected the social, political, economic, and religious spheres of Israelite society. Archaeological and extra-biblical textual materials from the ancient Near East have made significant contributions to our understanding of ancient metallurgy, but a number of the questions discussed above remain unanswered or at least in the realm of uncertainty.

This study does not aim to find the elusive answers to all of these questions. It does, however, depend on the information that is available and the theories that have been proposed to answer them in order to 'set the stage' for considering the symbolic representation of ironworking in the Hebrew Bible. Toward this end I have chosen to use a multidisciplinary/ integrative approach drawing on the disciplines of biblical interpretation, archaeology, and anthropology. The primary aim of the study is to illuminate in general terms the impact that the introduction of iron technology had in ancient Palestine after its adoption into general use at the beginning of the Iron Age, a time when Israelite society was moving toward centralization. More specifically, my aim is to shed light on how the adoption of this technological innovation later affected Israel's understanding of itself as a people and how this was expressed symbolically in the sacred stories and texts preserved in the Hebrew Bible.

Transforming iron from a soft ore to a metal of superior strength is a complex and mysterious process. The technical skills required for facilitating this transformation evidently did not begin to be understood until approximately the same time that Israel is thought to have become conscious of itself as a cohesive people. One of the questions further posed in this study is whether an understanding of this complex process and the transformation it brought about in the metal iron had any significance with respect to the way Israel viewed and presented its development as a distinctive people both nationally and religiously.

The hypothesis tested herein is that iron, ironworking, and the interrelationships of the various factors contributing to the production of iron—that is, the ironsmith and the various instruments that are necessary for successful production—functioned as dominant cultural symbols in Israel for expressing its understanding of itself as a people in relation to the past, present, and future.

Method and Procedure

Integrative approaches to studying human phenomena are becoming more and more common. Attention is being given to integrating information and models from such diverse disciplines as literary studies, psychology, anthropology, archaeology, history, science, and religion. Over the last several decades, for example, the anthropological sub-discipline of ethnohistory has gained increasing respect as a way of studying historical societies and cultures. Historians can supply anthropologists with invaluable, critically tested and interpreted materials and, conversely, anthropologists can provide historians with equally valuable records based on careful and detailed observations and universal structural forms that shed further light on history (Evans-Pritchard, 1973:368). Both oral traditions and traditional history, which form a part of peoples' thoughts and thus part of their social life and culture, are also becoming accepted as legitimate data for reconstructing cultures and their histories (e.g., Vansina, 1985).

Ethnohistory has been described as a kind of documentary ethnology, a set of methods and techniques employed for 'reducing all classes of documentation to raw ethnographic data applicable to the study of human behavior with an anthropological theoretical framework' (Spores, 1973:25). For the ethnohistorian, the document, either written or oral, plays the role that the informant plays for the ethnologist. In addition to the critical interpretation of documents, the ideal for the ethnohistorian is to keep:

> an open mind with regard to utilization of all types of graphic materials, oral history, conventional ethnography, archaeological data, geographical, geological, or biological data, or any other information that will aid in cultural reconstruction, analysis, or explanation. (Spores, 1980:576; cf., e.g., Carmack, 1972:233)

A similar approach in contemporary anthropological studies is ethnoarchaeology. Ethnoarchaeology utilizes ethnographic information from contemporary societies and anthropological models for reconstructing the structure and evolution of historical societies recovered through archaeological excavations.

Anthropologists whose interests lie in interpreting the culture and symbol systems, that is, structures of meaning, in contemporary and ancient societies are also considering the benefits of observing the relationship between societies and their oral and written literature. Victor Turner, for example, has investigated the interrelationship of social structure, behavior in observable social events, and genres of cultural performance, which include both ritual and literature (1981). Turner asserts that narratives are often grounded in what he calls 'social dramas' (sociocultural processes) and that there is an interdependent and dynamic relationship between social dramas and genres of cultural performance. Anthropologists with similar interests have turned to interpreting texts using methods similar to those used in literary studies in order to recover the cultural meaning conveyed in texts. Several anthropologists have even tried their hand at interpreting cultural meaning in biblical texts (see, e.g., Lang, 1985).

Although one must recognize the problems associated with attempting interpretations that cross disciplinary boundaries and with borrowing models from other disciplines in which one is not trained (see, e.g., Geertz, 1980), numerous studies, not the least being those pursued by biblical scholars, are contributing significantly to our understanding of human cultures. In biblical studies, there are clear signs of emerging interest in moving beyond recovery of the 'everyday social realia of Israel's social world' (Knight and Tucker, 1985:xvi) to utilizing approaches that integrate the sociological or anthropological study of Israel's history with studies of biblical texts (see, e.g., Culley, 1985; Knierim, 1985; Flanagan, 1988).

The general tendency among recent biblical scholars who have appealed to anthropology, sociology, and archaeology in their historical reconstructions has been to argue for the value of hypotheses based on models and theories of socio-political structure and process (e.g., Gottwald, 1979; Frick, 1985; Flanagan, 1988). My study differs somewhat from these in its emphases on the use of anthropological theories on symbols and the interaction between symbols and culture. In this respect it has more in common with earlier studies that depended upon anthropology for interpreting ancient Israelite myth, ritual, and symbols (e.g., Smith, 1894; Hooke, 1933; 1935; 1958).

From a methodological standpoint, the social scientific approach to studying ancient Israel incorporates methods and theories from the social sciences—sociology, anthropology, and psychology—along with other critical methods traditionally used in biblical studies. Oral history, ethnography, archaeology, geography, geology, and studies of technology have also informed these social and cultural analyses.

The significance of this type of approach to interpreting ancient Israelite history lies not in providing further evidence to the biblical scholar, but rather in introducing tools for analyzing the ancient information and applying theories about the way societies are organized and develop. From comparative sociology (that is, anthropology and sociology) biblical historians have drawn valuable information on structural and processual forms in other societies that can shed light on the social organization and institutions of ancient Israel and on the religious foundations underlying the biblical texts. The social scientific approach balances the tendency to concentrate on Israel's political and religious history with attention to economic, social, technological, and other aspects of daily life. It introduces a stronger concern for the general as well as the specific, for the social world as well as isolated events and single individuals.

The social sciences also illuminate the sociological dimensions of the interpretive process. That is, they provide ways of identifying the origins, transmission, and meanings of the texts and relating these to social roles, social groups, and social structures. They offer analogies from modern and historical societies that help us interpret the oral traditions underlying the biblical texts and the functions of the literary forms in the Hebrew Bible.

Historical Background
Although the social scientific approach to interpreting the Hebrew Bible is just beginning to enter main-stream biblical scholarship, early biblical scholars also appealed to the social sciences in their interpretations of ancient Israelite society, religion, and literature (see, e.g., Hahn, 1966; Leach, 1982; Wilson, 1984). William Robertson Smith was the first systematically to apply comparative methods and theories to interpreting the Bible (see Beidelman, 1974). Robertson Smith, a late nineteenth-century British scholar, had a significant impact on early twentieth-century scholarship in such varied fields as biblical studies, anthropology, sociology, and psychology. His work contributed to broadening the scope of Hebrew Bible studies to include comparative materials and social scientific perspectives. In his most influential work, *Lectures on the Religion of the Semites* (1894), Robertson Smith defined the essential nature of 'Semitic', and thus 'Hebrew', religious behavior. He concluded that sacrifice was the central and basic rite of all religions.

1. Introduction

Although Robertson Smith has been criticized frequently both for his methods of interpretation and his conclusions, his contributions cannot be ignored. In the field of biblical scholarship, for example, one of his basic questions, 'What is the nature and role of ritual in ancient Israelite society?', continues to be of concern. But his greatest contributions to biblical studies must be traced indirectly through the fields of anthropology, sociology, and psychology. Of special importance in carrying on Robertson Smith's ideas and conveying them to succeeding generations were the works of James G. Frazer, Emil Durkheim, and Sigmund Freud. These scholars were instrumental in developing schools of thought in anthropology, classics, folklore, sociology, and psychology. Through the works of subsequent scholars in these disciplines, Robertson Smith's ideas on such topics as totemism, sacrifice, and the close relationship between religion and society have filtered down to biblical studies, the history of religions, anthropology, and sociology. The fruit of the seed planted by Robertson Smith at the end of the nineteenth century is represented in many of the contemporary anthropological theories on symbolism and ritual that I depend on in this study. Although the specific details and conclusions in his work are outdated, modern anthropologists still laud Robertson Smith's theoretical and methodological contributions (see, e.g., Douglas, 1966:10-28; Harris, 1968:207-208). Of particular import were his emphasis on studying cultural systems as wholes and analyzing religion as part of these wholes, his awareness of spatial and temporal social context, his recognition of the need to view a culture from the participant's perspective, his cultural relativism, and his treatment of the relationship between social organization and ritual and belief. Especially important is his assertion that rituals contribute to the maintenance of social solidarity. The comparative approach advocated by Robertson Smith, although greatly modified, has returned to the social sciences as a valid analytical tool and has made an important contribution to my own interpretations. And finally, combining the comparative approach with historical study has become an accepted method for the study of culture and culture change, both in biblical studies and in anthropology.

Following Robertson Smith, the next major contributions to the social scientific study of ancient Israel were made by Max Weber in *Ancient Judaism* (originally published in 1917-19; English translation, 1952). Weber was the first to apply comprehensively to the study of ancient Israel the methods and approaches of sociological analysis. His aim was to identify the relationship between social organization and religion in ancient Israel, particularly the connection between religion and economics.[1]

Although not a biblical specialist himself, by drawing on the works of biblical scholars Weber was able to present an impressive analysis of the texts in the Hebrew Bible, while simultaneously applying sociological methods of inquiry. In addition to his evaluation of the relationship between religion and society, Weber's contributions include his analyses of Israel's cult, the covenant, early Israel's 'charismatic' type of leadership, the social role of the Levites, Israel's diverse socioeconomic groups, and the nature and role of prophecy as related to conflict between religious ideals and socioeconomic organization. Weber perceived relationships in the Israelite social world not previously recognized, and his work stimulated new insights into the changing economic and social conditions underlying the literary sources that had been identified by earlier scholars. Finally, he stimulated new ways of looking at the role of Israelite religion in maintaining economic stability and in transforming Israel's economic ideals during times of crisis. My direct dependence on the insights of Weber is clear in my discussion of the social location of metalsmiths in ancient Israelite society in Chapter 5.

Following these early attempts to reconstruct the social world of ancient Israel by appealing to the social sciences, there was a hiatus during which biblical scholars turned away from depending on social scientific approaches for reconstructing the sociopolitical and economic spheres of Israelite society, although there was continuing interest in the types of

---

[1] Weber's interest in the relationship between religion and economics was in part stimulated by his disagreement with Karl Marx's assertions that religion in society is subordinate to economic factors.

questions posed by social scientists. For example, studies by Johannes Pedersen (a 1926-40 psychological study of ancient Israel) and Roland de Vaux (a 1961 study of Israel's social institutions) emphasized the importance of ancient Israel's social institutions. Hermann Gunkel's interest at the turn of the twentieth century in identifying the *Sitz im Leben* of literary genres was continued by other scholars throughout this period (see, e.g., Hahn, 1966:119-56) and is still an important aspect of form-critical studies today (see, e.g., Knierim, 1985). However, after Gunkel there was increasing emphasis on identifying the social settings of the language used in biblical texts, with little attention given to the social roles that these genres played in Israelite life as a whole. Other examples of important early studies that emphasized social organization are those by Adolphe Lods and Antonin Causse (see Hahn, 1966:166-70). The works of Albrecht Alt, Martin Noth, and W. F. Albright also attest to a continued interest in trying to reconstruct the social organization of ancient Israel.

The move away from a direct dependence upon anthropology and sociology as potential contributors to reconstructing ancient Israelite history and society was a consequence of a number of interacting factors. Among these were an increasing dependence on archaeological material, a move toward greater concern with theological questions, and a recognition that the works of the early advocates of social scientific approaches shared the weaknesses of the contemporary sociological and anthropological research upon which they depended. Furthermore, in the mid-twentieth century anthropology turned its attention to synchronic and culture-specific studies (see, e.g., Harris, 1968). This movement was stimulated by the structural–functional interests of British anthropologists and the cultural relativism and historical particularism of American anthropologists. Each stressed detailed synchronic ethnographic studies. This was a move away from the traditional concerns of biblical scholars with the historical and diachronic dimensions of ancient Israel and did not allow for the comparative approach that had contributed so much to earlier reconstructions of ancient Israel's social world.

However, an interest in social scientific theories was kept alive by some biblical scholars concerned with reconstructing the religion of Israel. In the social sciences, particularly anthropology, theories of evolution had lost their appeal, and concern for the diachronic dimensions of culture and culture change had receded into the background. But some anthropologists continued to deal with questions of culture change by applying theories of diffusion. Out of this theoretical orientation developed the controversial British Myth and Ritual School that was influenced particularly by the notion of 'patterns' of culture proposed by anthropologist A. M. Hocart. S. H. Hooke, who had some training in anthropology himself, was the founder of the school and the editor of a series of volumes concerned primarily with identifying the connections among the systems of ritual and myth in the ancient Near East, especially as these related to the Hebrew Bible (1933; 1935; 1958). Applying Hocart's assertion that social institutions tended to conform to a limited number of 'ideal types' with fixed sets of component parts, Hooke proposed a common ritual 'pattern' for the ancient Near East. And in agreement with diffusionist theory, Hooke and others in the Myth and Ritual School asserted that culture change is the product of cultural contact rather than evolution and, thus, that the proposed ritual pattern had diffused throughout the Near East from one cultural center.

Although criticisms of the Myth and Ritual School have been numerous and harsh, it did make a number of lasting contributions to biblical scholarship. The School made a forceful critique of simplistic evolutionary schemes, emphasized the significant contributions of the comparative approach to studying culture, promoted awareness of the role of the king in the Israelite cult, and stimulated collaboration among scholars from different fields. The conclusions of the Myth and Ritual School remain controversial, but many of the insights of Hooke and others presage some of the more recent theories on myth and ritual proposed by anthropologists. The 'pattern' proposed by Hooke, for example, is quite similar in structure to the processual structure of rituals identified by Victor Turner and others (see Chapter 2), although they are explained in radically different ways. My

1. *Introduction* 29

dependence in the following chapters on the processual structure of rituals as a model for interpreting texts is somewhat similar to the concerns of the Myth and Ritual School.

Other studies from this period and later treated the subjects of social, political, and religious offices, practices, and institutions, but little attention was given to reconstructing their cultural contexts. In recent decades there has been renewed interest in applying social scientific approaches and theories to reconstructing the society and culture of ancient Israel. Biblical scholars have recognized the importance of relating the literature of the Hebrew Bible to its sociological contexts. Furthermore, there is a growing awareness that this literature was shaped by social, religious, and ideological factors that were influenced by social as well as historical phenomena. The availability of a wider range of social scientific data and approaches combined with methodological rigor has generated new theories with the potential of opening up new perspectives on biblical material. Especially significant is the emphasis on the importance of diachronic and processual studies for understanding culture and society, an orientation that is necessary both for understanding the nature of the biblical literature and the sociocultural contexts that underlie it.

In biblical scholarship, there have arisen more methodologically responsible studies of the origins of Israel and of the institutions of the Israelite monarchy. These appeal to sociological and anthropological models of nomadism, tribalism, and state formation. Advances in archaeological theory have contributed to these developments by giving more attention to the use of ethnographic analogies (ethnoarchaeology) and to such factors as settlement patterns and means of subsistence. Each of these contributes to the goal of attaining a more nearly complete picture of ancient Israelite society.

Much of this recent work focuses attention on reconstructing the social world of the enigmatic tribal period. Both the controversy over the mode of settlement of the Israelite tribes (conquest vs. peaceful infiltration) and the growing recognition that Martin Noth's amphictyonic hypothesis inadequately explained the organization of the tribes have contributed to a growing interest in appealing to social scientific models for possible insights.

The most comprehensive reconstruction of the tribal period that is grounded in the social scientific approach is Norman Gottwald's monumental and controversial *The Tribes of Yahweh* (1979). In this work Gottwald expands on George Mendenhall's earlier proposal of a peasant rebellion against the oppressive Canaanite city-state system (1973) and further postulates an intentional 'retribalization' that established a tribal organization made up of diverse social groups sharing a common egalitarian ideal and worshipping a common liberating God. Gottwald also examines the social processes that shaped Israel during the tribal period, and by appealing to sociological and anthropological studies analyzes the social world and religion of tribal Israel in the context of politics and economics. His primary goal is to delineate and conceptualize early Israel as a total social system.

Gottwald begins by assembling what he considers to be the most reliable information about Israel's rise as determined by traditional methods of biblical interpretation and by examining previously proposed hypotheses on the social characteristics of early Israel (e.g., pastoral nomadism, tribal confederacy, and peasant revolt). He then applies models from anthropology and sociology. He makes use of a structural–functional (synchronic) model to examine the relationship among the various elements in Israel's social organization and a historical cultural–materialistic (diachronic) model to explain the changes that accompanied Israel's emergence (1979:xxii-xxiii). For the latter model, Gottwald relies heavily on the stream of scholarship associated most closely with Karl Marx. According to this theoretical perspective, the forces underlying historical change are economic and social rather than ideological (as had been asserted by Mendenhall). Environmental and technological aspects of society such as metallurgy, agricultural methods, and water systems are also examined in the context of this model because they pertain to the materialistic perspective.

Among Gottwald's major conclusions are: 1. early Israel was a heterogeneous formation of marginal and oppressed Canaanite peoples that included 'feudalized' peasants, mercenaries and adventurers, transhumant pastoralists, tribally organized farmers and pastoral nomads, and possibly itinerant artisans and disaffected priests—social groups that were identified in the fourteenth-century BCE Amarna letters; 2. Israel emerged in a fundamental breach in Canaanite society brought on by a common opposition to Canaanite imperialism, not as the result of an invasion or immigration from outside; 3. early Israel's social structure was a deliberate and conscious 'retribalization' process; and 4. the Yahwistic religion was a crucial societal instrument for supporting political and economic equality at the individual and tribal levels (1979:xxiii).

Social scientific methods and theories have also been applied to interpreting the social world of the Israelite monarchy. In a 1981 article on the development of the monarchy, James W. Flanagan used anthropological theories on state formation to reconstruct the transitional period in Israel's history during which tribal organization began to move toward state organization and the establishment of kingship. Flanagan examined the transition in light of cultural evolution and social anthropological descriptions of the processes involved in succession to high office. He proposed an intermediate stage of chiefdom for the reigns of Saul and David as one stage through which Israel's sociopolitical organization passed as kingship emerged. As chiefs, Saul and David provided leadership for familistic, but non-egalitarian, social groups. Flanagan identified the principal prime movers that may have affected Israel's social organization during this transitional period and outlined the origins of hereditary inequality that eventually led to monarchy. In this study, Flanagan considered kinship and the political, religious, and economic factors that contributed to the rise of the monarchy.

Frank Frick also argues for a transitional stage of chiefdom in the evolution of the Israelite monarchy (1985). Frick uses an ethnoarchaeological approach. Based on his assessment of archaeological remains combined with what is known about the material culture of chiefdoms from ethnographic studies, Frick argues for an earlier date for the introduction of chieftaincy in ancient Israel. Of primary import in the studies of both Flanagan and Frick is the recognition that factors internal to the social world of ancient Israel may have played an equal, if not more significant, role in the adoption of a state form of sociopolitical organization as such external forces as the Philistine threat emphasized in the biblical narratives.

In a more recent study Flanagan (1988) builds upon his earlier proposal on the processes of state formation in Iron Age I Israel. Here, Flanagan extends his 1981 study on chieftaincy by including an analysis of the archaeological information and illuminating archaeological and literary images with comparative sociological studies based largely on Middle Eastern ethnographies.

Three new dimensions to the sociological approach to studying ancient Israel are presented in this study. First, Flanagan makes use of a common anthropological distinction between human actions and notions, domains that are usually only partially congruent. He suggests that the literary and archaeological information from the ancient world cannot be expected to agree entirely. Rather, texts and literature, which he treats as representing the domain of ancient notions, contain information from which we can infer images that differ from the images derived from archaeological information.

For analytical purposes, Flanagan assigns primary responsibility for interpreting the domain of notions to literary studies and responsibility for interpreting ancient actions to archaeology. By allowing disparate images to emerge *before* attempting to integrate and interpret them as ancient peoples might have done, Flanagan moves the focus from the images—whether similar or dissimilar—to the *relationship* between them. It is the relationship between the ancient domain of notions and actions that bears and communicates the primary *meanings* of the social world of biblical antiquity.

Secondly, and still within the analytical stage of investigation, Flanagan turns to the technology of holography and the images seen in holograms in order to explain how social world studies illumine the meanings of the past. Holography is used as a model for integrating the disciplines and images he treats separately in the first step within his analytical model. He also views the hologram as a metaphor for history itself and concludes that history *is* a hologram, that is, history consists of the meaning that we discover on the basis of information in ancient sources that is illuminated by modern hypotheses

1. Introduction

based on comparative sociology. The past, therefore, is reconstituted in the present.

I need not describe the technology of holography or holograms here, nor spell out the complexities of Flanagan's model. For my purposes, it is sufficient to note that holograms must be illuminated in order for the image to become visible. When illuminated, the visual information encoded on the holographic plate (which is only partial) and the relationship between the two sources of information (i.e., the relationship between two light sources) are clarified. The result is the reconstitution of a three-dimensional image of the object holographed. Flanagan uses this technology as a metaphor for identifying the relationship between the separate ancient sources of information once they are illumined.[1] Modern historians see images that were visible to ancient peoples but are now lost 'behind' the sources. Interpreters seek to understand the complexities of ancient societies and the meanings that were significant. In order to reclaim those meanings, the relationship between ancient notions and actions must be illuminated.

For Flanagan, the illuminating 'beam' in social world studies comes from comparative sociology. Using ethnographies of peoples who exhibit the same patterns of congruence and incongruence in their actions and notions, he explains the disparities and reconstitutes a clearer image of Iron Age I Palestine. For example, he detects a much more complex pattern of social movement during the period than was identified in earlier hypotheses and demonstrates the relative impact of differing economic and religious motivations at work at the time.

Thirdly, after establishing his analytical model, Flanagan turns his attention to a systemic model, that is, toward explaining the social processes that characterized Iron Age I. For this model, he draws upon ritual studies, primarily those of Victor Turner on rites of passage and social dramas and Roy Rappaport on systemic ecology.

---

[1] Flanagan's use of holography as a metaphor for sorting out and identifying relationships is similar to the ways in which societies construct and use metaphors based on technologies.

Here, again, Flanagan finds the processes operating in Iron Age I Palestine to have been more complex than those identified in previous interpretations. Whereas most explanations emphasize the demise of Canaanite cultures and the emergence of Israelite society as more or less sequential processes, Flanagan proposes that the processes of sociopolitical and religious devolution and evolution were simultaneous, continuous, and characteristic of a single, open society that was struggling to maintain its equilibrium in the face of enormous economic and political change. In his estimation, rituals functioned in these processes to regulate and mediate the metamorphoses by adjusting egalitarian religious values in relation to decreased economic resources during the turbulent Late Bronze to Iron Age I transition. Flanagan argues that the type of figure the biblical David represents would have been acceptable to most of the social groups of the time—if stripped of the Yahwist roles imposed by the biblical writers. The Late Bronze Age cultures sought to limit the decline of their influence by halting the devolution from monarchical statehood at the level of chieftaincy. Iron Age I cultures, on the other hand, found the limited centralization of chieftaincy to be compatible with their level of social development and their religious values. Flanagan hints that the real social role of the literary figure of David (or of the historical individual if such a person existed) is most at home within the Philistine traditions. He finds that the role of the Philistines as mediators and traders between pastoral and agrarian peoples and between nomadic and sedentary groups corresponds positively to ethnographic information on the Middle East. The biblical David figure, therefore, may have emerged from those traditions.

This review of recent social scientific research is by no means comprehensive. The studies cited above are those that in some essential way have influenced my own thinking and have contributed to my own orientation and approach to interpreting ancient Israelite literature and history. I depend on a number of them as background information for this study and have learned something from each of them about how to integrate archaeological and literary information and how to apply in a responsible way comparative information from contemporary ethnographic studies. I do not always agree with the methods and conclusions of these individuals, but I acknowledge the significant contributions they have made to promoting the social scientific study of the Hebrew Bible as a legitimate and acceptable approach to interpreting ancient Israelite society.

My own study also departs in some significant ways from the major emphases and trends in this still-developing field. My concern is not with proposing hypotheses about the nature of Israelite social structure or the processual development of Israelite society as a whole, but with analyzing a single aspect of Israelite culture, that is, technology. I also diverge from some of these studies in my emphasis on identifying the systems of *meaning* associated with technology and technological innovations rather than the impact of technology on the material environment of ancient Israelite society. The field of symbolic anthropology is a rich one that has yet to make major inroads in biblical studies. It is a perspective that is being taken more and more seriously by anthropologists who recognize that there has been an overemphasis on the material side of culture and not enough on the ways in which people think about their worlds and construct systems of meaning that are expressed through symbols (see, e.g., Geertz, 1973; Turner, 1977). Also important is the growing awareness that systems of meaning are not mere appendages to the material culture of human beings, but can also influence social and cultural change. Anthropology in recent years has been concerned not only with the behavior of human populations, but also with their models for perceiving and interpreting their material environment and generating behavior. What is emphasized in this interpretive orientation is attention to the interrelationship between modes of thought and modes of action. If anything I hope that this study of the symbolic representation of ironworking in the Hebrew Bible will encourage others to delve into this fascinating world of symbols.

Research Model

Because the project is multidisciplinary in scope, methodological issues are particularly important. Models and theories developed by anthropologists, archaeologists, and biblical scholars who have used a social scientific approach to interpreting the history and literature of ancient Israel are integrated in defining, sorting, and interpreting the various categories of information considered and then in integrating the conclusions drawn from each of these. The model proposed by Flanagan in his 1988 study (cf. 1985) has had the greatest influence on the approach I have taken in separating, analyzing, and relating categories of information. The archaeological and textual information from ancient Israel, the domains of actions and notions respectively, are treated as 'informants' of ancient Israelite society that can supply us with 'ethnographic' data. The comparative ethnographic material from contemporary African societies and anthropological theories on symbols serve as heuristic devices for illuminating the relationship between the archaeological and literary categories of information and for proposing hypotheses about systems of meaning. In considering the narratives from the Hebrew Bible, traditional interpretations are supplemented by and tested against proposals made by anthropologists about the ways texts convey meaning. Examples are Edmund Leach's application of the processual structure of rites of passage to interpreting the structure of texts and Victor Turner's application of 'social drama' and liminality as heuristic aids for understanding texts.

Organization

An overview and analysis of the relationship between iron technology and other spheres of culture in traditional African societies and the use of this technology to express cultural meaning through symbols (Chapter 2) precede my analysis of the information from the ancient Near East. African traditions are considered because of the availability of ethnographic information and analyses of the relationship among iron technology and other spheres of culture for that region. The analysis of this material provided a wealth of insights that made it possible for me even to consider analyzing the biblical symbols drawn from iron technology. Attention is also given in this chapter to reviewing anthropological theories on symbolism and how symbols function in society and culture. Particu-

1. *Introduction*

lar attention is given to theories that serve as heuristic devices for understanding how metaphors derived from technological processes in general and ironworking in particular contribute to a society's self-understanding.

Chapter 3 consists of a review and summary of the evidence and theories relating to the rise of iron technology in the ancient Near East from its earliest appearance in texts and archaeological contexts down to the beginning of the Iron Age (c. 1200 BCE). The material presented in this chapter establishes a background from which to view the evidence for the adoption of iron technology in Iron Age I Palestine.

In Chapter 4 the archaeological evidence related to the innovation and adoption of iron technology in Iron Age I Palestine is reviewed and considered in historical and sociological context. Artifact types, chronological and spatial distribution of artifacts, and the archaeological context of artifacts are included in the review and analysis. Questions are raised about what the archaeological information infers about the symbolism of iron during this transitional period and how the adoption of iron technology related to the evolution of the Israelite state.

The biblical information on the symbolic representation of iron is reviewed and interpreted in Chapter 5. These symbols are considered in relation to the archaeological information on the development of iron technology and the technological process of ironworking. The symbols are interpreted in light of the theories presented and the conclusions drawn in Chapter 2. Attention is given to how these symbols function in the context of Israelite culture and society, particularly how they are related to Israelite religious understandings. Where relevant, the literary structure of biblical narrative is also analyzed in order to interpret the meaning behind the symbols.

The concluding chapter gives particular attention to identifying the relationship between the archaeological and the literary information, and what this suggests about the interrelationship between the domains of actions and notions in ancient Israelite society. Also considered are shifts in the meanings conveyed by symbols associated with iron technology over time in relation to the development and adoption of the new technology and in the context of changing historical and social circumstances. The result is a picture of how iron technology as a 'defining technology' functioned in Israelite society as a dominant or key symbol, as a root metaphor, for expressing reaffirmation or reinterpretation of shared values and principles in relation to understandings about the people's past, present, and future.

Chapter 2

IRON TECHNOLOGY AND SYMBOLISM IN AFRICAN CULTURES

Introduction

I have argued in Chapter 1 that ethnographic information is useful as a heuristic device for interpreting the social world underlying the texts of the Hebrew Bible. In particular, I propose appealing to ethnographic examples as a means of illuminating the relationship between the ancient Israelite domains of *actions* (represented primarily in archaeological information) and *notions* (represented primarily in the literature of the Hebrew Bible) (see Chapter 1; Flanagan, 1985:302-304; 1988:88-103). The specific relationship this study is concerned with identifying is that between the introduction and development of iron technology and the impact of this new technology on the culture and religion of ancient Israel as expressed through symbols. Of central import is getting at the *meanings* underlying these biblical symbols.

Information from studies on iron technology in African societies serves as my point of departure for proposing hypotheses concerning the social world of ancient Israel. It is important to emphasize, again, that utilizing ethnographic information is meant only to raise questions and as a heuristic aid, not as 'evidence' for the situation in ancient Israel (see Flanagan, 1985:298-99; 1988).

Africa has been selected as the most useful source of information for several reasons. First, a great deal of information on iron technology in African societies has been recorded and evaluated by ethnographers. The sources include not only information on the technological processes involved in iron production, but also on the popular beliefs and perceptions about these processes that are expressed in social and religious beliefs and practices. The role of the primal smith or iron god in mythology and tradition, the social roles and statuses of ironsmiths, and the symbols associated with the ironsmith, the tools of the trade, the smithy, and the end product—iron—are examples. Secondly, in traditional African societies, iron technology is a defining technology that is crucial to social and economic well-being. The iron tools and weapons provided by the ironsmith are essential for agricultural production, for warfare, and, in some societies, for hunting. Finally, several recent studies (e.g., Coy, 1982; Margarido and Wasserman, 1972; Quirin, 1977) have explored the relationship between what we have defined as the domains of actions and notions.

Three major African culture areas have been selected for examination in order to provide a broad spectrum for analysis: 1. sub-Saharan West Africa; 2. East Africa; and 3. the African Horn. Within and among these culture areas are represented a variety of ecological zones, subsistence strategies, economic systems, and sociopolitical and religious organizations and institutions. Providing a broad spectrum of the beliefs and practices associated with iron technology is essential to the analysis of the symbols in the Hebrew Bible and the hypotheses proposed in Chapter 5. Although the manifestations of the social and religious beliefs and practices surrounding the ironsmith and the various elements of his work are unique in each society, they nevertheless communicate strikingly similar symbolic messages.

The information presented in this chapter is gathered from twentieth-century ethnographies and studies that span a time period from as early as the turn of the century down to the present. During these nine decades the character of African culture in many areas has changed dramatically. Some African peoples, for example, have held on tenaciously to their traditional beliefs and ways of life, while others have more readily accepted and incorporated elements of European culture. Technology in particular has been affected by the African encounter with European culture. Traditional technologies such as ironworking have been swept up in the tides of change. The smelting of iron, for example, has been abandoned in many societies because of the ready availability of scrap iron. Such changes pose a problem for interpreting the nature of ironworking in traditional societies, because many of the old practices are being abandoned. However, even in those societies that have experienced rapid technological change, traditional beliefs often endure. The reformulation of myth and religious beliefs and the modification of social sentiments are slow processes when compared to changes in technology and sociopolitical relations, because traditional myths and codes preserve patterns and social relations that are considered to be of intrinsic and overriding value, and are believed to be indispensable to the preservation of social cohesion and solidarity.

While recognizing the difficulties associated with separating old traditions from the effects of new technological innovations, my review of ironworking in African societies focuses primarily on how ironworking is perceived in *traditional* African culture. I use the 'ethnographic present' with an awareness that many of the traditions I discuss either have been abandoned altogether or are falling into disuse. In some cases I cite situations in which symbols associated with iron technology have been appropriated and reinterpreted to deal with culture change.

It is not my intention to make direct comparisons between contemporary African ironworking and ironworking in ancient Israel. Nor is it my intention to draw definitive conclusions about the symbol system of ancient Israel based on information from Africa. Temporal and spatial distance militates against making such assertions. Some interpreters have argued that the diffusion of Near Eastern culture was responsible for the development of West African civilizations (e.g., Lucas, 1948). Similar arguments have been proposed for the diffusion of iron technology (see, e.g., Trigger, 1969). Such claims may be valid for the African Horn and parts of East Africa, but they cannot be substantiated for West Africa. However, diffusionist arguments do not enter into the present evaluation, nor do they ultimately affect the conclusions I draw. The symbol system of any society, whether ancient or modern, must be interpreted in the overall context of that society's particular situation.

None of the African societies considered here is directly comparable to that of ancient Israel. Many of them are agricultural, some are pastoral, and some have mixed subsistence strategies dependent on both. Ecological zones range from the fertile zones of the West African savanna, forest, and wet forest regions and the Ethiopian highlands, to the more arid zones of Somali and East Africa. Sociopolitical organization ranges from the highly developed states of many West African peoples to the 'tribal' organization of such East African peoples as the Masai. Considering such a wide range of situations is particularly useful for a study of the beliefs associated with iron technology because the similarities in the essence of these beliefs are so striking. These essential similarities provide a foundation for assessing the nature of iron technology in ancient Israel, how this important technology was perceived by ancient Israelite peoples, and how these perceptions were translated into the many rich symbols present in Israel's sacred literature.

Organization

The ethnographic material in this chapter is presented under two major headings, divided according to major culture areas: 1. West Africa; and 2. East Africa and the African Horn. Within each section I discuss the roles of iron technology and ironsmiths in myth and ritual, the social roles and statuses of ironsmiths, and the symbolic significance of the ironworking process itself.

Despite the imbalance in the quantity of information available for each society in the representative sample considered here, enough information is available to assess the symbolic value of the ironworking process and to propose a common denominator underlying the varied symbolic expressions. The final section in this chapter defines this common denominator. The analysis of the ethnographic information is based on the nature of the ironworking process and anthropological theories on symbols. It is suggested that central to the symbolic expressions in all of these societies are the concepts of *transformation* and *mediation* (in addition to the traditional associations of strength, power, superiority, and so on).

Africa: The Introduction of Iron Technology

With the exception of countries of the Mediterranean basin, Nile Valley, and Red Sea Coast (e.g., Egypt and Nubia; see Chapter 3), a Bronze Age did not precede the Iron Age in Africa. Iron was the first metal produced (van der Merwe, 1980:463). The origins of this important technology are obscure, and the debate over whether it was the product of diffusion from the Near East or was an indigenous development remains unresolved. It has been theorized that a number of Sub-Saharan West Africa's cultural traits—for example, ironworking, brick architecture, and divine kingship—diffused across the Sudan grasslands from Meroe in Nubia. Although this theory has gained fairly wide acceptance, there is no solid archaeological evidence to substantiate it (see Trigger, 1969; Guggenheim, 1961; van der Merwe, 1980:474). Iron smelting appears to have been practiced there by c. 500 BCE, about the same time as Meroe, but there is no indication that the source of origins was the same. A stronger argument can be made for the diffusion of iron technology from Meroe into East Africa since the swamp region of the southern Sudan poses less of a barrier to population movements.

In Ethiopia, iron technology was present as early as the tenth to ninth centuries BCE and may have been influenced by technologies developed in the Near East. From c. 1000 BCE on, Semitic speaking peoples from southern Arabia were settling in northern Ethiopia, and close cultural contact was maintained between the two areas. The presence of locally manufactured iron at Hajar Bin Humeid in southern Arabia from the tenth to ninth centuries implies that iron was known in Ethiopia at the same time. Coupled with this is the fact that the word for iron in the Kushitic languages spoken by many Ethiopians is a Semitic one (van der Merwe, 1980:475).

Whatever its origins in each of these regions, the wide variety of approaches, furnace designs, and smelting products suggests that new inventions were added locally. Every conceivable method of iron production appears to have been employed in Africa, and a number of procedures do not fit the traditional categories of direct or indirect processes of production. In fact, the laborious procedures of carburization, quenching, and tempering (see Chapters 3 and 4) are rarely applied in any systematic way in Africa (van der Merwe, 1980:485-86).

General Surveys on Iron and Symbols

The sacred role of the ironsmith and that of the metal that is the source of his[1] livelihood, and the esteem rendered both, are evidenced from antiquity down through the Middle Ages (see, e.g., Fleming, 1986) and continue to exist in many contemporary societies. Much of the historical and ethnographic material relating to ironworking has been reviewed in the works of such historians and historians of religion as R. J. Forbes in a series of studies on ancient technology (1971; 1972) and Mircea Eliade in a study of alchemy (1978).[2] One can also find such information gathered in encyclopedias of religion and popular studies (e.g., Newall, 1970; Robins, 1953). From this literature it is possible to glean bits of information about myths in which the metalsmith plays a prominent role, the symbolic qualities of the metal iron, the social roles and statuses of smiths in various societies, the rituals associated with the ironworking process, and the power ascribed to the smith's tools and the smithy.

In mythology, the smith is most often portrayed as a crucial actor in mythic dramas about heavenly battles or as a civilizing or culture hero (see, e.g., Eliade, 1978:87-108; Newall, 1970:2616). For example, in Egyptian mythology the god Ptah, in the role of smith, assisted Horus in defeating Seth by forging Horus' arms. In a similar myth from India, Indra was able to overcome the demon Vritra by using weapons manufactured by the smith Tvashtri. In Canaanite mythology, the artisan god Kothar was responsible for supplying Baal with the weapons necessary to defeat Yam, the cosmic representative of chaos. Hephaestus in Greek mythology made the thun-

---

1 The masculine pronoun is used throughout this chapter to designate the smith. I use it intentionally because I have come across no references to women as smiths in these traditional societies.
2 On the philosophical and religious underpinnings of alchemy, see also Burckhardt, 1971.

2. Iron Technology and Symbolism

derbolt with which Zeus overcame Typhon. With a hammer forged by the dwarfs Thor vanquished the serpent.

The general studies cited above note the consistency with which the smith and his products are perceived in both ancient and contemporary cultures. In many societies the ironsmith holds a position of prestige. Although there are societies in which he is despised rather than honored, he seems always to be held in awe. According to the general interpretation, the pattern seems to be that among pastoral peoples he is perceived as a dangerous sorcerer, and thus is spurned or feared, but among agriculturalists is honored, often holding the position of counselor, and sometimes chief or priest. Among the latter, he is often looked upon as a wise and clever man who is an important go-between and trader, a man whose curse is taken seriously, a prophet, or a person with healing powers. In many societies he also serves as an important person in initiation rites, secret societies, and the religious life of the community in general (Forbes, 1971:71, 74-75; Eliade, 1978:98).

Also noted in these general studies is the smith's position within the organization and structure of society. Smiths tend to form groups apart that are in some way isolated from the rest of the community. This separation may be radical, especially in societies in which the smith is held in low esteem, or it may take the form of endogamous families, as seems to be typical of societies in which he is honored. The smith's trade is one that is generally passed on through heredity, handed down from generation to generation and recorded in long genealogies. Because the proficiency of the trade is acquired through generations of practice and discipline, smiths are normally (among agriculturalists) organized in guilds that jealously guard their secrets and adhere to a rigid system of ethics (Forbes, 1971:73, 83; Eliade, 1978:101-102).

The work of the smith is generally bounded by traditional rites and ceremonies. Among miners, rites of purification, fasting, meditation, prayers, sacrifices, and other acts of worship are normally strictly observed. Practically every operation of the smelting and forging processes (e.g., lighting the kiln, starting the fire, or beginning a new piece of work) must also be accompanied by specific rites. The work of the ironsmith must be undertaken in a state of ritual purity. Sexual taboos are typical, and in some societies women are forbidden to enter the smithy. The fire is especially important and must be kept burning and purified by regular offerings because in the fire resides the power that assists the smith in transforming stones into metal (Forbes, 1971:73-74; Eliade, 1978:53-70).

The material that is transformed in the smelting process and the tools of the trade also take on mysterious and powerful qualities among many peoples. Ambivalent feelings toward iron are common, and many taboos are observed in its manufacture and use. In folklore, iron objects are traditionally protective against witchcraft, evil spirits, and malign influences. The power of the metal is often ascribed to its connection with the earth, that is, it is believed to be a piece of earth that has been purified by fire.

Finally, there is the power ascribed to the smith's tools (particularly the hammer, anvil, and furnace) and the smithy. The smith's tools are often endowed with sexuality and assigned roles as such in the creation of iron. The furnace, for example, serves as a symbolic uterus where the ore completes the period of gestation. Often tools are credited with divine attributes, and great care is taken when handing them on during an initiation into the smithing trade. The smithy is often viewed as a ritual center or temple where the smith is priest and the furnace an altar upon which the rites are enacted (Eliade, 1978:34-52, 57).

Survey of Traditional African Societies

The general surveys cite most of these characteristics as typical in traditional African societies. The ambivalent attitude is present and tends to be somewhat regionalized. A despised smith caste and absence of smelting ritual are said to characterize the pastoral and hunting societies of the northern and eastern grasslands. Trade guilds, sorcery, association with secret societies, and a smithy that serves as a gathering place or temple are viewed as typical of smiths in West Africa where agriculture is practiced and arts and crafts are well developed. Ironsmiths in these societies are often 'priests' and are regarded as separate from the rest of the community. This

2. Iron Technology and Symbolism

separate status is manifest in the tendency for their families to be endogamous, marrying only within their own ranks. In the Congo there is often a close association of smiths with chiefs and hunters, complex rituals in which 'medicines' and spirits play major roles in the smelting and forging processes, and organization in guilds. Secrecy, the belief that sexual activity can in some way compromise the work, personification of hammer and anvil, and inheritance of the profession are general throughout Africa. In some parts of Africa smiths rate as 'shamans' or religious leaders (Cline, 1937:114, 140; Forbes, 1971:54-55; Parrinder, 1961:75, 180).

The general surveys are informative and provide a broad, although superficial, spectrum of the beliefs surrounding the processes of ironworking in Africa. However, they do not allow for the culture-specific variation that occurs within the major African culture regions. To identify this variation, it is necessary to look at some specific cultures.

West Africa
West African cultures are typically agrarian societies that have flourished for thousands of years and have developed great empires and highly complex cultures, often with centralized kingship and strong secret societies. These cultures extend from the savannas of northern West Africa into the forested area of the south where kingdoms were established in ancient times in such areas as Benin and Ile-Ife in Nigeria (Zuesse, 1979:152).

Smithing in many African cultures is a sacred process shaped by cosmological beliefs (Zuesse, 1979:96). This is reflected in a number of West African myths in which the first smith was the demiurge or agent of the creator god, the trickster, or the first culture-bringer. The role of the smith as civilizing or culture hero has been noted above. In this role the smith as god or as a semi-divine figure assists in the completion of creation, in organizing the world, and in educating humans.

The Dogon. The Dogon of the Volta area of West Africa have a particularly well-developed mythology that explicates such problems as their place in the natural world, the nature of the

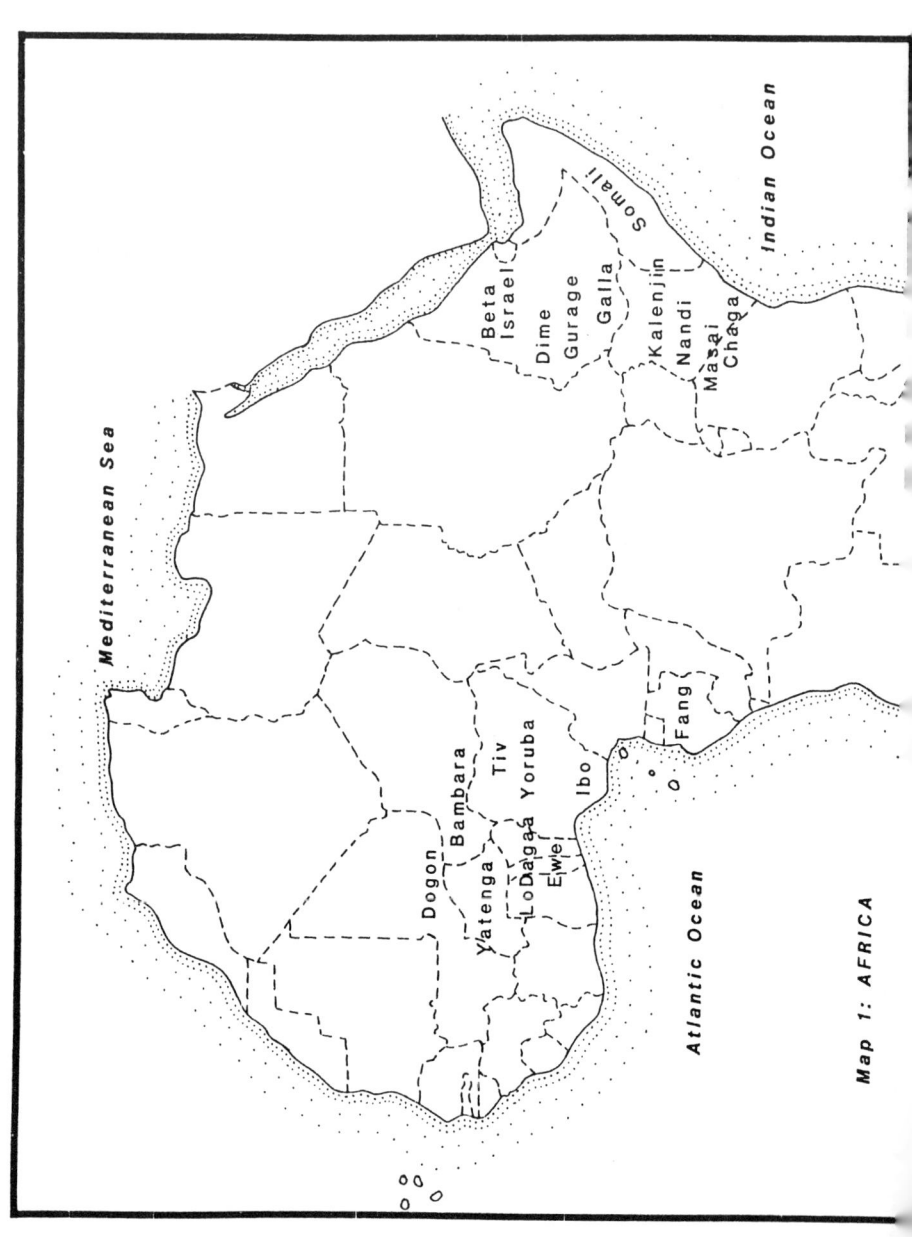

2. Iron Technology and Symbolism   49

individual, and the reasons for certain rituals. In their elaborate system of myths and symbols, the Dogon express a correspondence between their social organization and the world order as they conceive it. Social life is believed to reflect the working of the universe and, conversely, world order depends on the proper ordering of society. The social order is also projected on the individual, who is a microcosm of the whole and also affects cosmic order (Griaule, 1960:365; Griaule and Dieterlen, 1954:83-84).

The smith is a highly esteemed individual in Dogon society, and his tools have an important role in the cult. This is reflected in the essential place the first smith occupies in their creation myth. A number of variants of this myth have been recorded (see, e.g., Dieterlen, 1973; Griaule, 1960; 1965; Griaule and Dieterlen, 1954; Margarido and Wasserman, 1972), but the role of the first smith remains constant despite variations in detail. The myth is very long and its characters and symbols very complex. It will suffice for my purposes to focus on the smith's role in the myth. The first smith is said to have been created from the umbilical cord of the sacrificed Great Nommo or the blood of his castrated testicles (Dieterlen, 1973:45; Margarido and Wasserman, 1972:94). The Nummo (pl. of Nommo) are twin spirits who helped inspire and shape the first eight ancestors of humans. Sometimes the first smith is considered the Nommo's twin (Dieterlen, 1973:44-45). The principle of twinness is fundamental to Dogon cosmology and dominates the organization of society and the family.[1] All existence is conceived in an eight-fold pattern, and everything is 'twinned' with a male and a female half (Griaule and Dieterlen, 1954:86; Zuesse, 1979:160). The primal smith is said to have participated in the reordering of the cosmos following the activities of the rebellious and earth-defiling trickster figure (see, e.g., Griaule and Dieterlen, 1954; Dieterlen, 1973; Pelton, 1980), and to have introduced agriculture to the Dogon. In one variant of the myth, the first smith received specimens of the primary cultivable grains from the supreme deity Amma, which he placed in his hammer. He then sus-

---

1 On the concept of twinship in African symbol systems, see Southall, 1972.

pended himself by means of an iron chain, and Amma sent him down to earth. He is also said to have stolen grain from Amma and concealed it in his hammer. When he was subsequently sent down to earth, he became unclean and was unworthy to return to the sky.

Typically, the first smith is identified either as one of the first eight ancestors created from the sacrificed Nommo or as one who accompanied the Nummo in their descent from the sky to the earth in an ark. He was responsible for building and bringing to earth the first granary, symbolized by the smith's hammer (see Griaule, 1965:38-42). The granary and its contents reflect the world system of the new order established by the smith. When it was brought to earth, the granary was dispersed and became the primordial field, around which humanity came to be organized. This primordial field was distributed among the first eight ancestors, each of whom took a special craft. The celestial first smith was also the inventor of fire and taught humans about agriculture and animal domestication. In one variant of the myth (Zuesse, 1979:96), the fire was transported to earth in an ark that was also the smith's furnace and anvil. This ark was 'feminine', the smith's 'wife', and represented the female Great Nommo. When the first smith hammered this ark/furnace/anvil the vibrations produced life in all directions. The anvil, the blood of the sacrificed Nommo, is also said to be responsible for purifying the earth which had been polluted by the trickster (Dieterlen, 1973:46). Another report concerning the introduction of fire (Griaule, 1965:42) asserts that the ancestral smith stole a piece of the sun in the form of live embers and white-hot iron (cf. Dieterlen, 1973:48). He hid it in one of the skins of the bellows, exclaiming, *'Gouyo'* ('stolen'). This word also means 'granary' and is said to serve as a reminder that without the fire of the smithy and the iron of hoes there would be no crops.

The creation of the smith's tools and his workplace is also a part of the Dogon creation myth. The penis of the sacrificed Nommo was made into the tuyère and his testicles into bellows. The grains brought to earth by the primal smith were contained in his hammer, which is a symbol of the primal granary and represents the male Nommo. Iron ore was created from the blood of the Nommo's spleen (Dieterlen,

1973:46-48). The wooden beam in which the 'female' anvil is embedded is the bed of the two Great Nummo, and when the hammer strikes the anvil the two come together. With the sound produced when the smith strikes iron with his hammer, he reminds others of the supreme power of Amma and the Nummo, and assists in both prayer and appeasing the possible wrath of the celestial beings. Striking the iron with the hammer is also a means of restoring order among quarreling people and of requesting that the earth restore to the smith the strength of which he had formerly been emptied. As a descendant of the primal smith, who poured a large portion of his strength and life-force into the granary, the Dogon smith is characterized by a diminished life-force that removes him from the category of the 'living' (i.e., other Dogon). This enfeeblement constitutes a kind of uncleaness that sets the smith apart, although it is of a different sort than ordinary impurity. In one sense, he is diminished, but in another sense he is increased because he has given his energy for the common good (Griaule, 1965:86).

According to the myth, the primal smithy was constructed on the flat roof of the granary and the tools and implements of a forge assembled, because the future task of the smith was to teach humans the art of ironworking to enable them to cultivate land. The Dogon smithy is a model of this primal smithy (Griaule, 1965:84-86). In the primal field the smithy/granary was erected on the north side at the edge of the land that was to be cleared. Thus, Dogon smithies are always located on the north side of the central square which itself is always to the north of the village. The layout of the village is likened to a person, with the smithy as the head (Griaule and Dieterlen, 1954:96).

Smiths then became masters of fire. They were given the power to extract minerals from the soil and to smelt and transform them. Endowed with the capacity to make tools and weapons, both vital to humankind, the smith became a 'master of knowledge'. He carried out the rites of circumcision and excision on the first ancestors in order to render them fit for marriage and to prepare them to receive learning. Learning was transmitted to young people by the first smith, who survived the death of the eight primordial ancestors. The myth ends with his death and the celebration of his funeral, sixty-six years after his descent to earth. Events pertaining to the mythical smith, and their consequences, are symbolically reenacted whenever a new smithy is built or repaired (Dieterlen, 1973:49).

Germaine Dieterlen (1973:50-53) draws the following conclusions about the relationship between the creation myth and the Dogon smith's social status: 1. Since the smith is essentially a 'twin,' like all the first living beings created by Amma, he shares their privileges, their powers, and their 'sacred' character. For this reason he is able to invoke Amma when he prays for rain, the sperm of the sacrificial Nommo, his 'twin', whose sexual attributes he manipulates in his forge. 2. Ontologically, the smith is considered to belong to the same class as the members of the oldest generations. As such, he is 'seated' beside the chief priest during communal ceremonies. 3. Dogon smiths form an endogamous group and other Dogon will not mix blood with them in marriage. According to tradition, this is because smiths have 'mixed blood', one part of which derives from the blood sacrificed at creation by the Nommo. 4. The materials and tools used by the smith symbolize the organs and limbs of the sacrificial Nommo, who passed through the extreme stage of impurity (death) and triumphed over this impurity through resurrection. The smith works with both the 'pure' and 'impure'. He is associated with the breakdown of an earlier established order and the organization and maintenance of a 'new' world. 5. The 'sacrificial' blood of the smith derives in part from the sexual attributes of the sacrificed Nommo. Sexuality is incorporated into the work of the smith at his forge, which is likened to sexual activity and procreation. Taboos surround this activity because, as is characteristic of the smith in general, sex has ambivalent characteristics that involve the risk of impurity. 6. As one whose 'blood' derives in part from the castration of the sacrificed Nommo, the smith is responsible for performing circumcisions. In a sense, circumcision is understood to be a sacrifice presided over by the smith. The results of the rite of circumcision are similar to the changes wrought on the iron he extracts from the earth and works at the forge. It is a kind of rebirth. Circumcision changes a child into a man in the full meaning of the word. 7. The Dogon smith is one of the masters of initiatory knowledge and plays a prominent role during the ceremonies that commemorate the 'renewal of the world' that take place every sixty years. This role is reflected in the last episodes of the myth where he is identified as a purveyor of knowledge.

In the annual sacrifice associated with the cult of Lebe (one of the first ancestors), the smith also plays a central role. When the throat of the sacrificial victim is cut, he beats the ground with his hammer to facilitate the passage of the lifeforce of Lebe from the victim to the person who is to receive it (Griaule, 1965:133). In addition to his role as ritual specialist, the Dogon smith is considered to be the holder of technical secrets, is often a healer, is responsible for mediating conflicts, and is believed to have the ability to mediate between the living and the dead (Margarido and Wasserman, 1972:98).

The blacksmith's special position in Dogon mythology derives in large part from his importance to the success of agriculture, the dominant mode of production in Dogon society. He is excluded from agricultural work in the fields, but he nevertheless represents the determining factor in agriculture—it is he who manufactures the necessary implements. This separation from agricultural work is also manifest in the social separation of smiths who, in addition to being endogamous, live in separate villages or in separate areas within villages (Margarido and Wasserman, 1972:96).

The Bambara (Bamana). The Bambara are a Mande people of Upper Nigeria who at one time controlled an empire extending thousands of square miles over the savanna. They are neighbors to the Dogon with whom they share a history of economic, military, and diplomatic interaction. They also share with the Dogon a system of social organization that distinguishes artisans from other members of society, providing them with a prominent and honorable position (McNaughton, 1977:4).

The cosmology and religion of the Bambara also have much in common with those of the Dogon (Dieterlen, 1973:53). Like the Dogon, the Bambara conceive of the world as having been created in two stages, the first stage characterized by severe cosmic disorder.¹ Faro, the counterpart of the Dogon Amma, was responsible for reorganizing the universe and establishing the present order. The first ironsmith is said to have been created from the blood of the water spirit's castration, a belief that is similar to that of the Dogon that he issued from the twin Nummo, or water spirits, sacrificed in the sky by Amma. This is why the sacrificer in the worship of the guardian spirit of water must belong to a family whose ancestors are smiths descended from heaven. The primordial smith is said to have collaborated in creation by serving as Faro's intermediary and introducing agriculture to humans. He descended from the sky in an ark, holding in his hand a 'mass' containing the eight cereal grains. The celestial ironsmith is also the most important of Faro's auxiliaries, who participate in his ongoing maintenance of cosmic order, acting as a kind of 'secretary' (Dieterlen, 1960:75).

The ironsmith's forge and the tools of his trade are also attributed mythological significance, as well as sexual characteristics, among the Bambara (see Dieterlen, 1960:161-66). The forge, for example, is conceived as a living being surrounded by taboos aimed at protecting its material and spiritual integrity. Breaking these taboos is equivalent to attacking the virility of the ironsmith because the bellows, for example, are his testicles. The forges of a village are generally grouped together in a public square around a large anvil. In front of this communal anvil judicial affairs are settled, vows and promises are made, and purification for breaking taboos takes place.

According to tradition, Bambara ironsmiths have occupied central positions, undertaken important roles in their societies, and at times been at the very center of the history-making process from as early as the twelfth century CE down to the present (see McNaughton, 1977:19-48). Smiths are separated from the agrarian population by their profession and by the cultural components that constitute its special character. Among the Bambara, social differentiation is defined in relation to the materials one is able to manipulate.

---

1 For a more complete account of the Bambara creation myth, see Dieterlen, 1960:13-58; Cline, 1937:129; Zahan, 1979:123.

2. Iron Technology and Symbolism 55

This system is conceptualized in terms of relationships to agriculture, the forge, leather- and wood-working, and the art of speech. The major social distinctions are between those who devote themselves to working the earth and are able to provide for their own alimentary needs, often called 'nobles' in the ethnographic literature, and those whose skills are used for providing the farmers with what they need to fulfill their task. For example, ironsmiths extract iron and manufacture implements that are necessary for tilling the soil, other artisans provide utensils that are necessary for preparing and consuming food, and 'masters of speech' enhance the glory of farmers through compliments and praise. These artisans depend for their livelihood on what farmers exchange for their services. The social separation of smiths is also manifest in settlement and marriage patterns. Smiths live in separate enclaves within communities or in separate communities altogether. They are also endogamous and do not intermarry with 'nobles' (McNaughton, 1977:39, 55, 87). Interpreters have often identified this social differentiation as a rigid hierarchy that constitutes a kind of 'caste' system in which artisans, especially smiths, are 'despised' (e.g., Zahan, 1979:121-24; Paulme, 1973; on the Mande in general, see Vaughan, 1970).[1] This assertion has recently been challenged as a misinterpretation. According to Patrick McNaughton (1977:50-55), smiths are not differentiated on a *hierarchical* scale, but are simply perceived as *special* and *different*.[2] Bambara smiths, in fact, perceive themselves as 'a separate nation' (McNaughton, 1977:23; cf. Richter, 1980:40; Vaughan, 1970:77; 1973:167). In contrast to being 'despised,' as they

---

[1] The question of caste is one that is debated in the literature on African societies. Recent studies of both West and East African peoples have called 'caste' into question as an appropriate descriptive term. On the question of 'caste' among Mande peoples, see Vaughan, 1970; 1973; McNaughton, 1977:50-55; Richter, 1980. 'Castes' in East African and African Horn societies are considered below. For a survey of the issues associated with the question of caste in Africa, see Tuden and Plotnicov, 1970.

[2] The *special* and *different* nature of the smith, as opposed to *hierarchical* differentiation, is also treated in studies of other Mande peoples. On the Marghi, see Vaughan, 1970:79-80; 1973:167. On the Senufo, see Richter, 1980:40.

have so often been labeled, they are highly respected and feared among the Bambara and often hold important leadership positions, although they are barred from assuming direct political leadership as chiefs and kings. The fact that outsiders have often referred to them as 'despised' points to the ambivalent attitudes inspired by the awe and fear in which they are held. According to Mande beliefs, ironsmiths are born with the potential of securing high levels of energy, which they develop and learn to control and manipulate during an eight-year training period (McNaughton, 1977:i, 91-92). Smiths are called *numu* (pl. *numuw*) and are distinguished along with other artisans as *nyamakala* (see McNaughton, 1977:68-80; Paulme, 1973:91). *Nyama* has typically been defined as the power that animates and activates the universe, and *kala* as 'handle'. *Nyamakala*, then, means something like 'handle of power' (McNaughton, 1977:69). Marcel Griaule defines *nyama* as:

> instant energy which is impersonal and unconscious, shared by all animals, plants, and supernatural beings, things of nature; it is an energy which tends to support, in its being, the sustenance required either temporarily (mortal beings) or eternally (immortal beings). (quoted in Paulme, 1973:91)

Denise Paulme (1973:91) interprets *nyamakala* quite differently, and her interpretation points to the ambivalent attitudes with which artisans are regarded. According to her interpretation, by a play on words and a perhaps unconscious pun,[1] *nyama* ('pile of rubbish', 'manure') is linked to *n'ya-ma* ('life, personality, spirit, divine spirit, divinity'), whose essential source is blood. She points out that filth, *nyama*, is naturally very rich in *n'ya-ma*, since it is secreted along with waste matter, but continues to remain a part of the individual. 'Strength and filth—it is easily understood with what mingled feelings of fear and contempt the caste groups are treated' (Paulme, 1973:91).

---

1 Edmund Leach (1976:18) notes that punning is an important feature of symbolic forms of communication, especially in areas of social life that are the focus of taboo.

2. Iron Technology and Symbolism 57

The activities of the *nyamakala* among the Bambara involve the manipulation of *nyama*, that is, the transformation of matter by rearranging and radically altering it. They are bearers of profound power, having learned the laws of universal order and action, which they use to benefit others. Their distinguished social position is defined according to these principles (McNaughton, 1977:68-80). They hold important leadership positions, are indispensable to the proper practice of traditional Bambara religion, and are a primary source of economic and moral stability. The name by which a smith is called, *numu* (pl. *numuw*), identifies a person as a smith, but also as a sculptor, doctor, diviner, and a number of other occupational specialists.

The 'knowledge' smiths are said to possess provides them access to power and is therefore surrounded by secrecy. Without this secret knowledge, smiths could not forge iron into adequate tools, nor could they perform their other roles adequately (see McNaughton, 1977:104-57). Because of their secret knowledge of the *nyama* of the sky, they can provide rain. As 'persons who know', they are diviners who can tap the natural order and operation of the universe. Of the other responsibilities of the smith, the most difficult and potentially dangerous are those of circumcision and excision. Only smiths are permitted to carry out these important initiatory operations.

The Bambara smith's ritual functions extend to the rituals associated with the most important of Bambara religious societies—the Komo (see Dieterlen, 1960:187-216). Theoretically, the Komo society in each village is made up of all circumcised men, both living and dead, the sanctuary and its altars, the responsible chief (preferably a smith), and the Komo masks. The latter are made by smiths and are considered their most dramatic and powerful accomplishments because they are infused with the energy that the smiths are most qualified to use (McNaughton, 1977:ii). The Komo society, dominated and protected by the power of Faro, is involved in most of the activities of Bambara daily life—birth, circumcision, marriage, burial, the cult of the ancestors, agriculture, technology, and political and economic issues.

> The Komo is a society which unites the highest divine power, men [sic!], animals, and plants until the end of the world. It is the keeper of souls. When there is no longer life on earth, when there are neither men [sic!], nor animals, nor plants, the Komo will awaken the souls of the dead which have been in its keeping for eternity. (Dieterlen, 1960:215-16)

As the chief functionary in this religious society, the smith has considerable responsibility. He is guardian of the altar, which contains all the spiritual forces of the society. He is the only one able to manipulate these forces, and thus is in charge of all rituals that depend on them. As chief of the Komo, he is responsible for dispensing justice since the Komo is the repository of traditional beliefs and rules of solidarity. As Komo leaders, smiths are community arbitrators and personal advisers to political leaders (McNaughton, 1977:153-57; cf. Richter, 1980:41; Vaughan, 1970:86-87; 1973:168-69). They are a potent force in the community without holding the highest offices. They serve as advisers and interpreters, financial and social intermediaries, judges, spokespersons, and witnesses. The smith's anvil, which represents his authority, is the surface on which oaths are declared. Essentially, the role of the smith in Bambara society is maintainer of balance and harmony (McNaughton, 1977:159).

The Ewe. The motif of the smith as culture hero is also prevalent in the beliefs of the Ewe peoples of the Dahomean Kingdom of West Africa. The Ewe are scattered over a linguistically homogeneous area of over 8,000 square miles from what is now southern Ghana west through southern Togo into Benin (Verdon, 1983:21). Although there is much diversity among Ewe groups—for example, southern groups are more 'centralized' with a type of 'divine' kingship, while northern groups are more 'decentralized' with a chiefly type of leadership—they share common legends of origin and a common language (Verdon, 1983:21, 23). They have been greatly influenced by their Yoruba neighbors, particularly in the realm of religion (Mercier, 1954:210), and according to tradition migrated from Yorubaland (Verdon, 1983:21; on the Yoruba, see below).

2. Iron Technology and Symbolism

The Fon are an Eastern Ewe people who live for the most part in what is now Benin. Although the wealth of Fon religious and cosmological ideas represents a number of divergencies and contradictions, there is nevertheless a remarkable stability in the essential patterns of Fon myths, patterns that have correspondences in the social sphere. For example, the principle of dualism, so prominent in the religions of the Dogon and Bambara, is also found in Fon religion and society (Mercier, 1954:212-17).

The head of the sky gods, the dual Mawu-Lisa, was responsible for the present ordering of the world.[1] In the dual Mawu-Lisa, Mawu, associated with the moon, is female, and Lisa, associated with the sun, is male. Sometimes their relationship is expressed by the concept of an androgynous, self-fertilizing being. Their dual nature is said to express the complementary forces activated in the world. The concept of twins expresses the equilibrium maintained between opposites, which is the nature of the world (Mercier, 1954:219; Booth, 1977:161-62).

In the sky pantheon of the Fon, Gu, the *vodu* (god) of iron and war, often ranks first among the offspring of Mawu-Lisa. Gu is one of the two *vodu* who were not assigned a special domain. The other is Legba, the Fon trickster (see, e.g., Mercier, 1954:228-29; Pelton, 1980), who acts as an observer and interpreter among the *vodu*. Gu is the Fon culture hero, the agent of the introduction of civilization. He was charged by Mawu to make the earth habitable for humans. It is Gu who is believed to have supplied the tools for human beings to build shelters, hoe the ground, cut down trees for firewood, make boats and implements, and triumph over enemies. He also introduced the knowledge and practice of ironworking, a task he is believed to carry out down to the present. Among the Fon it is said that '*Gu* himself is not iron, but that property of iron which gives it the power to cut' (Booth, 1977:170).

Gu is regarded variously as a person or as an instrument in the hands of Mawu-Lisa (Herskovits, 1938:105; Mercier, 1954:223). As a person, he is the celestial ironsmith, patron of earthly ironsmiths, and inventor of all crafts (except weav-

---

1 On Fon cosmogony, see Mercier, 1954:17-33; Booth, 1977:161-62; Herskovits, 1933; 1938.

ing). As an instrument of Mawu-Lisa, Gu is conceptualized as a 'force' that took the form of a *gubasa*, a kind of ceremonial sword or wand of office. As a wand of office Gu is said to have been in Mawu's hand when Mawu created humanity or in Lisa's hand when civilization was established. He is also believed to have been largely responsible for organizing society. He is regarded as one of the first founders of families because on his visits to earth he mated and paved the way toward social, organized life.

The Yoruba. The Yoruba live in the savannas and forests of southern Nigeria between the lower Niger and the Gulf of Guinea. They are bounded on the west by the Ewe-speaking peoples of Benin. Although quite diverse in some respects, the Yoruba are bound together by common language, dress, symbolism, ritual, myth, and history. Before the advent of the British, the Yoruba were famous for their arts, including ironworking, in addition to their competence as agriculturalists. Today, most Yoruba identify themselves as either Muslim or Christian, but many continue to practice some aspects of their traditional religion.

Among traditional Yoruba gods, Ogun, the god of metal and war, is considered an indispensable deity and has maintained a particularly strong following in modern times.[1] Traditionally the god of iron and of those whose occupations are related to the use of iron (hunters, warriors, and smiths), Ogun is now also worshiped by chauffeurs and mechanics. He is also greatly respected by Yoruba farmers, who recognize that iron is essential to their work. Ogun is numbered among the *orisha* ('lesser deities') of the Yoruba, who are subordinate in classification to the 'Supreme God' Olurun or Olodumare. The *orisha* are associated with persons, places, functional concerns, and even diseases. Ogun is variously regarded as one of

1 On the role of Ogun in Yoruba religion, see, e.g., Booth, 1977; Lawson, 1984:61-62; Lucas, 1948:106-8; Parrinder, 1961; Awolalu, 1979; Zuesse, 1979:96; Idowu, 1962:85-89. Parrinder (1961:34) suggests that Gua, the Ga thunder god who is served by smiths, may be related to Gu and Ogun of the Ewe and Yoruba. On the religion of the Ga, see Field, 1937. On the survival and diffusion of Ogun's popularity, see, e.g., Barnes 1980 and 1989.

2. Iron Technology and Symbolism

the original gods or as a deified ancestor. He is considered to be the first forger of weapons and the first hunter, who used to descend from heaven on a spider's web. According to tradition, when the gods first came to inhabit the earth they came upon a thicket they were not able to cut their way through. A path was finally cleared through the mediation of Ogun and his metal axe. The Yoruba thus hold the belief that when one's path is obstructed, or when one encounters difficulties, appeal to Ogun will clear the way. They also believe that Ogun opens paths for communication between the heavenly and earthly spheres and that he mediates material and spiritual prosperity. For these reasons, an emblem of Ogun is often found stationed at the entrance of many shrines. He is said to be the possessor of two axes: one with which he prepares the farm and one with which he clears the road. It is also believed that Ogun put the finishing touches on the creation of human beings by taking charge of the work of circumcision, tribal marking, tatooing, and other surgical operations necessary for keeping humans in good health (Idowu, 1962:85-87; Awolalu, 1979: 31).

According to the religious traditions of the city of Ife, Ogun was its first king. Ife is considered to be the navel of the cosmos where the earth was established and humans created (Pelton, 1980:156). The fierce, warlike character of the iron god is emphasized in this tradition which claims Ogun to be the son of Oduduwa, a creator god, and a great warrior who assisted his father in battling enemies. Rulership of the city was given to him as a reward for his victories. The story speaks of Ogun as an explosive ruler who lost control when his subjects failed to show him proper respect. After killing a number of his subjects, he killed himself and disappeared into the earth, establishing himself as a mediator between the worlds of the living and the dead. His last words are said to have consisted of a promise that he would respond to all who call on him in times of great need (Lawson, 1984:61; Awolalu, 1979:31).

The discovery of metals and tool-making is considered by the Yoruba to have been a fundamental and creative step forward. The implements that are a product of this creative act are known to be both destructive (weapons) and constructive (tools) and are considered to have both divine and human attributes. Ogun's status as both god and ancestor reflects this duality. He is associated with both heaven and earth; his abode is both in the heavens and on (or under) the earth; he is both a living god and a dead ancestor. Because of his borderline status, Ogun stands for both the justice of the gods and the justice required in human actions. He is, therefore, called upon to witness covenants or agreements between individuals or groups. When an adherent of traditional Yoruba religion is brought to court, he or she is asked to swear by Ogun, represented by a piece of iron he or she must kiss. Anyone who swears falsely or breaks an agreement is believed to suffer serious consequences that normally result in accident or death. In addition, the smithy often serves as a place where pacts of friendship are sealed (Lawson, 1984:61-62; Awolalu, 1979:33; Parrinder, 1961:35).

Ironworking, the trade with which Ogun is most closely identified, is a traditional Yoruba craft, organized in guilds, which is hereditary and is passed down from father to son (see Lloyd, 1953). As in other West African societies, the smith is said to be a kind of 'magician' and healer (Margetts, 1965:116). The symbol of Ogun is iron, and the anvil and forge are regarded as sacred.

The LoDagaa. Among some West African peoples, the smith and his work are closely identified with the earth (see Eliade, 1978:43-52). This is the case among the LoDagaa, an agricultural people who live in the northwestern corner of Ghana. Until recently, all LoDagaa were farmers and hunters. The exceptions are a few specialists such as smiths, xylophone makers, diviners, and others who specialize in magico-religious activities. The territory of the LoDagaa is divided into ritual areas, each containing an Earth shrine. Those persons owing allegiance to a particular Earth shrine are in effect a local 'congregation,' bound together by the observance of certain prohibitions, particulary against shedding the blood of a fellow member.

LoDagaa smiths are organized in kin-guilds in which the traditions are handed down among their members. The smith's tools (*saa kpiera*) and the smithy are closely associated with the Earth shrine. 'The smithy is [the same in certain

2. Iron Technology and Symbolism 63

respects] as the Earth shrine (*saa in tenggaan*)', say the LoDagaa. This association probably derives from a common link with iron, which is dug out of the earth.

Since the smith works with the 'earth' (iron), his role in some respects parallels that of the Earth shrine's custodian. Like the Earth priests, the smith, who fashions the weapons of war, can also act as a peace-maker. Like the Earth priests, he can 'throw ashes and make things hot and cold'. His tools are attributed similar powers and can calm a person who is inclined toward self-violence. For example, a father who attempts suicide following the death of his son is forced to grasp a pair of smith's tongs. After this, it is believed, any further attempt at suicide would prove futile. This act is likened to forcing a suspected witch to swallow some earth—both acts are carried out under threat of force and both invoke the Earth shrine (Goody, 1962:3, 6, 91-92, 205; 1971:46).

Yatenga. The smiths of Yatenga also play an important role in relation to Earth shrines. Yatenga is one of four Mossi kingdoms that comprise a part of the West African Voltaic region. All Mossi are farmers. It is only during the season after the rain has stopped and the harvest is in that attention can be turned to more specialized activities.

Metalworking, woodworking, and the manufacture of pottery are the most specialized Mossi crafts and are almost exclusively confined to the smiths, *saba*, who form an endogamous 'caste' descended from the indigenous inhabitants of Yatenga (the Mossi population is made up of indigenous peoples and peoples who later migrated into the territory). The wives of the smiths are the potters among the Yatenga. The right of smiths to engage in their specialized work is ascribed on the basis of their separate social identity. Not all members of the smith descent groups work with metal, however, for it is a matter of choice.

A distinctive ritual aura surrounds both the smith and his work, and he often serves the Earth deity in a ritual capacity. The Earth priests are denied any sort of political power but are the principal intermediaries between the people and the natural manifestations of the deity. Along with smiths, the Earth priests, elders of the patrilineages, are descended from the 'indigenous' population.

The Bogaba (sing. Boga), most of whom are smiths, are subordinate and auxiliary to the Earth priests. Their ritual responsibilities consist of maintaining a balance in the society's relationship to the vegetal aspect of the deity. They are also responsible for such activities as assisting barren women to conceive. Many elements of their social status parallel those of the Earth priests. They are, for instance, always the elders of the founding lineages of their sibs (Hammond, 1966; Goody, 1971:46; Cline, 1937:130).

The Tiv. The mediatory role of the ironsmith is pronounced among the Tiv, a northern Nigerian people. The Tiv stress a kind of metaphysical relationship among iron, stone celts, thunderbolts, and the cult of the dead, and in Tiv magic there is a close association of heaven, thunderbolts, and the ironsmith's craft. Iron plays a role in making contact with deceased persons and functions as a mode of communication between the worlds of the living and the dead. The tuyère, one of their cult emblems, is employed along with iron in rites to secure the aid of household ancestors and to ward off their displeasure.

The power ascribed to iron also flows through the smithy, which serves as a kind of common meeting place, and all objects associated with it. This power is manifest in thunderbolts. Thus, for example, it is said that a member of a secret society who uses his power for destructive purposes and then enters a smithy will be struck by lightning. The power of a smith's tools or iron slag automatically brings death by lightning upon a sorcerer or witch who tries to bewitch a person who possesses it. For this reason, the things that the *mbatsav* ('witches') tend to shun are those most closely associated with smithing—fire, earth, slag from the furnace, the tongs, and the 'Axe of Heaven'. The slag of the furnace also serves as protection for boys immediately following rites of circumcision, and is thought to cause lightning to strike any offender. Oaths are sworn at the smithy and on the ironsmith's tools. In addition to its protective function, iron is said to connote power and prestige. This is why the Tiv chief wears a pair of iron for-

2. Iron Technology and Symbolism

ceps around his neck and why many chiefs possess complete sets of smith's tools (Cline, 1937:126-127; Bohannan, 1965:513-514, 538-539; East, 1939:36, 62-63, 254).

The Ibo (Igbo). Among the Ibo peoples of southeastern Nigeria, smiths are organized in hereditary sacred guilds[1] whose secrets are carefully guarded. They enjoy special economic and social status, are accorded a high social position, and as a rule must not be harmed (Cline, 1937:129; Neaher, 1979:90-91). The ironsmiths of Awka are especially notorious, not only for their skill in ironworking, but also for their religious, social, political, and legal influence. They travel extensively as smiths, doctors, purveyors of cults and cult symbols, circumcisers, teeth-filers, missionaries of the priest-chiefs of Nri, and, above all, as agents of the oracle of Agbala, which is a kind of final court of appeal in disputes (Neaher, 1979; Cline, 1937:129; Meek, 1970:18).

The Nri people of Ibo territory claim that they are not of Ibo descent but rather are descended from Eri, a man sent from the sky by the great God. The ironsmith plays a prominent role in the legend associated with this tradition. It is said that when Eri, the first king, found himself standing in the morass of the world surrounded by water, he complained of his plight to the great God. The great God responded by sending an ironsmith, who blew on fire with his bellows and made the ground dry. This smith then became the ancestor of the Awka Ibo, who since that time have specialized in ironworking (Henderson, 1972:59-60; Neaher, 1979). Thus, as among other West African peoples, the smith is perceived as having a primary role in establishing culture.

The metal iron plays a prominent role in the Ibo ritual performed during the building of *mbari* houses, temporary temples that are never repaired and eventually fall into ruin. The central figure in the *mbari* house is usually Ala, the Ibo earth goddess, in whose honor it is set up to invoke the blessings of prosperity and offspring (Parrinder, 1961:37-38, 61).

---

1 On guild organization in Africa, see, e.g., Nadel, 1942:257-94; Jaggar, 1973.

Before the date is set for sealing the ritual contract to build the *mbari*, a diviner searches the town for women who have passed child-bearing age. From among these women the diviners select the 'leaders of iron' or 'people at the head of iron'. These individuals are said to represent the deity for whom the house is being built. The ceremony of 'tying the head on iron' or 'establishing the leader of iron' follows this selection. This ceremony focuses on an iron bar that previously had been offered to Ala as an *osu* sacrifice (typically a living sacrifice in which a cult slave is dedicated to the goddess). The rod iron, which symbolizes strength, wealth, and supernatural power, also serves as a symbol that the *mbari* is to be built, and both the rod and the women are thought to be invested with the power of the god. During the ceremony the rod iron is ritually prepared for the next phase of the ritual, 'walking the iron'. It is during this phase of the ritual that the participants in the building of the *mbari* enter into a period of ritual seclusion in the compound where it is to be built. The ritual consists of entering into the compound by walking on long narrow iron bars laid down end to end. The iron bars serve as a bridge which conveys the workers to their ritual death, that is, into the liminal phase of this rite of passage, which is to last for three weeks. Once inside the fence of the compound the workers are secluded in a kind of communal living situation in which members of both sexes live together and cannot act normally until after the *mbari* opens. Before the initiates emerge from this seclusion, which prepares them for a change in status, or 'rebirth', each acquires a staff of iron that serves both as protection and to identify him or her with the god (Cole, 1982:75, 81-84, 185-186).[1]

The Fang. Similar kinds of symbols are associated with iron in the contemporary Bwiti cult[2] among the egalitarian Fang of the equatorial forest of West Africa (northern Gabon). Bwiti is

1 Iron rods are used in a similar mediatory fashion among the Bari of East Africa to induce rain, i.e., to mediate between heaven and earth. See Seligman, 1928:468-70.
2 Numerous symbols are manipulated in the Bwiti ritual process, of which forge imagery is one. On the Bwiti cult, see, e.g., Fernandez, 1965; 1966; 1973; 1977; 1982.

2. Iron Technology and Symbolism

a reformative cult that originated at the turn of the century and represents a reworking of the Fang ancestral cult, a cult with which traditional ironworking is closely associated.[1] Since World War II a substantial number of Christian elements have been absorbed in the cult liturgy and cosmology. Much of what is symbolized in the liturgy of the cult is related to the transition between the traditional ways and the modern world, the past and the present, toward which the Fang have an ambivalent attitude consisting of both regret and satisfaction. Through the Bwiti rituals and the sermons delivered in the context of the rituals, the Fang are able to derive some consistency in the distribution of traditional and modern values (Fernandez, 1966:48).

As is the case among other West African peoples, ironworking is an old and much respected craft among the Fang, although the smith is not accorded exceptional status (Tessman, 1959:257; Fernandez, 1973:198). This is reflected both in their mythology and their rituals. A good example is found in the Fang myth of the creation of human beings:

> Now Zame looked around and even though he was in the company of Nlona and Nyingwan he still felt lonely, so he reflected and made a hole in the earth—a smelting hole—and he made the Fang bellows, *nkom*, and he took the fire from the sun which belonged to him. He gathered together a ball of earth and he shaped it, for the body comes from Zame. Then he turned to Nyingwan who reached into her heart and took out the last drop of blood that always remains in the heart of any living thing even when it is dead and she placed that drop in the center of the body of the earth. For our blood is that of Nyingwan Mebege. Then he turned to Nlona who reached into his brain and took out the white substance, '*meyom*,' and placed it in the earth. Now the ball of earth was placed in the fire and Nyingwan Mebege began to pump the bellows while Zame turned the earth. Finally when it was red hot Zame reached in and removed it and struck it with his hands. It cracked open and out stepped Adam who resembled Zame in every particular. (Fernandez, 1982:328)

[1] Traditionally, ironworking among the Fang was closely associated with both the fire cult and the ancestral cult. See Tessman, 1959:245. For a discussion of traditional ironworking in general, see Tessman, 1959:243-62.

This type of forge imagery is also richly represented in Bwiti rituals in which the actions of forging are often simulated. It is used, for example, in the 'dance of Creation' when entering a Bwiti chapel. Represented in this dance is a move from disorder to order, obscurity to clarity, coldness to heat. There is a movement from a desolate lifeless place 'out there', where one is barely warmed by the creation fire, to the lively and orderly place, the 'forge' of the Bwiti chapel where one is heated and 'forged' by many fires (Fernandez, 1982:313).

The creation of human beings by Zame is also often ritually re-enacted. In the chapel of the Disumba branch of Bwiti the early part of the ritual focuses on the central circle of the chapel and the fire that is considered to burn constantly beneath it. Early in the evening the long clay pipe attached to the bellows is placed in the fire. One member of the congregation, representing Zame, pumps the bellows while another member on the opposite side of the fire bends forward slowly and lights a bundle of raffia slips. The latter then jumps over the fire, runs around it holding the torch high, and then runs out of the chapel into the night, eventually to return to the chapel where the entrance songs are begun. This is described as a re-enactment of the creation of the first human being, Adam, by Zame (Fernandez, 1982:329; cf. 1965:905, 909-10).

At midnight there is a pause in the Bwiti ritual, during which a sermon is delivered. Fernandez interprets this as a liminal period that serves as a bridge between two fundamentally different dramatic statements. This period occurs between the late evening, when the creation and origin of all things and the birth of Christ are being danced, and the early morning hours in which the death of Christ, the destruction of the world, and the hope for resurrection are enacted (Fernandez, 1966:47; cf. 1965:905-906). In the sermon itself, smelting images are often central. For example, the speaker complains that all the good things that were associated with Fang ironworking (strength in battle, cooperation among humans in production, order in the exchange of women, etc.) have been abandoned in the same way that ironworking has been abandoned (Fernandez, 1982:507). The furnace and the production of iron represent what the Fang have lost and need

2. Iron Technology and Symbolism

to regain, that is, they serve as mediators between the past, traditional way of life and that of the present, modern Fang.

This can be seen, for example, in one of the sermons recorded and interpreted by Fernandez:

> ... The Fang, he is bone. At the door of the slag furnace God himself did it. God knows the Fang, he made him there. Brothers argue at the furnace. But the bellows at the forge remain within it. God made the furnace. Iron was within it. Then Fang men made the iron for the bride price. The women sat peacefully. Our seed was abundant. Then manioc sticks came to be called *matudi*, and then money came to us from down-river. The women no longer multiply. The clan should not forget its seed. The antelope... is not the child of the elephant. God himself, he has made all things. (1966:52-53)

According to Fernandez, the iron represents the authenticity of the traditional way of life. Confronted by modern technology, the Fang are able to see in ironworking their own gratifying technology. It also represents masculine power because only men make it and use it in war. And its association with bride price represents lineage increase as well as obtaining in a just manner an agreement of a woman and her family to marriage.

In Fernandez's assessment, these symbols connected with ironworking are *key symbols* for the Fang people that have endured in both thought and action. As key symbols they are linked to three levels of human behavior: the physiological, the social (i.e., the system of interaction), and the cultural (i.e., the ideological system of beliefs and values). The bellows and the forge symbolize the penetration of the male organ into the womb to prepare the womb to receive and mold the child. The male (hot) thus brings the female (cold) to the proper temperature for creation, just as the bellows keep the fire hot. At the social level, the symbolism suggests the initiatory and dominant role of male over female and man over wife, a distinction that has been increasingly blurred and is considered to be in need of redefinition and stabilization. The cultural referent is the value of and belief in the male's dominance and his preparation of the female for procreation (Fernandez, 1966:61-62).

East Africa and the African Horn

The ethnographic literature on the ironsmith in West African societies emphasizes both the role of the first smith or iron god in myths about the creation and organization of the world and the smith's social status. In contrast, the literature on East African and African Horn societies focuses almost exclusively on the social status and roles of the smith. This contrast is in large part due to the fact that cosmogony in East Africa seems not to be as elaborately developed as in West Africa and that the smith has little if any role in creation myths. The peoples of the African Horn have turned largely to practicing Islamic and Christian traditions, in which there is no place in creation mythology for the smith. Much of the secondary literature on smiths in both of these major culture areas deals with the question of whether or not smiths can be considered to comprise 'castes' within the larger society. The issue of caste was touched on briefly in the discussion of West Africa but looms larger in the literature on East Africa and the African Horn. Earlier literature on the subject uses the word 'caste' to describe the social status of smiths without qualification. However, recent studies tend to suggest that this term is inappropriate for defining social status in African societies (see, e.g., Tuden and Plotnicov, 1970). Part of the problem has to do with the questions of how one defines 'caste' and whether caste is a social phenomenon that is limited to Pan-Indian civilization. The arguments are too extensive and complex to discuss in the present study, and my analysis does not depend on resolution of the problem. What is significant for my purposes is the fact that smiths are almost always somehow set apart from the rest of society in a way that makes them marginal groups.

East Africa and the African Horn consist of culturally heterogeneous and fragmented culture areas representing multiple ecological adaptations. Complexity of social organization ranges from the loosely structured social units of the Eastern Rift Coast region to the elaborate hierarchical structures of the Ethiopian Highlands.[1] The greater part of the area

---

1 The Ethiopian Highlands are often distinguished from the Horn (Somalia). Here, I follow Kesby (1977) in identifying the Ethiopian

is a vast plateau divided by a series of valleys known collectively as the Great Rift Valley. Rising from the plateau are a number of highland areas, some of which are crowned by high snow-capped mountains or mountain ranges (see Shorter, 1974; Kesby, 1977).

The major boundary between East Africa and the Horn, or the North-African-Near-Eastern region (NANE) (Kesby, 1977), follows the vegetational transition between the deserts of the Sahara and the Horn to the north, and the dry woodlands and grasslands to the south (Kesby, 1977:7). A number of cultural differences characterize these two major regions (Kesby, 1977:7-11). Historically, the NANE has been dominated by vast empires with high degrees of social differentiation and specialization. The exceptions to this pattern are desert peoples such as the Somali and Galla, who are organized on a smaller scale. In East Africa (Kesby's African Major Region), the largest social unit tends to be an autonomous village comprised of about three hundred people. The long influence of Christianity and Islam in the NANE also distinguishes it from the African Major Region, where these traditions are more recent. Differences in language, bodily appearance, architecture, and artistic style are also distinguished. Finally, there are also differences in material culture. For example, ironworking is much older in the NANE than in the Major Region, although it has been widespread in the latter for at least the last hundred years.

The Masai and the Nandi. The Masai, a cattle-raising people of southern Kenya and northern Tanzania, are often quoted as the typical example of a people who perceive the smith with complete loathing (Margarido and Wasserman, 1972:105). As was noted in the introductory section of this chapter, a distinction is often made between agricultural societies, in which the smith is typically honored, and pastoral societies, in which the smith is 'despised'. Although one must guard against making simplistic oppositions (Margarido and Wasserman, 1972:91), it does seem to be the case that smiths in East African pastoral

Highlands as part of the North-African-Near-Eastern Major Region and include them in my discussion of the Horn.

societies are not ascribed the same social prestige as smiths in West African agricultural societies. On the other hand, this seems to be the case among many East African agriculturalists as well.

Most of the so-called pastoralist peoples of East Africa also practice a certain amount of cultivation. The Masai are an exception in that they raise sheep and cattle to the exclusion of cultivation (Shorter, 1974:30). They live in a marginal dry plains area of the Eastern Rift Coast region where there are typically no states or kings. The largest social units in the area until recently were autonomous settlements of at most a few hundred people. Leaders of these societies are either hereditary priests or individuals who excel in conciliation or warfare (Kesby, 1977:19, 78; for a general overview of the Masai, see Hollis, 1905).

The Masai are the culturally dominant people of the region (Kesby, 1977:72). There are three major groups in Masai— Masai warriors, Masai smiths (Il-Kunōno), and the Dorobo, the latter variously described as hunters (e.g., Huntingford, 1931; Margarido and Wasserman, 1972; Cline, 1937:114) or 'serfs' who provide the Masai with cereals and vegetables (Shorter, 1974:33). Neither the Il-Kunōno nor the Dorobo are considered to be Masai, and both form endogamous clans, often defined as 'castes'. The Il-Kunōno have a language of their own, although they speak Masai, and are thought to be of a different race from the Masai (Huntingford, 1931). They live among the Masai but have separate kraals and war parties. The Masai avoid contact with them, as do the Dorobo, who themselves are held in low esteem (Cline, 1937:114). Contact with a smith or anything he has touched is considered to be contaminating (Huntingford, 1931), and settling too close to a smith village is thought to bring death and disease to the livestock (Margarido and Wasserman, 1972:107).

Smiths are also feared for other reasons. For example, sexual contact with an Il-Kunōno woman is believed to cause a man to lose his reason, father defective children, or be slain in the next raid. To pronounce the word *Il-Kunōno*, a term of insult when applied to a non-smith, after dark is to invite nocturnal attacks of lions or human enemies.

2. Iron Technology and Symbolism

The Il-Kunōno are partially excluded from the prestige-building activities considered most essential by the Masai—warfare and cattle-raising (Cline, 1937:115; Margarido and Wasserman, 1972:108-9). Although smiths are allowed to participate in warfare and raids as long as they are not against other Masai, only Masai warriors are allowed to carry weapons. Smiths are also allowed to own cattle and to keep cattle acquired in raids, but they are limited in the number they can possess, and therefore in the acquisition of wealth. If they go beyond this imposed limit, the Masai eliminate them.

The reason given by the Masai for the low status they attribute to smiths is that they are 'impure and inauspicious' because they make weapons that shed blood, and God abhors and forbids the shedding of blood (Cline, 1937:114; Margarido and Wasserman, 1972:105). This assertion introduces an interesting paradox in Masai ideology because warfare is such an essential part of their way of life. Not only is warfare a prestige-building activity, but it is also essential to the economy of the Masai. Without warfare and raiding, the Masai would not be able to ensure the increase or replacement of their livestock. So, in spite of the Masai assertion that God forbids bloodshed, Masai warriors nevertheless use the weapons provided by smiths.

The smiths (Kitoñgik) of the Nandi, a neighboring people of the Masai, are of Masai origin, belong to the Il-Kunōno, and speak both Nandi and Masai (on the Nandi, see, e.g., Hollis, 1909:36-37; Huntingford, 1931; 1953). In contrast to the Masai, however, each Nandi clan has its own smiths who are, for all practical purposes, members of the clan and are treated almost as equals. Nandi smiths have no clan of their own. Nevertheless, very few of the Nandi clans will openly intermarry with smiths or allow their cattle to be herded or bred with cattle belonging to smiths. Fear of the smith's powers is also felt among the Nandi, who spit into their hands before they handle anything a smith has made. The curse of the smith is also greatly feared because he has the power to cause death.

The Chaga. In addition to the Il-Kunōno, the Masai depend on the smiths of the neighboring Chaga for their weapons (Margarido and Wasserman, 1972:110). The Chaga are intensive cultivators who live to the east of the Masai in the wet highlands of the Eastern Rift Coast (Kesby, 1977:87). Chaga smiths are said to come from Masai (Cline, 1937:115) and in some respects have a social status similar to that of smiths among the Masai. Although not 'despised', they are feared because they manufacture deadly weapons, because they possess the secret of 'binding iron together', because their hammer and bellows possess supernatural powers, and because of the dangerous potency of their blood (see Cline, 1937:115-17). Intermarriage with smiths, or their daughters, is strongly discouraged, although not forbidden. In some districts smiths are forbidden to participate in warfare because, as makers of deadly weapons which God hates, their presence is likely to bring death. As is so often the case in African societies, the curse of the smith is greatly feared, especially by thieves.

In contrast to the status ascribed to smiths among the Masai, Chaga smiths are honored as well as feared. They and their tools guard against thieves, they interpret omens, and they make efficacious amulets and medicines from iron. Iron arm and neck bands made and ritually blessed by the smith are believed to promote fertility and protect against illness. Chaga smiths are perceived as sociable individuals who do not exploit their powers for purposes of evil magic or deception. The Chaga often gather at the smithy to gossip and often confide in the smith things that are otherwise only confided to shamans or diviners.

The Kalenjin. To the north of the Nandi live the Kalenjin, a people related to them linguistically. The Kalenjin practice agriculture and raise cattle. Among these peoples, attitudes toward smiths vary according to ecological zones (Coy, 1982:137-38). In the highlands and agricultural areas, smiths are both feared and greatly respected for their power and their work. In the lowlands and areas unsuited to agriculture they are disliked and subject to harrassment. However, they and their tools are viewed by all Kalenjin as possessing special powers and attributes that are considered mysterious and dangerous (Coy, 1982:83-93).

The social marginality of Kalenjin smiths is manifest in several ways: 1. they are consistently members of minority clans; 2. intermarriage with them is believed to be inauspicious; 3. they are not given equal access to commodities in the local arena of reciprocal exchange; 4. they are excluded from a number of social activities; 5. they are not allowed to own cattle; 6. during periods of war with neighboring peoples they are exempt from threats by either side (they provide tools and weapons for both sides); and 7. the smithy is always set off from the living space of the larger community (Coy, 1982:131, 152-53).

In spite of their position of social marginality, smiths play important political and religious roles in Kalenjin society. They serve as advisers to local elders in decision-making and in situations of conflict resolution, and often sit on the local elders' council (Coy, 1982:132-33). The smith's curse also has an important function in maintaining social order, especially in dealing with theft and asocial behavior. In the realm of religion and ritual, smiths provide articles for protection and rituals, as well as status markers. They perform protective services and are able to ward off illness and enemies (Coy, 1982:110-13).

Michael Coy's 1982 analysis of Kalenjin smiths provides an interesting and important perspective on the roles and status of the smith. First of all, he is careful to distinguish between the attitudes of the Kalenjin smiths themselves and those of the dominant group. Secondly, he notes the dialectical relationship between role and status, between actual behavior and perceptions or the 'emotionally charged attribution of affective feeling' (p. 25) (the domains of actions and notions respectively).

Coy notes that the perceptions of the dominant group do not always reflect reality and that, in fact, there are a number of discrepencies between what it is said smiths do and what they actually do (pp. 148-51). For example, it is generally said that the smith's craft is restricted to access by particular clans and is passed on from father to son. For an outsider to take up the craft would mean certain supernaturally sanctioned death.

Although smiths are consistently members of minority clans, in reality the craft is not confined to particular clans, and with the smith's blessing, it is possible for an outsider to learn the craft (pp. 75, 103-105). On the basis of the situation among the Kalenjin, Coy suggests that assertions of clan-relatedness among smiths in other societies are probably an 'ideal' expression.

Beliefs about marriage with smiths are subject to similar contradictions. It is commonly believed that marriage to smiths is inauspicious because they possess attributes that make them poor marriage prospects. In spite of this ideological reinforcement, however, the objective reality is that Kalenjin women do marry smiths (pp. 142-48).

Smiths themselves actively reinforce the attitudes held about them by the larger population.

> The smiths engage in purposeful efforts to surround their craft with secrecy, mystery, and supernaturalism in order to maintain effective monopolies over the production of iron goods in their exclusive market area. Restrictions placed on the recruitment of new smiths limit the proliferation of craftsmen, further reinforcing economic monopoly and related social control... This results in specific social status attributions on the part of the non-craftsmen as seen in... economic/ecological complexes... (Coy, 1982:iv; see also p. 69)

What is described by many early studies as the 'despised' status of the smith, then, is probably only the surface ideology manipulated by craftpersons to their own ends (p. 14). The common explanation for the supernatural association of smiths and ironworking—that ironworking is an intrinsically mysterious and magical process—is perhaps to some extent true, but without some effort on the part of smiths to sanction the mysterious nature of their work, the mystery would no longer prevail (p. 30).

The Somali. Herbert S. Lewis has noted that 'virtually every Ethiopian Cushitic- or Semitic-speaking society for which evidence exists contains within it at least one endogamous group of hereditary occupational specialists' (1970:183). This characterization holds true for the Somali of Somalia and

Ethiopia, among both pastoral and agricultural peoples and both societies that are basically egalitarian and those that are highly centralized. The African Horn proper (comprising Somalia, Southeastern Ethiopia, and Northeastern Kenya) is a desert-like dry woodland with low and unreliable rainfall (Kesby, 1977:8, 15). In this area, cultivation is largely confined to the river valleys and is carried out with the hoe, as is typical of most of Africa. Livestock (camels, sheep, and goats), however, assume greater importance (Kesby, 1977:24). Over most of the region range nomadic pastoralists such as the Somali and Galla, who either grow no crops at all or occasionally plant crops in favorable situations. There are typically no kings or centralized governments, although there is some degree of specialization in the form of endogamous groups of hunters and smiths, who are clients to both pastoralists and cultivators (Kesby, 1977:24, 52-64).

Among the segmentary pastoral nomadic Somali (see I. M. Lewis, 1955; 1961), smiths (Tumal) and hunters are quite distinct from other Somali (Huntingford, 1931:264; I. M. Lewis, 1961:14; H. S. Lewis, 1970:183). They are distinguished from 'noble' Somali by their practice of specialist crafts, which Somali pastoralists abhor. They are segmented into small lineages on the Somali pattern and are typically attached in servile status to various Somali lineages. In addition to a restriction on intermarriage with the Somali, Tumal are also excluded from full participation in Somali social relations.

The Galla. A similar social status applies to smiths among the agricultural peoples of southern and southwestern Ethiopia. Among the ethnic groups of southern Ethiopia, the largest is the Galla. There are many Galla-speaking societies, some pastoral and egalitarian and others agricultural and monarchical (H. S. Lewis, 1965:xiii-xiv; 1970:163).[1] In the Galla kingdom of Jimna Abba Jifar, a centralized monarchy, almost all artisans and craftspersons form endogamous marginal

---

1 The empire of Ethiopia as it exists today is an amalgamation of the ancient kingdom of Abyssinia and a number of other ethnic groups, tribes, and kingdoms (H. S. Lewis, 1965:xiii; see also Kesby, 1977; Quirin, 1977).

groups, as in most of Ethiopia and Somalia (see H. S. Lewis, 1965:53, 97; 1970). Among these are groups of smiths, potters, tanners, weavers, and beekeepers. Although they engage in agriculture (in spite of the fact that the Galla say it is forbidden) and do not live in separate regions, their members are considered to be ritually impure, and anyone who comes in contact with them is in danger of being polluted. As a rule, smiths are believed to be associated with the supernatural and as such are considered to be bearers of the evil-eye, are often suspected of being were-hyenas, and are believed to be capable of sorcery, magic, and the preparation of efficacious charms.

The marginality of smiths and other craftspersons is also expressed socially. They are forbidden to intermarry with or enter the homes of non-artisans, they are not allowed to own land, and they are normally not allowed to participate in the regular political and judicial life of the larger society.

The Gurage. An almost identical situation obtains among the Gurage, a Semitic speaking people of southwestern Ethiopia (see Shack, 1964; 1966), although they are segmentary societies lacking centralized leadership. The marginal occupational groups among the Gurage are called Fuga, and all of the distinguishing features of the similar Galla groups are present (see Shack, 1964; 1966:8-12). However, the Fuga are also ritual specialists and play an important role in Gurage religion, particularly in rites of passage.[1]

The Fuga perform circumcisions, prepare and dispense ritually prepared 'medicines', distribute amulets, and collect fees for services rendered by the religious dignitaries for whom they are agents. Their principal ritual functions, however, are performed in the rites of passage for Gurage girls and the religious association connected with these rites. They are also responsible for leading the annual rituals for the major deities.

Both men and women among the Fuga participate in important religious activities, particularly in the two major

---

[1] The Konso of southwestern Ethiopia are very similar to the Gurage in conferring ritual responsibilities on the *hauda*, the Konso marginal craft groups. See Hallpike, 1968.

Gurage cults, the annual Cešt festival honoring the sky-god Waq for men and the annual Dämwamwit festival for women (see Shack, 1966:172-98). The principal religious specialists in the male cult are female, and those of the female cult are male. Aside from these specialists, no persons of the opposite sex are allowed to take part in these festivals. Other ritual specialists are Fuga women and men. In the Cešt cult, Fuga women act as intermediaries between Gurage men and their chief priestess, and in the Dämwamwit cult, Fuga men mediate between Gurage women and the male representative. Beyond this important role, the Fuga ritual agents are responsible for organizing and regulating ritual activities. These two major Gurage cults mirror the conflict between men and women in Gurage society and through ritual are able to bring about temporary resolution. Because Fuga are marginal individuals, they are in a position to mediate this conflict manifest in the polar opposition of the sexes.

The Dime. Among the Dime of southwestern Ethiopia, who practice slash and burn agriculture on extensive terraces, D. M. Todd (1977) distinguishes seven 'castes' ranked hierarchically according to considerations of purity, non-purity, and impurity. The chief and priest castes are pure, the commoners non-pure, and the ritual servants, hunters, smiths, and tanners are impure. Ideologically, each of these 'castes' is endogamous. The largest impure group is that of the smiths. The usual social prohibitions already discussed also obtain for Dime smiths. They do not own land or cattle, are prohibited from setting foot on farmland, and cannot eat or drink with ordinary Dime or enter their homes. These prohibitions apply because the smith himself, his house, and his personal effects are considered to be polluting. The ritual system of the Dime defines the impure as parasites on the country, depleting its resources but playing no part in their renewal.

The Beta Israel (Falasha). In the highland regions of northern Ethiopia are scattered marginal groups of people called Falasha by the dominant Amhara and Tigre peoples. The economy in the three sub-regions occupied by the Amhara, Tigre, and Falasha (highlands, plateau, and lowlands) is based on mixed plow cultivation of cereal and animal husbandry (see Quirin, 1977:1-6). Although the development of the relationship between the dominant Amhara and Tigre and the marginal Falasha is historically complex (see Quirin, 1977), today the Falasha are physically, linguistically, and culturally indistinguishable from the Amhara and Tigre among whom they live. However, Falasha differ in significant ways from the dominant groups. They are primarily known as artisans, especially ironsmiths, potters, and weavers.[1] They possess many of the characteristics that have been cited for other marginal Ethiopian groups—traditionally they do not own land, they live in either separate villages interspersed among those of the Amhara and Tigre or in separate quarters of Amhara and Tigre towns, they do not intermarry with the Amhara and Tigre, and in general they are socially shunned. They are a people who have been institutionally, but not socially, incorporated into the dominant society. Hence, they occupy a social position both inside and outside of the dominant society, that is, they are marginal (see Quirin, 1977:9-31; Shack, 1974:51-55).

But the Falasha are distinctive in one way that is quite unique. In contrast to the dominant Ethiopian Orthodox Christianity, the Falasha practice a syncretistic religion that is comprised predominantly of an ancient form of Judaism, combined with some elements of Ethiopian Orthodox Christianity.[2] The Falasha refer to themselves as 'Beta Israel' and trace their origins back to ancient Israel. According to one tradition, the Beta Israel migrated to Ethiopia with Menelik I, the alleged son of Solomon and the Queen of Sheba. Other

---

[1] Although they claim to have been artisans since their alleged origins in ancient Israel, the Falasha have not always been artisans. Occupations such as ironsmith and probably potter and weaver were adopted in the fifteenth century CE (Quirin, 1977:68).

[2] On Falasha religion, see Quirin, 1977:219-32; Shack, 1974:62-64; Leslau, 1979. For a translation of Falasha sacred texts, see Leslau, 1979. The Falasha are not the only Ethiopian peoples who practice an ancient form of Hebraic religion. The related Qemant, for example, follow similar religious traditions (see Gamst, 1984). In contrast to the Falasha, however, the Qemant are farmers rather than artisans and, like the Amhara and Tigre, fear the Falasha as possessors of *buda*, the 'evil-eye'.

2. Iron Technology and Symbolism 81

traditions hold that they are descended from a group of Jews who left Egypt at the time of the exodus or who entered Ethiopia following the destruction of the first or second temple. Most scholars, however, suggest that they are descended from a segment of the indigenous Agau population that was converted to Judaism, possibly by the Jews of Elephantine or Yemen sometime in the first centuries CE (Shack, 1974:52, 62; Leslau, 1979:xlii-xliii). The antiquity of the Beta Israel religious traditions is presumed on the basis of their religious literature, for which the chief sources are the Hebrew Bible and the Book of Jubilees, not the Talmud.

Historically, the religious leaders of the Beta Israel attempted to maintain the purity of their people by self-imposed religious isolation. Today the marginality of these people is reinforced by both the Beta Israel themselves and by the dominant groups who call them Falasha. There are very clear rules regulating social interaction between the two groups which are reinforced by sanctions imposed by each side (Quirin, 1977:218). The Beta Israel are concerned with maintaining their own purity and consider contact with others to be polluting. Some Ethiopians call them 'do not touch me' (Leslau, 1979:xl). The dominant groups, on the other hand, fear the Beta Israel and avoid them except for the necessary exchange of goods in the market place.

Much of the fear exhibited by non-Beta Israel groups is reinforced by the belief that the Beta Israel are possessed by the *buda* or 'evil-eye' (see Quirin, 1977:213-16; Reminick, 1974). A *buda* is considered to be both the spirit that possesses a person and the person who is capable of causing the spirit to possess another individual. It is believed that the *buda* turns into a hyena at night and roams about digging up graves and devouring corpses. During the day, a *buda* is capable of possessing another person and turning him or her into a hyena, a donkey, or some other animal or object. Death or illness can also be caused by a *buda* who enters into a person's body and consumes his or her blood or entrails.

James Quirin (1977:215-16) suggests that the roots of this attitude may lie in the mystery surrounding the processes of transforming earth into clay and 'rock' into iron in a technologically simple society, the assumption being that the craftspersons have supernatural assistance. The social implications in Amhara society, according to Quirin, are that the *buda* phenomenon has functioned to maintain social solidarity during times of crisis and to enable threats of rivalry to be projected outward, thereby strengthening internal social and psychological solidarity (cf. Reminick, 1974).

Analysis and Interpretation

> Knowledge is transmitted by traditional art through its symbolism, its correspondence with cosmic laws, its techniques, and even the means whereby it is taught through the traditional craft guilds which in various traditional civilizations have combined technical training in the crafts with spiritual instruction. (Nasr, 1981:258)

This survey of iron technology in traditional African societies raises a number of questions that deserve analysis in terms of how and why iron technology is appropriated and translated into symbols that are essential elements in cultural systems of meaning. In the analysis that follows I consider the following questions: 1. How are these symbols related to the process of ironworking and the physical characteristics of iron? 2. How can the varied symbols associated with iron technology be classified according to the definitions of anthropologists? 3. How is the symbolic role of the smith related to the symbol system? 4. What is the symbolic role of the smith in society, myth, and ritual? 5. How is the symbolic role of the smith interrelated with and reinforced by his position in the social structure and the attitudes directed toward him? 6. What is the symbolic role of the smith's tools? 7. What is the significance of the sexual imagery associated with ironworking? 8. What is the primary social function of these symbols?

Essential to interpreting the complex cultural, religious, and social symbols associated with iron technology in African societies is an understanding of the nature of the craft itself and the transformation that is effected by means of the complex smelting and forging processes (see Chapters 3 and 4). It is useful to draw an analogy between the ironworking process and the transformation that is effected when the process is brought to a successful conclusion and the processual struc-

2. Iron Technology and Symbolism

ture of rites of passage (on rites of passage see, e.g., van Gennep, 1960 and Turner 1969). Rites of passage mediate transitions in space, social status, social position, or age. There are three phases in the processual structure of these rites: separation, margin (limen), and aggregation (in van Gennep's terminology the preliminal, liminal, and post-liminal stages). In a social setting, separation consists of the symbolic detachment of an individual or group from an earlier fixed point in the social structure or from a particular set of social conditions (a 'state'). It is a kind of symbolic 'death' in preparation for the ritual transformation. The marginal or liminal phase marks the entrance into a cultural realm that has few of the attributes of the past or forthcoming phase, a move from structure to anti-structure. The participants in the ritual are 'betwixt and between', and their characteristics are ambiguous (see Turner, 1979). For example, symbolically, they are neither living nor dead, and they have no status, property, or position in the kinship system. It is during this phase that reorientation and transformation are undergone and the initiates are prepared for re-entry into society in a transformed state. In the third phase of the process, the initiates are reincorporated into the normal structure of society, whereby a symbolic 'rebirth' represents their change in status.

A processual structure similar to that in rites of passage can be identified for the complex and mysterious technological process of iron production. This process corresponds in structure as follows: In the preliminal phase, the iron ore is a relatively soft metal. When the ore is introduced into the furnace, it is separated from its previous state and moves into the liminal or marginal phase during which it is transformed by the fire with the assistance of the smith and the smith's tools. As it undergoes the transformation, it possesses neither its previous attributes nor those it will ultimately acquire. It is 'betwixt and between'. It is during this crucial phase that it is 'reoriented' through carburization (see Chapter 4) and forging and is prepared to move into a higher state as a strong metal superior to that which entered into the process. By the end of the process, the substance is 'reborn'. It takes on a new set of characteristics that allow for its use in the form of tools and weapons. In this state iron is recognized for its significant social and economic contributions to maintaining life in the community. In the form of tools it contributes to providing both food and shelter. In the form of weapons it contributes to providing food (hunting) and to protecting the community from internal and external disturbances (e.g., warfare).

This model establishes a frame of reference for interpreting the varied symbols associated with the metal iron and the tools, smithy, and smith which are all instrumental in facilitating its transformation. While focusing my analysis on the mysterious and complex process that facilitates transformation, I am fully aware of the argument that this explanation is too 'simplistic' in its own right, especially for illuminating the social status of the smith. Those who have considered in detail the social roles and statuses of smiths (e.g., Coy, 1982; Vaughan, 1973; cf. Margarido and Wasserman, 1972) caution against making simplistic assumptions based on the 'magical' nature of the technological process and emphasize, rather, that the explanation lies in the socioeconomic position of the smith (or other craftspersons) vis-à-vis the primary economic activities of the larger community (e.g., farming or cattle-raising). I agree that this is an essential consideration. However, one factor cannot necessarily be distinguished as *the* primary causal factor in considering the social perceptions, beliefs, and attitudes that tend to be associated with the smith. The symbols that arise from one (the mystery and transformation) reinforce those that arise from the other (the socioeconomic role of the smith and his work) and vice versa. To assert that one is primary and the other secondary throws us into the realm of the chicken vs the egg dilemma.

I use as a starting point Fernandez's assertion that forge imagery functions as a *key symbol* in Bwiti rituals and sermons (1966:61-62). In an article on key symbols, Sherry Ortner (1973) distinguishes two basic types which operate at many different levels: summarizing symbols and elaborating symbols (cf. Foster, 1980). According to her classification, summarizing symbols sum up, express, and represent for individuals in a society in an emotionally powerful and relatively undifferentiated way what the system means to them. They operate to compound and synthesize a complex system of ideas (1973:1339-40). Elaborating symbols, on the other hand, serve as 'vehicles for sorting out complex and undifferentiated feelings and ideas, making them comprehensible to oneself, communicable to others, and translatable into orderly action' (p. 1340). These symbols are essentially analytical and are accorded key status on the basis of their capacity to *order experience*. They can be identified primarily by their recurrence in cultural behavior or cultural symbolic systems.[1]

Ortner further identifies two modes through which symbols can be viewed as having elaborating power (p. 1340). The first is the conceptual mode in which symbols are valued as a source of categories for conceptualizing, encoding, and expressing the ordering of the world, as a means of orienting oneself in the world, and as a way of understanding the relationships of parts in a whole. The second mode is related more to action. In this mode symbols are valued as implying mechanisms for successful social action and therefore provide a means of strategy. One of the primary characteristics of symbols with conceptual elaborating power is the use of metaphors as a mechanism of communication. They are, therefore, sometimes referred to as 'root metaphors'. Ortner proposes that a society recognizes that many aspects of human and social experience can be likened to and illuminated by comparison with this type of symbol. Unlike signs or signals, in metaphoric symbols the human imagination is used to associate two entities or sets of entities, to translate experience from one domain to another by virtue of a common factor or factors that can be generalized from the experiences in the two domains, either material or abstract, that ordinarily belong to quite different contexts (see, e.g., Leach, 1976:39; Fernandez, 1986:12, 37; cf. Laughlin and Stephens, 1980). The symbol, then, provides a set of categories (a metaphor) for conceptualizing other aspects of human experience. More specifically, a root metaphor allows for conceptualizing and expressing the interrelationships among various phenomena by analogy to the interrelations among the parts of the root

---

1 Similar distinctions are made in other analyses of symbols. For example, Fernandez's (1977) textual and structural metaphors and Sapir's (1977) internal and external metaphors are roughly equivalent to Ortner's summarizing and elaborating symbols.

metaphor. Although often there is no literal connection between the symbol and its referent, that is, no 'natural' link, it is nevertheless possible to identify a formal congruence of logical structure between them. The congruence is determined by factors specific to the communities for which the symbol operates (Firth, 1973:70-71). By virtue of the fact that symbols can pick up meaning from many contexts and come to represent many things (Fernandez, 1986:30-31) and that many aspects of experience can be likened to a 'root metaphor', it provides a kind of unifying cultural orientation (Ortner, 1973:1341).

A similar evaluation of symbols in ritual contexts is represented in the work of Victor Turner. Victor Turner's 'dominant' symbols are similar in definition to Ortner's 'key' symbols, as are his definitions of the two basic subtypes—condensation symbols and referential symbols (Ortner's summarizing symbols and elaborating symbols respectively). Referential symbols are cognitive in nature and serve as economical devices for purposes of reference. Dominant symbols can be identified by virtue of their appearance in many ritual contexts, sometimes presiding over the whole procedure and sometimes over particular phases. The meaning content of these symbols possesses a high degree of constancy and consistency throughout the total symbolic system, and because of their properties they are readily analyzeable in a cultural frame of reference (Turner, 1967:29-31).

An analogy has been drawn above between the processes of ironworking and rites of passage. If we recognize the *transformation* that occurs in both of these processes as of central importance, we can further postulate that the analogy, whether made consciously or unconsciously,[1] is also made by peoples in the communities in which iron technology plays a significant technological and economic role. Furthermore, I propose that symbols associated with ironworking function primarily as 'elaborating' or 'referential' symbols of the

---

1 As used here, conscious and unconscious metaphorical analogies are understood to be tacit or implicit. In the former case, individuals are able to make this implicit knowledge explicit. In the latter, they are not able to make it explicit (Dan Sperber's 'implicit knowledge' vs 'unconscious knowledge'; see Sperber, 1974:17-50).

2. Iron Technology and Symbolism

'structural' type (see Fernandez, 1977; 1986:12) for which the translation between realms is based on some structural similarity of the relationship of parts in a whole. As such, they are essentially conceptualized in reference to the transformation the metal iron is known to undergo when it is smelted and forged, in addition to the interrelationship of the various elements that are instrumental in facilitating the transformation. In the following analysis, I first consider how the various elements involved in the process operate on a symbolic level, and then evaluate how the entire process is conceived as a 'root metaphor' as represented most clearly in the Bwiti cult of the Fang.

The ironsmith plays the most essential role in effecting the technological transformation of iron. It is the smith who takes what is 'potential' in the iron ore and makes it 'actual' through smelting it and giving it the form of tools and weapons. He is, in a sense, imitating the formation of cosmos out of chaos (cf. Burckhardt, 1967:45). It is through his intervention and mediation that it is possible for the transformation to occur. The smith's broader mythical, religious, social, and political roles are illuminated by drawing an analogy between his role as a craftsperson and the role of ritual specialists in rites of passage. In the rituals directly associated with mining and working iron, for example, there is commonly an emphasis on ritual purity and correct ritual procedures.[1] In an analogous social or religious rite, those who participate in facilitating the ritual passage must also undergo ritual purification. By virtue of his function as *mediator* in the 'mysterious' transformation of iron, the smith is also assigned a number of other quite varied roles in which he also functions as a mediator. In other words, his role as a craftsperson serves as a cognitive or analytical model, as a metaphor, for mediating relationships.

---

[1] There are a number of studies that give detailed accounts of the technological process and rituals associated with this process in African societies. See, e.g., Brown, 1971; Wise, 1958; Cline, 1937; Jeffreys, 1952; Eliade, 1978:53-64; Gardi, 1969:16-20; Kense, 1983; Tylecote, 1965; Fagg, 1952; Sasoon, 1964; Adéníji, 1977; van der Merwe and Avery, 1987.

The mediator has been identified as an essential element in myths (see, e.g., Lévi-Strauss, 1963:206-31; Leach, 1969).

> In every myth system we will find a persistent sequence of binary discriminations as between human/superhuman, mortal/immortal, male/female, legitimate/illegitimate, good/bad... followed by a 'mediation' of the paired categories thus distinguished. (Leach, 1969:11)

It is the role of mediator that is played in West African myths by the first smith or the iron god. Furthermore, myths themselves often refer to crucial points of passage or transition in the lives of individuals or groups (Turner, 1974:254). The smith's role is essential to effecting the transformations portrayed in myths. In his mythological role as culture- or civilizing-hero, he serves as a facilitator of the formation of order out of chaos between the first aborted creation and the present world; as both a descendant of the gods and the first human ancestor, he mediates between the heavenly sphere and the earthly sphere and transmits to humans crucial knowledge associated with social organization, agriculture, animal domestication, technology, and so on; his abode is both in heaven and on or under the earth, and he sometimes serves as a link between the living and the dead; he is believed to be the one who can clear the way ('mediate') in times of difficulty and make it possible to attain material and spiritual prosperity; and he is able to maintain a balance between justice in the divine and human spheres and resolve the internal and external controversies of the community. Sometimes conceived as having been created from the umbilical cord or blood from the testicles of the great water spirits (portions of the body that mediate life and nourishment), the mythological smith is the mediator *par excellence*.

The religious, social, and political roles attributed to the smith can also be understood in relation to his mediating function in the process of ironworking. By virtue of his ritual function in the technological 'rite of passage', he is well-suited to play the same role in other ritual functions, thus his central role in many initiation rites. This role is reinforced by the belief that he possesses special spiritual knowledge, whether positive or negative. For the same reasons the smith is often recog-

2. Iron Technology and Symbolism

nized as a mediator in settling disputes and as an upholder of social justice and harmony. He is a significant actor in what Turner calls 'social dramas' (see Turner, 1974). All of these offices can be related to his role as craftsperson in facilitating the 'death' and 'rebirth' of the material he works in the smelting and forging processes.

The ambivalent attitudes expressed about ironsmiths in the social sphere are also implicit in the mythological role attributed the first smith or iron god. As mediators, ironsmiths are individuals who are marginal, who 'exist' on the boundaries. For example, as both first ancestor and divine being, the first smith does not belong fully to either the earthly or the heavenly realms. He is 'betwixt and between', to use Turner's phrase. In his analysis of the structure of myth Edmund Leach notes:

> 'Mediation'... [of binary discriminations] is always achieved by introducing a third category which is 'abnormal' or 'anomalous' in terms of ordinary 'rational' categories. Thus myths are full of fabulous monsters, incarnate gods, virgin mothers. This middle ground is abnormal, nonnatural, holy. It is typically the focus of all taboo. (1969:11)

The marginality of smiths and their families is reinforced by the fact that they are marginal in the economic realm. As individuals whose responsibilities lie in providing tools and weapons to their communities, they do not participate fully in the primary economic activities of their communities, whether they be farming or pastoralist. Even in societies in which smiths are honored, they are not included among those who are considered 'noble' by virtue of their role as farmers. Smiths, then, are socially located on the boundaries or margins of their communities. Thus, the typical social separation of smiths and their families, both socially and spatially, can also be understood in light of the craft with which they are so closely identified. It is precisely their role as smiths, as marginal mediators in many realms, that sets them apart from the rest of society.

Victor Turner has noted the tendency for artisans to be included among peoples such as prophets, shamans, priests, hippies, Gypsies, court jesters, and others who are often considered to be structurally inferior or 'marginal' in society (1969:96ff.; 1974:231-33). Not only do groups of marginal peoples tend to play major roles in myths and popular tales as representatives or expressions of universal human values, but they also tend to function socially as arbiters in disputes, as representatives of what Turner calls 'communitas', as a kind of check on the normative system of bounded, structured, particularistic groups.

> A fairly regular connection is maintained between liminality, structural inferiority, lowermost status, and structural outsidership on the one hand, and on the other, such universal human values as peace and harmony between all humans, fertility, health of mind and body, universal justice, comradeship and brotherhood, equality before God, the law, or the life force of men and women, young and old, and persons of all races and ethnic groups. (Turner, 1969:134)

The socially marginal position traditionally associated with the smith, then, is closely related to and connected with his function as mediator. It is no wonder, therefore, that the smith is so often accorded the role of judge, arbiter of disputes, mediator between heaven and earth in his ritual functions, and so on.

As ritual specialists, smiths specialize in activities that are directly associated with other types of margins. An interesting example is the role smiths play in the bodily 'mutilation' that is often carried out in rites of passage to symbolize passage into a new state. Edmund Leach suggests that these physical symbols are also associated with boundaries:

> Most mutilations involve a removal of a part of the body boundary—foreskin, clitoris, hair, teeth... and the rite of removal is very commonly seen as one of purification. The logic of the situation here is related to... the ambiguity of boundaries and their association with taboo. (1976:61)

We have yet to resolve the problem so often raised in the literature on African smiths, that of the distinction between those who are 'honored' within their communities and those who are 'despised'. The marginality of the smith also enters into this dichotomy in attribution of social status. Edmund Leach (1976:33-36) has noted that markers of spatial and

2. Iron Technology and Symbolism

temporal boundaries are implicitly ambiguous and are a source of conflict and anxiety. Boundaries separate zones that are *normal, time-bound, clear-cut, central*, and *secular*, but the markers that actually serve as boundaries are *abnormal, timeless, ambiguous, at the edge, sacred*. He has made a similar argument in his interpretation of mediating categories in myth (1969:11). Not only are these boundary markers or mediating categories perceived as sacred or holy, but, because of the ambiguity and ambivalence associated with that which is abnormal or un-natural, they are also taboo. Although Leach's discussion of boundaries focuses on time and space, it applies equally to social margins.

But marginality, as Mary Douglas has made so clear (1966; 1975:47-59), is often also identified with pollution and impurity. According to Douglas, all margins, including marginal social states, the edges of all boundaries that are used in organizing social experience, are treated as dangerous and polluting (1975:56). Margins are associated with danger and are regarded as sources of power. The social status of marginal, socially ambiguous individuals, of which there are many variant types, reflects this association of marginality and power.

> Where the social system requires people to hold dangerously ambiguous roles, these persons are credited with uncontrolled, unconscious, dangerous, disapproved powers—such as witchcraft and the evil-eye. (1966:99)

> Witches for example are the social equivalent of beetles and spiders who live in the cracks of the walls and wainscoting. They attract the fears and dislikes which other ambiguities and contradictions attract in other thought structures, and the kind of powers attributed to them symbolise their ambiguous, inarticulate status. (1966:102)

The opposing interpretations of Leach and Douglas suggest that there is a fine line separating 1. beliefs that margins are associated with that which is holy and 2. beliefs that margins are associated with impurity and pollution. Both realms, in fact, are the target of taboos. We see here the ambiguity of distinguishing between the sacred and the impure that was noted a century ago by William Robertson Smith (1889; published in 1894) and later by James G. Frazer (1981

[1890]:169-72) and Emil Durkheim (1965 [1915]). In West African societies, where smiths are feared but tend to be honored, their social status appears to reflect an emphasis on the sacredness associated with margins, whereas in East African and African Horn societies, where smiths tend to be 'despised', their social status reflects an emphasis on the marginal as polluting. In the latter, cultural intolerance of ambiguity is expressed by avoidance and discrimination. The difference may have to do with the degree to which the power structure in a society is articulated. Douglas suggests that where a social system is well articulated, articulate powers are vested in the points of authority, whereas where the social system is ill-articulated, inarticulate powers are vested in those who are a source of disorder (1966:99). It is possible, therefore, that smiths in West African society are more fully integrated into the social system and consequently are more closely associated with 'articulate' controllable power, and that smiths in East African societies, not well integrated into the social system, are associated with 'inarticulate' uncontrollable power.

We must not, however, overlook the fact that even in societies in which smiths are honored some type of avoidance and discrimination is typical. Rules of endogamy and rules against their attaining roles of direct leadership are examples. Ambivalence remains a characteristic attitude toward ironsmiths whether they are feared and honored or feared and despised.

The symbols associated with the smith's tools and iron itself also express the concept of mediation. They typically serve as vehicles by which to understand such oppositional relationships as heaven/earth, living/dead, justice/injustice, male/female. They are essential actors in the dramatic transformation of iron as it 'dies' and is 'reborn' in the forging process. The smithy is thus conceived spatially as the place where sacred and profane meet, as a spatial mediator between heaven and earth. When one enters a smithy, one is entering 'sacred space'. Therefore, throughout traditional Africa it is often a place of worship, where the ground is sacred and one enters barefoot to guard against introducing impurity. It is a place of peace and often a place of refuge, and connected with it are notions of fecundity, life, and liberty (Zahan, 1979:30);

thus the designation of the smithy as temple or as the place where oaths are taken or judgment rendered. The location of the smithy in most African societies also symbolizes the marginal, and thus mediatory, character of the smith's craft. Without the necessary tools the technological transformation would likewise not be successful. The smith's tools assist him in his role as mediator and therefore take on similar symbolic qualities—oaths are sworn on them, they deliver justice when justice is called for, they have the ability to calm people down, they assist in communication with the dead, they protect the defenseless against those who would harm them. And by virtue of its having undergone the transformation itself, iron takes on these same symbolic referents in addition to those representing power, prestige, status, and strength, derived from the qualities it attains upon 'rebirth' from the forge.

An especially strong image of the symbolic mediation performed by iron is represented in the Ibo *mbari* ritual where it is used as a bridge from the structure of the preliminal phase of the ritual into the anti-structure of the liminal phase. Because iron is known to have undergone a similar transition, it serves as a metaphor, as a vehicle, by which it is possible to express the transition that occurs in this part of the ceremony. During the liminal phase iron, in the form of a staff, identifies the initiates with the gods.

These symbolic representations of iron technology are supplemented and clarified by the sexual imagery that is attached to them. Mary Douglas has shown that human physiology can often serve as a model for social, cosmic, and religious ideas (e.g., 1970), and Victor Turner has noted that the body as a microcosm of the universe is a variant of the widely distributed initiation theme (1979:241). In the Dogon myth of creation, for example, both the granary and the primal smithy are endowed with human attributes, and both are believed to represent the social and cosmic order. Sexual imagery also helps to clarify how iron is 'born' in the technological process that creates it (see Eliade, 1978:34-42). The hammer and bellows, for example, representing the male role in procreation, are said to impregnate the furnace, that is, the womb in which the final product is formed. This type of sexual imagery is clearly represented by the Fang portrayal of the creation of human beings by using forge imagery.

In addition to this cosmic dimension which is metaphorically represented through forge imagery are, as Fernandez has indicated, a number of social dimensions. Because of the characteristic 'multivocality' of ritual symbols, that is, their susceptibility to many meanings (see, e.g., Turner, 1969; 1973; 1979; Firth, 1973:81), it is possible for them to condense a number of references all at once. There is also a tendency for the referents of ritual symbols to polarize between physiological phenomena and a 'normative' or 'ideological' pole of meaning which can refer to either values or principles of organization (Fernandez, 1966:61-62; cf. Turner, 1969:52-53; 1974:55; 1979:237). Thus it is possible, for example, for forge imagery to represent what the Fang have lost and what they need to regain, that is, it mediates between the past traditional way of life and the present modern way of life, the relationship between males and females in Fang society, and social values all at one time. It is also significant that the sermon in the Bwiti ritual, in which forge imagery plays a dominant role, functions as a bridge between the two major phases of the ritual drama.

The primary function of symbols associated with ironworking in Africa, then, is that of mediation. They operate as models, as metaphors, or as 'storage bins' of information for understanding and expressing beliefs about cosmologies, values, and cultural axioms. They serve as concrete examples of the more abstract social and ritual transitions, the relationship between structure and anti-structure, between male and female, between heaven and earth, between divine and human, between justice and injustice, between past and present, and so on. On the basis of their capacity as key symbols to order experience, they function as 'vehicles for sorting out complex and undifferentiated feelings and ideas, making them comprehensible to oneself, communicable to others, and translatable into orderly action' (Ortner, 1973:1340).

The relevance of this analysis of African symbol systems to interpreting the symbolic representation of ironworking in the Hebrew Bible is explicated in Chapter 5. First, it is necessary to set the stage for evaluating the Israelite attitudes

2. Iron Technology and Symbolism 95

toward iron technology as they are represented in the Hebrew Bible. Chapter 3 lays out the archaeological and textual information for the development of iron technology in the ancient Near East before the advent of the Iron Age. Chapter 4 relates the development and adoption of iron technology in Iron Age I Palestine to the transition from tribal organization to statehood in ancient Israel.

Chapter 3

BACKGROUND TO THE DEVELOPMENT OF IRON TECHNOLOGY IN THE ANCIENT NEAR EAST

Introduction

> The study of the scientific background to the development of metallurgy adds an objective dimension to the reconstruction of ancient systems—a tangible reflection of human desires and ways of life. (Wheeler and Maddin, 1980:125)

The historical background of the development of iron technology in the ancient Near East is as yet little understood. Even less clear is the impact that the transition from a bronze- to an iron-based metal technology had in the social, political, economic, and religious spheres of ancient Near Eastern culture. Because the development of metallurgy itself was such a slow process, we must guard against exaggerating its impact on the development of ancient societies. But we can assert with some confidence that it did have a profound influence. It has been recognized as a crucial factor in the process of early urbanization and the rise of civilization, accompanied and stimulated by such developments as writing, mathematics, and the calendar. Although it is neither the prime nor the most important factor, its impact has been compared to other sciences that contributed to the rapid evolution of civilization and the centralized state, and it is recognized as having contributed significantly to the technological and economic character of early urban life (e.g., Forbes, 1971:5-7; Muhly, 1980:26). Although less directly, metallurgy's impact was also felt in the political, social, and religious spheres of culture. And as one of many interacting elements in urban culture, the acceptance and use of metals were also *determined* by a combination of social, economic, technological, political, and religious factors and by the ecology of the ancient Near East.

In a recent study based on evidence from Iranian sites, Dennis Heskel and Carl Lamberg-Karlovski (1980:230) note that 'the absence of systematic correlations between the development of metallurgy and the changes in other aspects of the cultural system has been a serious drawback in previous research on metallurgical development'. They emphasize, in opposition to materialist or economic determinist theories, that it is not technological innovations themselves that lead to rapid and major changes in social institutions. Rather, it is the social milieu into which the innovations are introduced that is the background of the causes of such change. Based on both ethnographic studies of egalitarian societies and material evidence from Iranian archaeological sites, Heskel and Lamberg-Karlovski conclude that a technological innovation must be accepted by the society into which it is introduced before it can have any effect on that society. As we have seen in Chapters 1 and 2 of this study, the introduction of new technologies is often accompanied by suspicion and ambivalence on the part of a society's members, an ambivalence that is often maintained for an extensive period of time once the innovation has been accepted and established. A close examination of ethnographic studies, for example, reveals that acceptance of an innovation in an egalitarian society depends on its acceptance by the society's members, especially those who are more respected because of wealth, age, or wisdom. Individuals of high status tend to control the acceptance or rejection of technological innovations. Social changes in the form of wealth and social-status separation and the establishment of an elite group result from the successful acceptance and continued production of the particular innovation (p. 261). In other words, it is not until it is socially determined that the innovation is acceptable that the door is open to the possibility of its contributing to social change. At Tepe Yahya in Iran, excavations have revealed that the introduction of technological changes in metallurgical production at that site did not lead to any immediate observable changes in the social system throughout the fourth millennium BCE (p. 262).

3. The Development of Iron Technology 99

Thus, a more adequate understanding of early iron technology and of the advent of the Iron Age must be sought with an awareness of all aspects of culture and their interrelationships; that is, attention must be given to developments in a broader context than isolated early occurrences of iron artifacts (Snodgrass, 1980:336). Theodore A. Wertime has noted:

> What stands out in this story of the complexities of the advent of iron amid a maze of other fire-using industries were the interconnectedness and massiveness of the thrust toward a literate, trading and communicating, road-building and seafaring, urban, pyrotechnologic civilization emerging in the Fertile Crescent and Eastern Mediterranean. (1980:9)

In addition to our caution against viewing the development of technology in general and iron technology in particular as isolated and independent processes, we must also guard against making definitive assertions on the basis of the available information. Problems in interpreting the information derive from: 1. the nature of the archaeological evidence for the numbers and distribution of iron artifacts; 2. the nature of the ancient literary information; and 3. the problematic interrelationship of the artifactual and literary evidence (see Waldbaum, 1978).

1. Although the tabulation of numbers and types of artifacts and their relative synchronic and diachronic distribution are the major means of determining when and where iron took precedence over bronze as the dominant metal used for domestic, agricultural, and military purposes, they are necessarily inaccurate. Absolute numbers of artifacts that are recovered in excavations are dependent on the intensity of archaeological activity at individual sites and in particular regions and on the publication of such artifacts (and/or access to unpublished materials). What can be ascertained about the synchronic and diachronic distribution of iron depends also on these limiting factors and on the types of sites excavated and the accuracy with which chronological levels are dated. Although published summaries of known iron finds from the

Near East are helpful,[1] their contents vary depending on the size of the areas considered and the times at which the studies were undertaken. Exact numbers of artifacts change constantly as new examples are added following excavation at both previously excavated and unexcavated sites. The Early Iron Age material from Palestine reviewed in Chapter 4 may present an especially distorted picture of iron usage because of both the lengthy and intensive archaeological interest in the area and the willingness of excavators and museum curators to make published and unpublished materials available to colleagues (Stech-Wheeler et al., 1981:246). An additional problem with working from summaries is that they often cite artifacts that are now considered to be of dubious date, context, or even attribution as iron (Waldbaum, 1980:69). In the summary of iron artifacts dating from the prehistoric through the Bronze Ages presented later in this chapter, I have depended on a number of these summaries, but have given primary consideration to those of more recent date (e.g., Waldbaum, 1978, 1980).[2]

Further contributing to the inaccuracy of the artifactual evidence are the tendencies for terrestrial iron to rust away[3] and for iron artifacts to deteriorate to the point that they often look more like lumps than artifacts (Stech-Wheeler et al., 1981:246). The former problem is especially acute for attempting to determine the relative values of bronze and iron since iron corrodes more readily than bronze. Pliny notes this characteristic of iron when he contrasts the strength of iron in the form of weapons with its short life: 'The foe of iron is the customary benevolence of nature which decrees that that which inflicts most loss on short-lived humanity shall be of all materials the most short-lived' (Pliny, *Nat. Hist.* 34.141).

---

1 See Waldbaum, 1980:91, n. 1, for a list of published summaries for the prehistoric and Bronze Ages and Waldbaum, 1978, for a summary of the Early Iron Age material.
2 Much of the information presented below is drawn from summaries that have already been published since it serves primarily as background material for the central concern of this study—the Early Iron Age and the biblical material.
3 Meteoric iron is more resistant to rust because of its nickel content. See, e.g., Forbes, 1972:208.

3. The Development of Iron Technology 101

However, rust is a very stable material that can be easily identified, and archaeologists today are more intentional than their predecessors about recording deposits of rust. But it is a problem that remains when considering the evidence from earlier excavations. What this all adds up to is that the abundance of any metal in the material record, especially iron, cannot be considered to be accurately representative of its relative utilization in earlier times.

2. The ancient literary evidence for the development and utilization of iron in the ancient Near East prior to the advent of a full-blown 'Iron Age' must also be approached with caution. For the texts that date from the Bronze Age, we must take into account the many problems that accompany interpretation and dating. These include such considerations as discerning the meanings of particular terms and their relative contextual meanings, in addition to the meanings and intentions behind the texts themselves. For most texts to be useful, they need first to be interpreted by historical-critical methods, though such methods yield only tentative, hypothetical results that need to be related to other types of evidence. Perhaps most frustrating is the fact that in most regions of the ancient Near East the adoption of iron technology coincides with a period of severe cultural recession in which literary records are temporarily deficient (Snodgrass, 1980:335). Because of this literary hiatus, it is not possible to appeal to textual evidence for information that might enlighten us about how and why iron technology developed during this critical period.

3. Finally, we must note the frustrating fact that the textual and artifactual remains do not always offer compatible evidence (Waldbaum, 1978:17; cf. Flanagan, 1988). Certain texts seem to imply a far greater degree of technological competence than the actual finds seem to warrant, although, as we have noted above, the known finds may not be accurately representative either. On the whole, most experts on ancient metallurgy view the material evidence as reflecting more clearly the actual situation and the textual information as somewhat misleading. The latter, however, is accepted as a useful supplement to the artifactual and scientific evidence

(see Waldbaum, 1978:17; Snodgrass, 1980:335; cf. Muhly et al., 1985).

Bronze, the Precursor to Iron

In order to paint an adequate picture of its complexities, the development of iron technology and its impact on the ancient world must be investigated in the context of the early development of metallurgy. Here, a brief overview of metallurgical developments, emphasizing copper and bronze technology, are presented to set the stage for unfolding the story of iron. This overview is necessarily brief and does not by any means cover the extent of the complexities involved in interpreting these earlier developments. It serves primarily as a point of orientation for presenting the evidence for the development of ironworking in the ancient Near East and as a reminder that the technological means for producing iron implements were not created in a vacuum but were interrelated with broader developments.

The ancient historian Pliny noted almost two millennia ago:

> We cannot but marvel at the fact that fire is necessary for almost every operation. By fire minerals are disintegrated and copper produced, in fire iron is born and by fire it is subdued, by fire gold is purified! (Pliny, *Nat. Hist.* 36.200)

Pliny's observation indicates the importance of pyrotechnology for the development of metallurgy. However, the history of metallurgy is older than the subjection of metals to the transformative powers of fire. Prior to this discovery, native metals such as copper, gold, silver, and meteoric iron were hammered or cut without the assistance of fire. The turning point in metallurgical and pyrotechnologic development was sometime during the sixth or fifth millennium BCE when ancient Near Eastern peoples were able to produce a temperature of 1083 degrees C., the casting temperature of copper, and learned that under the right chemical conditions earthly gangues or impurities could be removed from metals as slags and that ceramic products could be vitrified to glaze or glass (Wertime, 1973:875). By the late fourth millennium BCE, a polymetallic metallurgical technology had emerged. Before

3. The Development of Iron Technology   103

that time, copper predominated, although there is evidence of an occasional piece of worked lead or silver and even a rare bead of gold (Muhly, 1980:25).

By the advent of the third millennium BCE, all the metals known to ancient peoples were present in great variety and combination (Muhly, 1980:25), and metalsmiths were remarkably sophisticated in their knowledge of metallurgical techniques. They were aware of the effects on metals of hammering, annealing (heating the metal to a high temperature and allowing it to cool slowly), oxidizing, melting, and alloying (reducing the purity of a metal by mixing it with another element). They must also have understood the phenomena of the simple decomposition of ores, their reduction, double decomposition and metathesis (the exchange of impurities), and perhaps the miscibility and immiscibility of solutions (Wertime, 1964:1264).

The reasons behind the extraordinary developments in metallurgical techniques during the course of the third millennium BCE are not clear. Some interpreters have argued quite convincingly that developments in metallurgy were closely interrelated with those of the ancient potter and that the metallurgist and the potter utilized and gained inspiration from each other's products and wastes (e.g., Wertime, 1964:1265; 1980:8-9). Since metals or the oxides of metals were the primary materials used by the potter for coloring in pottery and glazes, the metallurgist may have learned much from the potter about the character and reducibility of oxides. And it was probably from the potter that the smith borrowed the crucible, the heat-resistant vessel in which molten metal is collected. The potter, on the other hand, may have learned something from observing the slags of the metallurgist's reducing hearth about glazes and glass. Common to both the potter and the metalsmith is the knowledge that: 1. oxidizing and reducing atmospheres are almost as important as temperatures; 2. slagging of glass-like impurities is the crucial condition for the successful smelting of most ores; 3. unrestrained temperatures might be disadvantageous; 4. admixtures of other elements lower melting points; and 5. heat has highly variable chemical accompaniments (Wertime, 1964:1265).

Whether this widespread knowledge of metallurgical techniques was a product of independent regional invention or of the diffusion of ideas and techniques is disputed. The basic pattern in scholarship over the last two decades has been to emphasize local origins and independent technological development by indigenous cultures. This pattern has been described as a 'healthy reaction to the basic methodology of past years, when every new style and every new technique was interpreted in terms of diffusion' (Muhly, 1980:30). Such anti-diffusionist theories arose in opposition to diffusionist claims such as that of R. J. Forbes in his comprehensive survey of ancient technologies that 'every artifact that consists of a series of discoveries is more likely to have been diffused than reinvented' (1971:11; see also p. 17). James D. Muhly's suggestion that the truth must lie somewhere between these two poles, and that we should think more in terms of the transmission of ideas than of people or groups of objects, is a more likely explanation (1980:30; see also Wertime, 1973:876).[1] As he so astutely observes, much of the contemporary anti-diffusionist scholarship seems to imply that nobody ever went anywhere during the Bronze Age (1980:30). Certainly this was not the case since there is overwhelming evidence for extensive trade during this period.[2] On the other hand, we cannot deny to individuals or to independent areas the potential for creativity and innovation. Whatever their origins, the extraordinary developments in metallurgical technology during the course of the third millennium BCE must be viewed as interrelated with other developments such as the invention of writing, the growth of trade (especially trade by sea), and the advent of a proto-urban world within the area of Greater Mesopotamia (Muhly, 1980:27).

Copper thoroughly dominated metallurgy from c. 7000 to 1200 BCE. By the end of the fourth millennium BCE, the coppersmith was capable of producing such objects as a group of ten copper crowns discovered at the cave site of Nahal-Mish-

---

1 Heskel and Lamberg-Karlovsky assert that the evidence from Iranian sites suggests a variety of developmental schemes at each site and in each region (1980:230).
2 For a good concise discussion of international trade in the Bronze Age see Muhly, 1980.

mar near the west bank of the Dead Sea. Included in the hoard discovered in this cave were eighty 'scepters', 240 pear-shaped mace-heads, and twenty chisels or axes (Wertime, 1973:879).

The development of copper metallurgy falls into three broad phases: 1. the working of native copper (hammering and annealing); 2. the evolution of casting and smelting copper from ores; and 3. the origins of bronze (Wertime, 1973). Metallurgy advanced from the first phase of hammering and annealing native copper to the second phase of casting and smelting when metalworkers crossed the boundary of the melting temperature of copper—1083 degrees C. When it became possible to attain temperatures of this degree in the fifth and fourth millennia BCE, puddling of native copper also became possible.

The second great advance in copper metallurgy occurred during the course of the fourth millennium BCE when an arsenical alloy of copper was developed that contained from two to four percent, and occasionally up to ten to twelve percent, arsenic. Impurities of arsenic and occasionally antimony or bismuth, introduced into the metal from the casting of native copper or the smelting of ores, contributed to the ease of casting and shaping the metal. The best examples of this arsenical alloy of copper come from the hoard of over four hundred copper objects from the cave of Nahal-Mishmar cited above. The mace-heads and most of the ornaments were high enough in arsenic to suggest an origin in the smelting of sulfide ores in which copper and arsenic occur together naturally (see Wertime, 1973:879-81; Muhly, 1982:43).

The greatest advance in copper metallurgy, however, came with the development in the third millennium BCE of a true tin-bronze, consisting of about ninety percent copper and ten percent tin (Muhly, 1980:28). Why arsenic was replaced by tin and where the tin was obtained are questions that have been difficult to answer with any certainty. Although there is abundant textual evidence for tin trade within the ancient Near East (e.g., between Assyria and Anatolia and Mari and Susa; Muhly, 1980:37; Wertime, 1973:884), there is no extant information on where the peoples of the ancient Near East obtained it. Sources of tin throughout the world are scarce, and apart from three sources identified in the eastern desert of Egypt (for which there is no evidence of exploitation in antiquity), there are no known sources of tin anywhere in the Aegean, Eastern Mediterranean, or Near East.[1] Thus, the spread of tin-bronze as the predominant metal in the ancient Near East beginning in the third millennium BCE implies the existence of some type of long-distance trade.[2]

In any case, in the third millennium BCE, an elaborate bronze casting technology was developed. This operation is graphically depicted on the walls of Egyptian New Kingdom tombs. The most famous of these is that of the vizier Rekhmire (first half of the fifteenth century BCE; Muhly, 1982:43). We are also afforded a glimpse of the operation in the biblical passage describing Hiram's manufacture of the bronze implements for Solomon's temple:

> Now the pots, the shovels, and the basins, all these vessels in the house of the LORD, which Hiram made for King Solomon, were of burnished bronze. In the plain of the Jordan the king cast them, in the clay ground between Succoth and Zarethan. (1 Kgs 7.45-46)[3]

---

1 Wertime (1973), however, accepts the implications of the Greek geographer Strabo and Arab geographers that tin once existed in Iran, but asserts that it must have been exhausted by the earliest makers of tin-bronze. Tin is only known in a few areas of the world today, for example, in Cornwall, Thailand, and Malaysia. J. E. Dayton (1971) argues that the secret of tin-bronze was discovered in the Bohemian branch of the 'Finno-Ugrian-Hurrians' and diffused to the Near East over trade routes. He further argues that the most probable ores exploited by the peoples of the ancient Near East were those of central Europe and that tin was imported in the form of bronze, carried by way of the Danube and eastern Anatolia. Cornwall has also been suggested as a possible source of tin (e.g., Wertime, 1973:884; Muhly, 1980:40), as have Thailand and Malaysia. The latter suggestions are problematic because of distance and obscurity in relation to the Near East (Muhly, 1980:31). The biblical reference to tin from Tarshish (Ezek. 27.12) has not been useful in locating the source of ancient tin because Tarshish cannot be located (Muhly, 1982:43).
2 For a more thorough discussion of the problem of tin, see, e.g., Muhly, 1973; 1976; 1980:30-32; Dayton, 1971; Wertime, 1973:884-85.
3 All quotations from biblical passages are from the Revised Standard Version unless otherwise noted.

3. The Development of Iron Technology

At least two types of furnaces were required for such operations—those used for extracting metals from suitable ores (smelting) and those utilized for remelting (in the case of bronze casting) or forging the metal produced in order to form it into artifacts (Tylecote, 1980:183). Early metalworkers of the ancient Near East commonly smelted copper by filling a stone furnace (which need only be a hole in the ground) with alternating layers of charcoal and ore mixed with a flux. Close and intimate contact between the ore and the charcoal was necessary in order to obtain the reducing conditions necessary to separate the metal from the oxygen with which it is combined in a simple oxide mineral. The flux served the purpose of removing from the copper ore the elements that were not desired in the finished product, that is, the gangue. In the hot furnace the flux combined with the gangue, normally silica, and removed it from the metal. The appropriate flux for the ores typical of the Near East was the iron oxide hematite. The heat of the furnace combined with the silicon in the ore and the iron oxide to form an iron silicate. In some furnaces the heat of the fire was increased by the natural draft provided by a flue, and in others the air was forced into the top, sides, or bottom of the furnace with skin- or pot-bellows through clay pipes called tuyères. As the charge in the furnace got hotter, reaching about 1100 degrees C., the charcoal was oxidized to carbon monoxide, which flowed upward through the mixture of ore and flux, chemically reducing both. The resulting molten copper trickled down to form a puddle at the bottom of the furnace, leaving the gangue behind as slag. Although the temperature of the furnace could be regulated with blasts of air from bellows, early metalworkers could not have accurately predicted or measured the furnace temperature. Presumably, if no puddle of copper appeared, the furnace would have been allowed to cool and the process repeated with a different charge or more draft (Tylecote, 1980:183ff.; Maddin et al., 1977:123).

The Discovery of Iron[1]

As R. J. Forbes has noted, 'the beginnings of the iron industry are still very dark from the technical point of view' (1972:215). Although iron did not begin to play a major role in the metallurgical traditions of the ancient Near East until after 1200 BCE, there is ample evidence for earlier experimentation with and use of the metal to manufacture a variety of objects. Most of these objects appear to have been made for ornamental or ceremonial purposes. Iron ores seem initially to have been used as precious stones, amulets, and medicinals (Wertime, 1980:10-11). Magnetite was often used in early dynastic Egypt as an amulet, and in the Old Babylonian dynasties of Mesopotamia hematite was employed for cylinder seals. Hematite was similarly employed in the seals of Susian Elam and in Middle and Late Minoan Crete.

Much of the evidence indicates that iron obtained from meteorites was used in these early periods (see, e.g., Rickard, 1941), but there is also evidence that some smiths were able to smelt iron from ores. Natural iron occurs in two forms: meteoric and telluric. Of the two, meteoric iron is more common and is normally easy to identify because of its nickel content. Occasionally, however, it may be low in nickel content, and thus more difficult to distinguish from iron smelted from terrestrial ores. In contrast, nickel is not a common element in terrestrial iron ores, and if it is present it is usually only in very small amounts.[2] The nickel iron obtained from meteorites is

---

1 The development of a true Iron Age was earlier in the Mediterranean world than in other areas. Europe seems to have been a zone of secondary development where the Iron Age did not begin until c. 700 BCE (Pleiner, 1980). The Iron Age in China and India began at roughly the same time—in China during the seventh century BCE (Needham, 1980; Temple, 1986:42-50) and in India c. 700 to 600 BCE (Forbes, 1972:248-49). The history of the development of iron technology in China is especially interesting because by the fourth century BCE the Chinese had developed techniques for casting iron. In Europe, techniques for casting iron were not developed until the fourteenth century CE.
2 In a recent article on the Hittite iron industry, J. D. Muhly, R. Maddin, T. Stech, and E. Özgen (1985:74) note that smelted iron can also be nickel-bearing and, thus, that iron cannot be identified as

3. The Development of Iron Technology

also superior in quality and strength to the earliest wrought iron produced by smelting terrestrial ores. But nickel iron would almost certainly have been more difficult than smelted terrestrial iron for the ancient smith to forge (Coghlan, 1956:24-29).

It is doubtful that either meteoric or telluric iron played a significant role in the development of iron technology. Telluric iron is very rare, and although iron may first have come to be known through meteorites, the scarcity of attested meteoric iron artifacts makes it difficult to determine whether or to what extent meteoric iron may have influenced the discovery or development of smelting iron.

How smelting was learned has in the past been another subject of much debate, as has the question of whether this knowledge was acquired independently in the various regions in which it has been discovered or whether it was the product of diffusion from one central region. One of the older theories, which accounts for the discovery of smelting as accidental, suggests the campfire as a possible locus. This theory has been rejected on the basis of experiments that indicate it is not possible to obtain smelted iron from a campfire (Coghlan, 1956:45). More recently, R. J. Forbes (1972:213) proposed that smelted iron was originally produced as a by-product of the crucible process of gold-refining. This would, he argues, account for the fact that only small quantities of iron seem to have been produced, for the peculiar association of small pieces of iron with gold in early jewelry, and for the 'pygmy character' of early iron objects (e.g., the small models of tools, amulets, etc., found in the tomb of Tutankhamen; see Table 4).

H. H. Coghlan (1956:45) points to the complexities involved in smelting iron and outlines three important factors that contribute to the production of a useful metal by the direct process employed in the ancient Near East: 1. the ore to be smelted must be sufficiently protected by the fuel-bed against rapid oxidation caused by excessive exposure to air; 2. some form of smelting furnace is required that may or may not have a forced or induced draft; and 3. the furnace tempera-

---

meteoric simply because it contains nickel. It must also be shown to have the grain structure characteristic of a meteorite.

ture must be high enough for the metal to reach the semifused or plastic condition necessary for obtaining a workable bloom. Coghlan (1956:46) suggests that it is *possible* that certain types of pottery furnaces that could attain the temperature necessary for the reduction of iron ore may have contributed to the discovery of smelted iron. He cites as possible examples the large and elaborate pottery kilns discovered at Uruk, Susa, and Arpachiyah. Since red ochre, or red oxide of iron, was widely used for decorating pottery from very early times, reduction of the ochre to metallic iron may have taken place. But it is perhaps laboring the question to associate the pottery kiln too closely with the discovery of iron smelting (p. 47). The following are relevant considerations: 1. the discovery of iron smelting was preceded by a long tradition of copper smelting, and by the time iron was discovered ancient metallurgists had become highly skilled in this operation; 2. the knowledge of how to construct and operate large high-temperature furnaces had long been in existence; and 3. it was not altogether unusual to find a deposit of rich iron oxide in a weathered outcrop of a copper lode. Such a difficult operation as the development of ironworking techniques could only have been successfully undertaken by smiths familiar with the production and working of copper and bronze. Coghlan suggests that at a very early period copper smelters may have occasionally come across iron in small quantities, but without knowing how to make use of the soft metal. It is possible that hematite was accidentally collected and smelted. Since iron, with its slag and charcoal inclusions, could only be consolidated to yield a workable iron and then forged with great difficulty, it was therefore regarded as a costly metal without practical application. Coghlan inclines toward the view that the discovery of iron smelting most likely resulted from the accidental smelting of some iron oxide such as hematite found in a weathered outcrop of a lode being mined for copper (p. 48; see also Waldbaum, 1978:65). Certain Mediterranean copper ores in fact are quite rich in iron, particularly those in Cyprus and Anatolia. It is possible, then, that conditions were present in some Bronze Age cultures for metalworkers to experiment with iron at their leisure (Snodgrass, 1980:340).

3. The Development of Iron Technology

A related but more fully elaborated theory, first proposed by Theodore A. Wertime and Cyril S. Smith (Wertime, 1980:15; cf. Maddin and Stech-Wheeler, 1976), is that iron smelting is an inevitable by-product of copper and lead smelting. Smelted iron, it is argued, was first discovered accidentally in the form of high-iron slags occasionally produced in lead or copper furnaces (Wertime, 1980:2). The argument behind this theory is that iron, in the form of hematite or gossan (an oxidized pyrite), was directly involved as a flux in the development of consistent techniques for smelting copper and lead (see, e.g., Wertime, 1973:878-82; 1980:15-17; Charles, 1980). Although the smelting of ores could in some cases have been self-fluxing, deliberate fluxing, the product of a long process of experimentation, was in general a more crucial factor in the development of metallurgy. The most readily available and useful fluxes would have been found in the iron oxides that were often present in the gossans associated with copper deposits. Reduction of the flux to metallic iron would have occurred in situations in which the gangue content of the ore was low or in which there was no juxtaposition with other gangue material. In such cases the iron oxide would not have been reduced in combination with gangues such as silica, but rather as metallic iron. The presence of some form of metallic iron in the raked-out fire would presumably have caught the attention of the ancient smith. In cases where the initially produced copper was remelted in a crucible, iron would also have been noticed as a separate rim of distinctive material (Charles, 1980:165-66). Another possibility for the discovery of iron in connection with copper smelting, although less likely, is that hematite occasionally was mistaken for cuprite (a type of copper ore) because of their similarities in appearance (Charles, 1980:166). The presence of occasional non-meteoric iron artifacts in the earliest periods of the Bronze Age is cited as evidence that fits this theory—either the chance development of metallic iron through the erroneous selection of similar materials or the use of iron oxide base fluxes that were themselves sometimes reduced. Furthermore, as the Bronze Age proceeded, efforts to increase the efficiency of copper smelting would have led to the improved operation of furnaces. More efficient use of fluxes and greater control of combustion and heat conservation in furnaces would have led to an increased incidence of metallic iron in the spent charge material and association with the solidified copper. Eventually, an upsurge of interest in iron for its own sake would have developed (Charles, 1980:166-67).

Wrought Iron and the Early Processes of Smelting and Forging

Early iron workers produced iron from ores, mostly hematite and magnetite, by a smelting process much like the one used to produce copper. There are two processes by which iron can be smelted: direct and indirect. The direct, or bloomery, process, which only produces iron in small quantities, was that generally used by the ancient smiths.[1] The indirect process, now associated with the blast furnace, produces cast iron and is a much more recent development.

But, in spite of the general similarities, the ancient techniques for working iron differed fundamentally from those used for other ores in antiquity, and smiths accustomed to working other metals such as bronze had to acquire new knowledge and skill. The amount of heat required and the temperatures necessary were much greater for iron than for copper and its alloys—the melting point of copper is 1083 degrees C., while that of iron is about 1537 degrees C. This difference is crucial. Since the highest temperature that could be reached in a primitive smelter appears to have been about 1200 degrees C. (Maddin et al., 1977:123), iron could not be melted and cast. The temperature at which reduction takes place in an iron smelting furnace has an important bearing on the smelting process. When iron oxide is reduced at temperatures below 900 degrees C., a dark gray and very porous substance that would be impossible to forge is formed. If the temperature range is between 1000 and 1050 degrees C., the product is a loosely coherent mass that would still be very difficult, if not impossible, to forge. It is not until the temperature is increased to 1100 to 1150 degrees C. that iron begins to flow together to form a bloom (a semi-solid spongy mass) that

---

1 China, where cast iron was produced, is an exception.

3. The Development of Iron Technology   113

can then be hammered and forged into wrought iron. Thus, in order to obtain a useful bloom, a sufficient temperature in the furnace and a good reducing atmosphere that promotes the exclusion of oxygen from the ore are essential (Coghlan, 1956:39). Smelting iron ore at this temperature yields not a puddle of molten metal, but a spongy mass (the bloom) mixed with iron oxide and silica gangue (which collectively represent slag).

The smelting process, also termed reduction, is the heat and chemical process by which metallic iron is extracted from the parent ore (Coghlan, 1956:13). Under the right conditions, a chemical change is effected in which the ore is robbed of its oxygen and metallic iron is produced. If charcoal is the fuel used, the carbon of the fuel combines with the ore to release metallic iron. In a simple reduction furnace the carbon of the charcoal burns to carbon monoxide, and this gas takes the oxygen from the ore to form carbon dioxide. But a certain balance must be preserved.

> To produce usable iron the metallurgist must employ only iron oxide together with both heat and carbon, the latter performing an essential chemical function in the operation. There must be a sufficient excess of carbon so it will burn to carbon monoxide, not dioxide; whenever the ratio of dioxide to monoxide rises above a number that varies with temperature, metallic iron reoxidizes. (Read, 1934:384 [quoted in Coghlan, 1956:39])

The resulting semi-solid mass of spongy iron (the bloom) then has to be withdrawn from the furnace, reheated in a forge, and hammered to squeeze out the impurities. At the same time, hammering turns the bloom into a continuous network of iron grains interspersed with slag that had not been eliminated. Iron objects are made by further heating and hammering the bloom.

The product of this process, wrought iron, is not very useful and is generally inferior to bronze, especially tin-bronze, as it is both softer and less durable. Wrought iron is a soft, ductile, and fibrous product contaminated by small amounts of slag and largely free from carbon. It is the carbon content of iron that determines its hardness and strength and distinguishes wrought iron from steel (see Chapter 4). When carbon is present in wrought iron, it varies throughout the object, and the purified bloom is only partially and unevenly steeled. The process by which carbon was introduced into iron to increase its strength and durability was not consistently and intentionally applied until the advent of the Iron Age. A mild steel contains as little as 0.08 percent carbon, and it is not until 0.2 to 0.7 percent carbon is present in the material that it is fully in the domain of steeled iron (Wertime, 1980:13). Even for most of the Iron Age and for the periods before c. 1400 CE, ironsmiths worked with smelting conditions that could generally only produce a spongy iron low in carbon content and much interspersed with slag (Wertime, 1980:13). In part, this was due to the fact that the ancient smith was rarely able to attain the melting point of iron (1537 degrees C.), which is substantially above the melting point of the enclosed slag. Much heating and forging were thus necessary in order to extract a workable metal.

This primitive reduction process was also quite wasteful in material. A great deal of charcoal fuel was used, and much of the iron was lost in the slag, which is not easily separated from the iron. In the modern reduction process, lime is normally added to the charge as a flux to render the slag more fusible so that it readily separates from the iron. As is the case for smelting copper, productive efficiency is greatly increased by the selection and use of a suitable flux. It is the flux that, when added to the furnace charge, gets rid of extraneous matter to form a slag. The complexities involved in separating the iron from the slag are compounded by the fact that the fluxes need to be adjusted according to the type of ore being smelted (Coghlan, 1956:40-41).

Sources of Iron Ore

Deposits of iron ore are widely distributed throughout the Near East. Major deposits are located in the Taurus and anti-Taurus region of southeastern Asia Minor that extends from Cape Anamur in the west to the borders of Syria, and in Syria to Aleppo, the Euphrates, and Lebanon. In Asia Minor, the deposits are particularly rich in the regions of Caucasia, Transcaucasia, and Armenia (Forbes, 1972:195; see also

3. The Development of Iron Technology

Muhly et al., 1985:74). It is recorded that Ashur-nasir-pal (885–860 BCE) obtained iron in the neighborhood of Carchemish (Coghlan, 1956:15). Cappadocian iron was also famous in antiquity (Forbes, 1972:195). In Syria, there are some fairly rich deposits near Alexandria, and there is evidence of deposits that were exploited near Germanicia, located near the Taurus mountains (Forbes, 1972:194). In Iran, there are major sources in the mountains to the northeast of Nineveh and in the neighboring area of Kurdistan, in northern Iran near Persepolis, and in the Karadagh district where extensive mounds of iron slag have been found (Coghlan, 1956:15-16). Forbes refers to old mines in the Elburz mountains of northern Iran near Resht and Massula, where the inhabitants are still mainly blacksmiths (1972:195).

The Hebrew Bible describes Palestine as 'a land whose rocks are iron' (Deut. 8.9), but Palestine actually has few deposits of rich iron ores, although the poorer ores are quite common (Forbes, 1972:193; Muhly, 1982:45). In 1935, when Nelson Glueck published the results of his extensive survey in Eastern Palestine, he identified numerous centers of copper mining and smelting operations dating from the Iron Age, but only a few deposits of iron ore. 'Numerous veins' of iron ore were recorded in the vicinity of the Wadi es-Sabrah south of Petra (Glueck, 1935:49, 80; Har-El, 1977:76), and large heaps of iron slag have been noted near the town of Ajlun north of the Jabbock River (Har-El, 1977:76). Today, following several surveys carried out since those of Glueck, Mugharat el Wardeh in the Ajlun hills, about twenty miles north of Amman, is recognized as containing the only major deposits of iron ore in Palestine (Stech-Wheeler et al., 1981:259; Muhly, 1982:45). Other minor deposits have been identified in the Makhtesh southwest of the Dead Sea, in the Galilee, in the Negev along the Wadi Arabah, and rather small deposits in Transjordan and Lebanon (Har-El, 1977:76; Waldbaum, 1978:59; Stech-Wheeler et al., 1981:259; Muhly, 1982:45).

Whether, and to what extent, any of these sources of iron were exploited in antiquity is difficult to ascertain. Although iron deposits are more available locally and are more easily exploited than those of copper, no definitive evidence of mining has been recovered, and what little ambiguous evidence exists is difficult to date. This is probably due to two primary factors: 1. the fact that continuous mining in a given location may eliminate traces of previous workings (Waldbaum, 1978:59); and 2. the fact that many iron deposits are found on the earth's surface and evidence of surface mining would be difficult to spot (Muhly, 1982:44; Coghlan, 1956:17). The latter is possibly reflected in the passage in Deut. 8.9 that refers to 'stones of iron' and 'hills [that] may be quarried for copper'; that is, copper mining requires underground shafts and galleries, but iron mining utilizes surface deposits (Muhly, 1982:44-45).

The Artifactual Information[1]

Although iron did not begin to be utilized consistently for practical purposes such as agriculture and warfare until after 1200 BCE, iron objects are known from as early as the fifth millennium BCE. The following survey of the archaeological and textual information for the use of iron before the Iron Age spans a time period from the fifth millennium BCE down to c. 1200 BCE. Areas of the eastern Mediterranean related to Palestine through cultural connections or trade, that is, Anatolia, Iran, Mesopotamia, Egypt, and Syro-Palestine are surveyed.[2] To facilitate comparisons, lists of artifacts and their origins have been summarized in tables.

The Bronze Age in the Near East was characterized by increased urbanization, the formation of empires, and the development of writing systems. The civilizations of this

---

1 The following survey of artifactual and textual material is drawn primarily from previously published surveys and is meant to provide a background for the development of iron technology and ancient beliefs about it. The original reports and publications on these artifacts and texts are cited in the surveys noted here.
2 Although there were obviously trade relations with Greece during this period, and Greece plays an important role in the story of the rise of iron technology, it is necessary to draw boundaries in order to keep the coverage of the background material at a manageable level. Therefore, Greece has not been included in this survey. On the development of iron technology in Greece see, e.g., Waldbaum, 1978; Snodgrass, 1980.

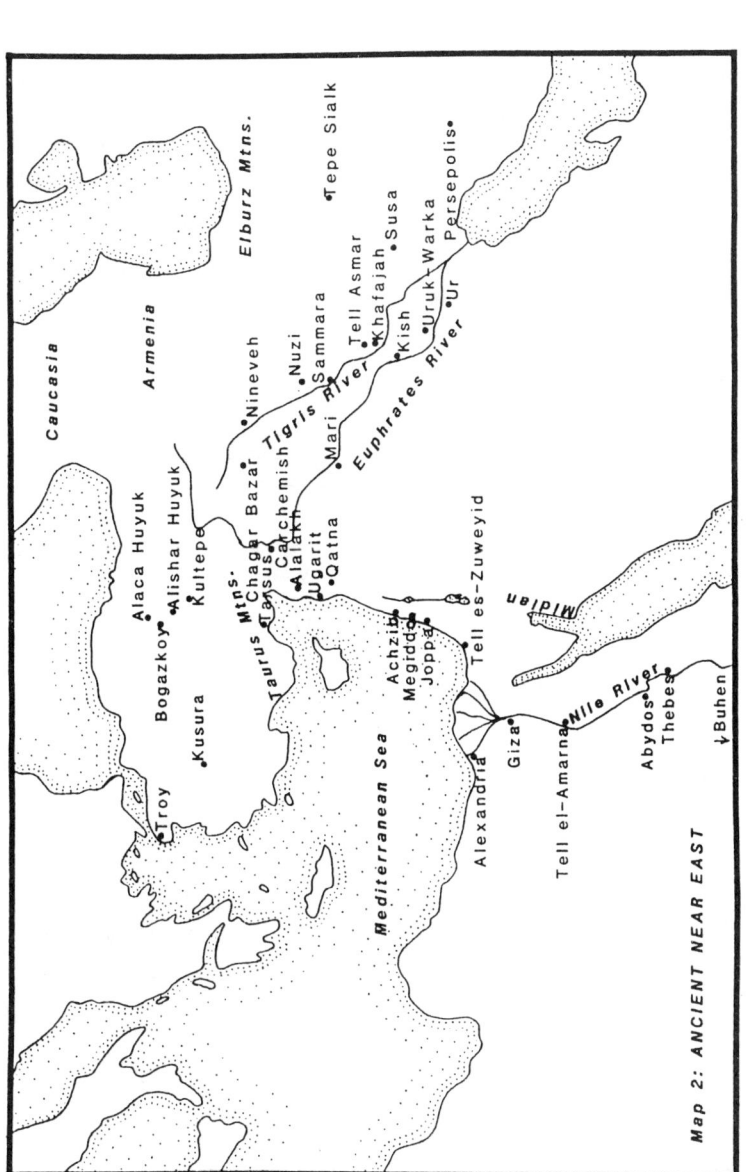
Map 2: ANCIENT NEAR EAST

period depended on bronze for the manufacture of tools, weapons, vessels, and other items including jewelry and ornamental objects. Archaeological and textual studies have provided evidence that iron was also used as early as 5000 BCE, although on a much smaller scale than bronze.

The archaeological information for iron metalcraft in the fourth and fifth millennia BCE is scarce, but a few examples from this period can be cited. Fourteen iron objects from four sites (one in Iran, one in Mesopotamia, and two in Egypt) dating to this period have been recovered (Table 1).[1] Of these objects, the ten recovered from the two Egyptian sites are ornamental. The functions of the remaining four objects from Iran and Mesopotamia are uncertain.

Table 1: *Iron Artifacts: Fifth and Fourth Millennia BCE*

Site	Date	Artifacts	Context
		Iran	
Tepe Sialk	4600–4100 BCE (Period II)	3 small spherical balls (apparently used as polishers)—meteoric	occupation level
		Mesopotamia	
Samara	c. 5000 BCE	4-sided 'chisel-like' object—smelted	Grave A
		Egypt	
el-Gerzeh	pre-dynastic (c. 3500–3300 BCE)	9 beads strung together with gold and stone beads—1 bead analyzed, probably meteoric	Graves 67 and 133
Armant	c. 3500–3100 BCE	ring	Grave 1494

[1] For inventories of pre-Iron Age iron objects, see Waldbaum, 1978:21; 1980:69; Wainwright, 1936; Coghlan, 1956:32; Wertime, 1973:878; Forbes, 1972:227-66.

3. The Development of Iron Technology

Table 2: *Iron Artifacts: Third Millennium* BCE

Site	Date	Artifacts	Context
		Mesopotamia	
Uruk-Warka	c. 3100–2800 BCE (Early Protoliterate period)	meteoric fragment	between 2 temples (D&E) of the Anu ziggurat
Khafajah	c. 2800–2600 BCE (Early Dynastic II)	unidentified 'lump'	—
Kish	c. 2800–2340 BCE (Early Dynastic II or III)	3 'button-like' pieces of iron inlay	Palace A, room 61
*Tell Asmar (Ur)	c. 2450–2340 BCE (Early Dynastic III)	fragments of a flat tool blade—meteoric	Royal Cemetry, tomb PG/580
Chagar Bazar	c. 2450–2340 BCE (Early Dynastic III)	fragment—smelted	Grave G67, Level V
	c. 2450–2340 BCE	2 smelted fragments	occupation
Mari	c. 2450–2340 BCE (Early Dynastic III)	unidentified number of fragments	near pre-Sargonid Temple of Ishtar
		Anatolia	
Troy	c. 2600–2400 BCE (EB II)	macehead or finial—probably meteoric	Treasure L, Troy II or III
Alaca Hüyük	c. 2400–2100 BCE (EB III)	2 pins with gold heads—1 meteoric (A 1/a MA 34, A 1/a MA 30)	Tomb MA, Period III
	c. 2400–2100 BCE (EB III)	crescent-shaped plaque—meteoric (A 1/a MC 33)	Tomb MC, Period III
	c. 2400–2100 BCE (EB III)	fragments of a knife that 'seem to be iron'	Tomb TM
	c. 2400–2100 BCE (EB III)	pendant	Tomb MA, Period III

Site	Date	Artifacts	Context
	c. 2400–2100 BCE (EB III)	'fitting' in the shape of an 'N' (A 1/a MA 23)	Tomb MA, Period III
	EB	dagger with iron blade and gold hilt, pommel, and rivets—non-meteoric	Tomb K
Tarsus	c. 2100 BCE (EB III)	corroded 'lump'	small treasure in a cooking pot, room 74
**Dorak	c. 2400–2300 BCE (EBIII)	sword with an obsidian hilt carved in the form of 2 leopards—inlaid with gold and amber spots	'royal tomb'
		Egypt	
Giza	c. 2565–2440 BCE (Dynasty IV)	deposit of rust on a flint wand—terrestrial iron	Valley Temple of Mycerinus
Abydos	c. 2345–2181 BCE (Dynasty VI)	rust corroded to a group of copper tools—terrestrial iron, perhaps a wedge	foundation of a temple
Deir el-Bahari	c. 2133–1991 BCE (Dynasty XI)	blade of a *pesesh-kef* amulet with a silver sphinx's head—meteoric	tomb of Princess Aa Shait

*'The temple service, a closed find, to which the knife belongs, was buried at the very end of the Early Dynastic Period, say between 2450 and 2350 BC. It is relevant that this blade of terrestrial iron was mounted in an openwork handle of bronze, while the other objects of the hoard, some 75 pieces, were made of copper. The knife may therefore not have been of local manufacture' (Frankfort, 1950:n. 160).

**This tomb was 'clandestinely' excavated and the sword has since disappeared. It is said to have been found with a treasure and has been tentatively dated to EB III by an associated cartouche of Pharaoh Sahure of the Fifth Dynasty (Waldbaum, 1980:71).

3. The Development of Iron Technology

During the third millennium BCE the use of iron appears to have increased (Table 2). Archaeological sites yielding iron artifacts from this period are limited in distribution to thirteen, located in Mesopotamia, Anatolia,[1] and Egypt, with larger concentrations in Mesopotamia and Anatolia than in Egypt. The twenty-three-plus objects found represent a variety of forms, primarily ornamental, and most were found in contexts that suggest either ritual or ceremonial functions, or some precious or special status, that is, tombs, temples, graves, and palaces.[2] The few objects that have utilitarian forms—the tool blade from Tell Asmar, the macehead from Troy, the knife fragments and dagger blade from Alaca Hüyük, and the sword from Dorak—were presumably used for ceremonial purposes and/or as indicators of status (rather than being intended for everyday use). This assumption is based on the contexts in which they were found (royal tombs and treasure hoards) and the fact that the precious metals silver and gold were combined with iron in their manufacture. Gold also decorates the two pins from Alaca Hüyük.

1 For a recent review and analysis of the artifactual and textual material from Anatolia, see Muhly et al., 1985.
2 In addition to those items listed in Table 2, reference should also be made to a number of artifacts that were assigned to this period in earlier publications, but are thought to be questionable according to more recent evaluations (see, e.g., Waldbaum, 1980:71; Coghlan, 1956:65-66). Objects from Egypt include: a rusted tool of terrestrial iron that had been smelted, found in a joint of the stones of the pyramid of Cheops at Giza—it is thought that this tool possibly belonged to one of the workmen; pieces of chisels from Saqqarah ascribed to the fifth dynasty; pieces of a pick-axe from Abusir ascribed to the sixth dynasty; broken tools from sixth dynasty Dahshur; and the rust from Abydos listed in Table 2. Also of interest is a third millennium BCE piece of white cast iron from Geoy Tepe in Iran, possibly the result of the serious overheating of a high-temperature furnace. This piece of iron would have been useless because it would have been impossible to work at the time (Coghlan, 1956:62). R. J. Forbes (1972:27) notes that the use of hematite for seal stones was widespread during this period and that fragments of a hard metallic variety of hematite were found in a smelting site near the ziggurat of Ur. For details concerning the objects listed in Table 2, see Waldbaum, 1978:19-21; 1980:70-71; Coghlan, 1956:32-33, 61-66.

In the third millennium BCE, then, iron was used sporadically and treated as a precious metal in almost every instance. According to the analyses of the objects, meteoric iron and smelted iron were used simultaneously during the third millennium in all of the major geographical areas, although whether one type or the other was predominant cannot be determined. Neither is it possible to determine on the basis of the analyses whether the smelted terrestrial iron was the product of accidental or deliberate smelting nor whether all smelted objects were of soft wrought iron or whether any show evidence of carburization or heat treatment.

Table 3: *Iron Artifacts: Middle Bronze Age (c. 2000–1600 BCE)*

Site	Date	Artifacts	Context
		Anatolia	
Alishar Hüyük	c. 1900–1700 BCE	small piece of decorative inlay set in bronze head of a pin (e 1555)	occupation, Stratum II
	c. 1900–1700 BCE	small piece of 'wire' used to fasten an arrowhead to its shaft (d 2948)	occupation, Stratum II
	c. 1900–1700 BCE	unidentified number of fragments	occupation, Stratum II
Kusura	c. 1800–1600 BCE	fragment	—, Period C
		Egypt	
*Buhen (Nubia)	c. 1991–1786 BCE (Dynasty XII)	spearhead with flat, leaf-shaped blade and cylindrical socket—smelted and hammered (?)	Grave K32, associated with a skeleton

*The Buhen spearhead is of doubtful antiquity. Forbes (1972:240) notes that it is very similar to weapons still used by the natives of Nubia. Both its size and shape make this find extremely doubtful (cf. Coghlan, 1956:65).

Evidence for the use of iron in the Middle Bronze Age (c. 2000–1600 BCE) is scarce. Only five objects are known from this period, four from Anatolia and one from Egypt (Table 3;

3. The Development of Iron Technology

Waldbaum, 1978:20, 22; 1980:74). Three of the four Anatolian finds come from an occupation level at Alishar Hüyük, and all four of the objects from Anatolia are very small or are preserved only as fragments. The object from Nubia, a weapon, comes from a grave (as is typical of ceremonial weapons from previous periods), but its antiquity is doubted.[1]

The first half of the second millennium BCE contrasts with the third millennium in the paucity of iron finds attributed to it. There are no examples from Mesopotamia, only four from Anatolia, and one doubtful example from Egypt. Whether this is an indicator of a temporary decline in iron usage or reflects the arbitrary nature of excavations cannot be determined. The proposal that this decrease is associated with the introduction of tin-bronze, which checked the development of iron technology because of its superiority over soft wrought iron (e.g., Coghlan, 1956:69), does not hold up under scrutiny. It implies that iron was used for utilitarian purposes during the Early Bronze Age, an implication for which there is no evidence. Although certainly some of the third millennium objects have the *form* of tools or weapons, there is no evidence that they in fact *functioned* as such. The contexts all suggest some kind of association with ceremony or status.

By the Late Bronze Age iron was used in increased quantities and distributed over a wider geographical area. A greater variety of types and functions occur, but jewelry, ceremonial weapons, and ornamental objects remain dominant. Iron is again combined with other precious metals. There is evidence of possible occasional utilitarian use, but such use seems to be limited when compared to that of non-utilitarian objects. The contexts of iron objects from this period are still most often royal or wealthy tombs, palaces, and sanctuaries. A total of at least fifty-six objects come from sites in Mesopotamia, Egypt, Anatolia, and, for the first time, Syro-Palestine (Table 4).[2]

---

1 Although the antiquity of this object has often been called into question, Davis, Maddin, Muhly, and Stech (1985:44) note that the burial in which it was found had apparently not been disturbed.
2 Other objects mentioned in the literature but not included in Waldbaum's 1978 and 1980 surveys are: a ring and two axe blades found in the Gezer water tunnel and assigned a Late Bronze Age date by the excavator (MacAlister, 1912). The tunnel is now considered to be

Table 4: *Iron Artifacts: Late Bronze Age (c. 1600–1200 BCE)*

Site	Date	Artifacts	Context
		Mesopotamia	
Nuzi (Yorgan Tepe)	15th century BCE (Hurrian period)	dagger with copper blade and iron hilt and rivet	floor of Temple A, Stratum 2
	15th century BCE (Hurrian period)	small spherical bead	Temple, Stratum II
		Syro-Palestine	
Ugarit (Ras Shamra)	c. 1450–1350 BCE	battle axe with cast-on copper socket in the form of a boar's forequarters and 2 lions' heads with gold decoration—perhaps meteoric or a mild form of steel	votive offering in a sanctuary attached to a 'residence', Stratum I.2
Minet el-Beida	13th century BCE	'rings' buried with silver and gold	Tomb 3
Alalakh	c. 1450–1370 BCE	'lumps' mixed with copper (one fragment possibly an iron knife blade with copper handle)	Niqmepa palace, Level IV, room 8; possibly a foundry hoard
	c. 1350–1273 BCE	arrowhead (39/294)	occupation, Level II
	c. 1350–1185 BCE	arrowhead (39/324)	occupation, Level I-II

of uncertain date. Coghlan (1956:62) and Forbes (1972:244) make reference to a gold-plated iron amulet found in a royal tomb at Byblos from the time of Amenhotep III. Waldbaum (1978:18) states that this object is in fact published as limonite, a mineral ore of iron. Both Coghlan (1956:62) and Forbes (1972:260) also cite 'iron weapons and tools' from the Kapara period at Tell Halaf found in association with a moveable hearth. And Coghlan cites 'iron objects' from Tepe Giyan I and Tepe Sialk A in Iran.

For an updated assessment of the artifactual material from Anatolia, see Muhly et al., 1985.

3. The Development of Iron Technology

Site	Date	Artifacts	Context
	c. 1270–1185 BCE	spatula with long plain handle and single, flat splayed blade (39/283)	occupation, Level I
Megiddo	c. 1400–1200 BCE (LB II)	ring (M3094)	Tomb 912B
	Late Bronze Age	tool with iron handle	—, Level III?
Tell es-Zuweyid	c. 1400–1230/1170 BCE	2 arrowheads and a handle	occupation, Level N 204-209

Anatolia

Site	Date	Artifacts	Context
Alaca Hüyük	c. 1500–1300 BCE	fragment (possibly of an armor scale) and a circular plaque (A1.t 142)	occupation, Stratum 3a
	c. 1800–1200 BCE	stamp seal, 2 nails (A1.d 226, A1.e 41), a needle (A1.e 48), an arrowhead (A1.e 55), a dagger (A1.m 71), a bracelet (A1.e 39), a plaque (A1.g 78), a fragment (A1.g 174), a socketed handle (spearbutt?; A1.e 35), and an 'axe-like' object (A1.g 301)	Strata 4-2 (Hittite levels)
Bogazköy	c. 1450–1200 BCE	a fragment (1246), a chisel (1295), and a lugged axe blade (1255)	Lower city Level II or Ib (Hittite level)
Bogazköy (Büyükkale)	c. 1450–1200 BCE	a fragment (1247), a lugged axe-blade (1256), and a spearbutt (1276)	Level IVb or III (Hittite level)
Bogazköy	c. 1300–1200 BCE	conical spearbutt (1277)	Lower city temple, Level I (in Hittite debris)

Site	Date	Artifacts	Context
		Egypt	
Thebes	c. 1417–1379 BCE (Dynasty XVIII)	arrowhead	Middle palace of Amenhotep III
	c. 1350 BCE (Dynasty XVIII)	*Urs* amuletic head-rest found under a mummy's mask (meteoric), 'eye-of-Horus' amulet on a gold *uzat* bracelet found near the lower part of the mummy's thorax, a dagger blade (meteoric) with a gold and jewel encrusted haft and sheath*, 16 miniature chisel blades set in wooden handles (all in one box; 6 different blade types)	Valley of the Kings, tomb of Tutankhamen
**Tell el-Amarna	c. 1379–1362 BCE (Dynasty XVIII)	2 masses of rust found under a bronze axe-head	floor of a house
Abydos	c. 1567–1320 BCE (Dynasty XVIII)	small pin used as a fastening for an ivory box	—

*There were two ceremonial daggers found in the tomb of Tutankhamen, one with an iron blade and one with a gold blade. J. D. Muhly makes the interesting observation that all the touring exhibits of the collection from this tomb have only included the gold dagger. The iron dagger remained in Cairo, being regarded as too precious to ship around the world (Muhly, 1980:37).

**Forbes (1972:241) refers to a pair of iron bracelets roughly worked with dogs' heads from XVIII Dynasty Tell el-Amarna.

Several of the finds from the Late Bronze Age are significant enough to warrant further discussion. The battle-axe from Ras Shamra in particular has received a great deal of atten-

3. The Development of Iron Technology

tion from metallurgists. At issue is the question of the type of iron used to manufacture the blade (see, e.g., Richardson, 1943; Coghlan, 1956:34). Tests have indicated that the blade has a high carbon content. Therefore, it was initially considered to be a very early example of steeled iron. It was later argued, on the basis of nickel content, that it is more likely that the blade is made of meteoric iron. But since the nickel content is low, it must be a type of meteoric iron that is difficult to distinguish from terrestrial iron. Most iron meteorites are known to contain carbon, phosphorous, and sulphur, which could account for the high carbon content. The low nickel is considered to be unusual, but not conclusively significant. It is possible, according to this interpretation, that in the process of heating and forging the characteristic structure of the meteoric iron was altered. Unfortunately, the question of whether the axe was manufactured from meteoric iron high in carbon content or from 'steeled' terrestrial iron has not been conclusively determined. If, in fact, the axe is made of terrestrial iron, it is one of the earliest examples of steel. The fact remains, however, that the axe is a ceremonial, not a utilitarian, weapon. The iron blade is crumbly and brittle, and the axe is not a formidable weapon in size, weight, hardness, or soundness. 'In a finish fight, the bronze socket would be far more dependable than the iron blade' (Richardson, 1943:72).

Also of special interest is the inventory of iron artifacts from the tomb of Tutankhamen. The tomb contained an unusually large number of iron artifacts with an interesting variety of forms. Based on the assumption of a Hittite monopoly on ironworking and a lack of technological know-how on the part of the Egyptians (see, e.g., Forbes, 1972:241; Coghlan, 1956:32), the large number of iron artifacts has sometimes been attributed to either contact with the Hittites or importation. Others assert on the basis of their unique forms that the objects are probably types of local manufacture that are peculiar to Egypt (e.g., Waldbaum, 1978:22; 1980:79). As will be discussed below, the issue is one of the origins and transmission of ironworking. However, since most of these objects were manufactured from meteoric iron, they do not provide information on iron smelting, a process that was essential to the origin and development of ironworking.

The types of iron objects recovered from Tutankhamen's tomb are also intriguing and have stimulated much speculation about function. The amulets obviously served some magical purpose and the dagger was presumably a prestige item. But what of the sixteen miniature tools included in the tomb inventory? They are too slight and too fragile to have been intended as utilitarian tools. It has been suggested that they too may have had some magical intention (e.g., Forbes, 1972:238, 241) and may have been used in the Egyptian 'opening of the mouth' ritual. Instruments used in this ritual are identified in Egyptian texts as *bia'*, the Egyptian term for iron (Wainwright, 1936).

Finally, the inventory of iron artifacts from the two Late Bronze Age Anatolian sites is interesting when compared to previous tendencies and to contemporary inventories from surrounding areas. For the first time, utilitarian forms, both tools and weapons, predominate for iron objects, presumably situated in occupation levels (since no specific locales are identified). Whether this indicates a move toward using iron for practical purposes, however, must remain inconclusive. To make such an assertion on the basis of two isolated sites would be premature and would not stand up 'in court'. As we will see later in this chapter, there has been a tendency on the part of previous interpreters to point to the Anatolian information as conclusive evidence of a Hittite 'monopoly' on ironworking in the ancient Near East. However, without further information, especially evidence for the actual manufacture of iron (e.g., furnaces and ironworking tools), this hypothesis cannot be upheld. Another reason for not jumping to such conclusions is that both iron tools and iron weapons were also recovered from occupation levels in Late Bronze Age Syro-Palestinian sites.

It is also necessary to keep the archaeological information on ironworking in perspective by recognizing that at no Late Bronze Age site does the number of 'utilitarian' iron objects even begin to approach their bronze counterparts. The majority of iron objects continue to be treated as precious, and iron is often combined with other precious materials. As before, this is indicated by contexts such as royal or wealthy tombs, palaces, temples, and sanctuaries. Meteoric iron continues to be used, but because the majority of artifacts have not been analyzed, it is not possible to determine the relationship of meteoric to smelted terrestrial iron.

Table 5: *Iron Artifacts Predating the Iron Age from the Near East*

	Iran	Mesopotamia	Egypt	Anatolia	Syro-Palestine	Total
Pre-third millennium	3	1	10	–	–	14
Third Millennium	–	10+	3	10	–	23+
Middle Bronze Age (c. 2000–1600 BCE)	–	–	1	4+	–	5+
Late Bronze Age (c. 1600–1200 BCE)	–	2	23	20	11+	56+
	3	13+	37	34+	11+	98

As for previous periods, there is little evidence for the production of smelted iron for the Late Bronze Age. The exceptions may be a few objects from Anatolia (Muhly, et al., 1985).

The Textual Information

A number of ancient Near Eastern texts refer to iron or meteorites. They are an important source for reconstructing the earliest stages in the manufacture and use of iron. Most of the texts date from the second millennium BCE, but some probably reflect an earlier understanding of the nature of iron (Bjorkman, 1973:91).

Because archaeological reports on Middle Bronze Age sites record few iron finds and because the iron objects found are poorly preserved, the contemporary literary documentation is particularly valuable (Waldbaum, 1980:75). Middle Bronze Age texts that mention iron include the Cappadocian texts of the Old Assyrian trading colony of Kültepe in central Anatolia (c. 1900–1800 BCE), the Hittite Anitta texts from approximately the same time, an Old Kingdom ritual text, the Alalakh texts (eighteenth century BCE), the Mari texts (c. 1700 BCE), and the Susa texts (eighteenth century BCE).[1]

---

[1] An updated list of Hittite texts that refer to iron can be found in Košak, 1986.

The Old Assyrian texts speak of the activities of an out-post of Assyrian traders in Anatolia. They provide some indication of the role of metals in society and of the relative values of the metals in use (Muhly, 1980:36). They further suggest that in Kültepe and its satrapies there was organized production of sulfide copper, large-scale trade in the rare metal tin, manufacture of bronze and silver, experimentation with iron, and extensive use of banking, credit, and complex written records (Wertime, 1973:875). Two terms for iron are used in these texts, Akkadian *amūtu* and *aši'u*. The distinction between them is not known, but it has been conjectured that the former may be the term for meteoric iron and the latter for terrestrial iron (Bjorkman, 1973:110-12). Another proposal is that *amūtu* refers to bloom iron and *aši'u* to iron ore (Maxwell-Hyslop, 1972:160; cf. Muhly, 1980:35).[1] Judith Bjorkman (1973:110-12) hypothesizes that *amūtu* may refer to meteoric iron or perhaps, although less likely, a rare deposit of telluric iron. In support of this hypothesis, Bjorkman suggests that: 1. the fact that meteoric iron can be polished to a bright luster and that some types resist rust may account in part for its high cost in relation to other metals; and 2. since the texts speak of the difficulty of finding *amūtu* on the market in Anatolia, meteoric iron is more likely because terrestrial iron ores are more readily available.

Rachel Maxwell-Hyslop's proposal (1972) that *amūtu* refers to bloom iron and *aši'u* to iron ore is based on her study of the contexts in which the two words are used in the texts. For example, she translates *Kültepe* text *CCT* 4 4a as follows (1972:159):

> You wrote me (concerning) 1 mina of (bloom)-iron (?) which PN and PN2 brought here saying (thus), sell it for silver or gold, for copper do not sell it. PN and PN2 said 'the (bloom)-iron (?) to GN bring'. The (bloom)-iron (?) to the head man I brought and he said 'I will forge it'. I said 'for forging I will not give permission'. He said 'when you have gone I will

---

1 Muhly (1980:35) states that the translation of *amūtu* as bloom iron is convincing, but he is less certain of the translation of *aši'u* as iron ore. The latter is among the materials offered to a local Anatolian leader as a gift, and Muhly finds it difficult to believe in an offer of a lump of ore.

3. The Development of Iron Technology

forge it'. The (bloom)-iron (?) he forged and a lump (or bar) 2/3 shekel (in weight) resulted through forging and I suffered (?) a loss of 4 shekels. For the rest of the (bloom)-iron (?) 8 shekels of gold per shekel he offered me, I said 'it is too little'.[1]

The apparent loss of weight during forging evidently resulted from cleaning the slag from the bloom (cf. Bjorkman, 1973:112), which resulted in wrought iron. This text indicates that *amūtu* was expensive, eight times the value of gold.

In BIN 4 45:11, *amūtu* and *aši'u* occur in the same text. Maxwell-Hyslop translates:

if the (bloom)-iron which you took from PN is still there with you go and send me the (bloom)-iron here... should there be any iron ore anywhere, write.

Examples of the occurrence of *aši'u* in the Kültepe texts are found in a group of texts concerning a partnership of four traders financed by a certain Inaa of Kanesh for the purchase of iron (*CCT* II 48; Maxwell-Hyslop, 1972:161). In one example, the agent writes from Hurama that the four individuals had 'brought the silver and the gold into the heart of the country but could not find any *aši'u*'. More silver and gold is then requested and the agent gives assurance that *aši'u* will be available 'in the neighboring area', that is, at Hurama.

Maxwell-Hyslop notes that one important difference in the usage of the two terms is that *aši'u* is never given a weight or price as is *amūtu*, an expensive metal forty times the value of silver and at least eight times the value of gold (1972:159). This distinction, she suggests, may derive from the fact that it was not deemed necessary to quote a weight or price for iron ore (*aši'u*) unless it had been smelted (*amūtu*) (1972:161). Another significant characteristic of the references to *amūtu* is that it was apparently traded in small quantities that could only have been used for manufacturing jewelry, decorating small objects, or for making knife blades or small tools (Maxwell-Hyslop, 1972:159-60).

---

[1] Maxwell-Hyslop's translation also requires that *ṣarapu* denote the forging process rather than smelting as is translated in *CAD* (*amūtu*, p. 98a).

Amūtu and *aši'u* disappear almost completely from cuneiform texts after the demise of the Assyrian trading colonies in Anatolia. Whether this is due to the eclipse of meteoric iron because of the gradual discovery of steeling (if Bjorkman's suggestion is correct), a depletion of sources, or the disruption of trade routes is not known (Bjorkman, 1973:112). Unfortunately, Hittite texts cannot help solve the dilemma of how these two terms should be translated correctly because they do not make a distinction (Maxwell-Hyslop, 1972:61). Nevertheless, the texts do indicate that iron (*amūtu*) was expensive, eight times the value of gold and four hundred times the value of tin, even though iron was local and tin imported (Muhly, 1980:35). Iron was so precious, in fact, that there was an interdiction against its being taken from the country. Muhly believes that the high value of iron can only be explained by supply and demand and by the rarity of the metal whose methods of production were not really understood (1980:36).

The Hittite term *AN.BAR GE nepišiš*, literally 'black iron from heaven' (Maxwell-Hyslop, 1972:162), is used in the Anitta texts to describe a throne and possibly a scepter (Waldbaum, 1980: 75, 79). *AN.BAR* is also the Sumerian term for iron, but it seems to lack the celestial connotations of the Hittite word. It cannot be determined from the content of the Hittite text, however, whether the throne was made only of iron. An iron throne is also referred to in an Old Kingdom ritual text from Egypt of roughly the same age (Waldbaum, 1980:75) where the Egyptian term for iron, *bia' n pet*, also seems to reflect a cosmic origin, although it is used in association with all iron.

An Alalakh text, also Hittite, refers to four hundred weapons (*ŠUKUR*) of iron (*AN.BAR*) that have been taken by Ammitaku along with a host of other objects from 'those who opposed him'. The reference has often been cited to support the claim that the Hittites had a monopoly on iron. But, as Forbes (1972:244) indicates, the number of weapons captured may be exaggerated, as is typical of ancient war records. The material record does not even come close to supporting this claim. Later Hittite documents list statues of iron, iron weapons, iron cult objects, and simply 'black iron'. Despite the

3. The Development of Iron Technology

variety of types referred to (including weapons), most of these references occur in ritual texts or temple inventories, and the objects are listed for their ceremonial or intrinsic value rather than for any apparent utilitarian purpose (Waldbaum, 1978:21).

From the region of Syria, the Mari texts speak of the precious nature of iron and its use as an item of trade (Waldbaum, 1980:75). One text mentions an iron bracelet sent to Mari by the king of Carchemish, a single item of jewelry worthy of being traded among kings, together with other expensive objects. This text contains the earliest reference to iron as an item of trade. Iron is also portrayed as a luxury item that was not readily available and was more costly than gold. An eighteenth-century Susa text that mentions iron and gold rings is the last on our list from the Middle Bronze Age (cf. Forbes, 1972:260).

From the Late Bronze Age there are more texts dealing with iron use and trade than with its manufacture. Most of them are Hittite, but some are from Assyria, North Syria, and Egypt (Waldbaum, 1980:80). The texts come from Bogazköy, Susa, Mari, Alalakh, Qatna, El Amarna, Mitanni, Ugarit, and Nuzi. Many of them refer to iron jewelry and ceremonial weapons, to the exchange of small iron objects among monarchs, or to the use and storage of ceremonial objects in palaces and temples.

One of the most controversial Late Bronze Age texts is a letter found at Bogazköy from the Hittite king Hattusilis III (c. 1250 BCE) probably to Shalmanesar I of Assyria. It is the only Late Bronze Age text alluding to the manufacture of iron (Waldbaum, 1980:80). Although the circumstances in which the letter was written are obscure, it is apparently an attempt to put off Shalmanesar's demand for a shipment of iron and to appease him with a gift of an iron-bladed dagger. It explains that iron will be produced, but that the present time is not good for production. The letter speaks of iron manufactured within the boundaries of the Hittite empire, stored in Kizzuwatna (probably in Cilicia), and exported to other monarchs (Waldbaum, 1978:21). Waldbaum (1980:80) suggests that the letter may indicate either that iron was only produced seasonally or that the process of manufacture was slow and unreliable. The letter may further indicate that the gift of a single iron dagger blade was still considered in the Late Bronze Age to be worthy of royal exchange. This letter has been used along with the Alalakh text mentioned above to support the claim that the Hittites monopolized iron, an assertion that is not supported by the archaeological evidence.

There are more texts dealing with the trade of iron and its utilization in the Late Bronze Age than its manufacture, even among those of Hittite origin. Iron is mentioned frequently in Hittite inventories and ritual texts (Waldbaum, 1980:81; cf. Forbes, 1972:265). In the latter, it is often listed with other metals. References are also made to objects made of several metals. For example, mention is made of an iron kettle with a lid of lead used to trap evil spirits and a statue composed of a tin (?) frame and an iron head. There is also a text that lists foundation deposits of metals and stone, including iron. Among the iron objects mentioned are two pair of oxen, a hearth, props (?), and a door, each weighing one shekel. Lists of foundation deposits referring to iron buried with other precious materials in Middle Assyrian temples and Hittite palaces are also cited in the literature. Excavations have confirmed this practice (Waldbaum, 1980:80-81). A Hittite ritual for erecting a house states:

> The diorite they brought from the earth. The black iron of heaven they brought from heaven. Copper (and) bronze they brought from Mt. Taggata in Alasiya... (Bjorkman, 1973:110)

It is again the ceremonial or symbolic, rather than the utilitarian, function of iron that is reinforced by these texts.

Other Late Bronze Age texts from outside Anatolia include: a text from Nuzi that refers to a coat of iron scale armor for a horse (Muhly, 1980:50); a fifteenth-century BCE temple inventory of Qatna in Northern Syria referring to seven precious iron objects (six of them overlaid with gold) belonging to the goddess Nin-Egal (Waldbaum, 1978:18; 1980:80); and some Ugaritic documents that cite iron as a precious material worth sixty times the value of copper and twice the value of silver (Waldbaum, 1978:17; cf. Fensham, 1969).

3. The Development of Iron Technology 135

From among the Amarna letters is one from Tušratta, king of Mitanni, to Amenhotep III and Akhenaton of Egypt, mentioning daggers with iron blades, arrowheads, and iron rings overlaid with gold being sent as royal gifts to the pharaohs (Waldbaum, 1978:18; 1980:80; cf. Forbes, 1972:268). One of the daggers, among the objects sent to Amenhotep III as a bridal gift for his daughter Tadu-Kheba, is described as having a wooden hilt overlaid with gold and a pommel of rock crystal or lapis lazuli (Stech-Wheeler et al., 1981:264; cf. Forbes, 1972:268).

Finally, note should be made of the assertion that the thirteenth-century BCE Papyrus Anastasi I describes the activity of ironworkers at Joppa. According to Snodgrass (1980:3; cf. Forbes, 1972:241), this is an arbitrary interpretation and, in fact, the text does not mention iron specifically.

A number of early textual references to iron seem to indicate that meteoric iron was a primary source for the metal. In particular, the terms used suggest a meteoric source and indicate that the peoples of the ancient Near East were aware of its celestial or extraterrestrial origins. The Hittite term *AN.BAR GE nepišiš* means literally 'black iron from heaven', and the Egyptian term for iron, *bia' n pet*, also seems to reflect a cosmic origin. The Hittite ritual text cited above supports this interpretation. According to Judith Bjorkman, 'black iron' seems to be a technical term for meteoric iron in Hittite texts, 'black' probably indicating the black fusion crust with which meteors are covered. In three texts both iron and black iron are mentioned in the same list (Bjorkman, 1973:110). Bjorkman (1973:113) cites several other texts that suggest a meteoric origin for iron. One, an Old Babylonian hymn (c. 1800 BCE) refers to 'the fall of iron to the ground', evidently an epithet. The other lines in the hymn contain additional epithets referring to other natural phenomena. Another is a Sumerian hymn:

> The lord (king), who is the light for family and clan, going in front of them, iron (*AN.BAR*) (coming) from heaven, who could wander with you, what could vie with you.

Forbes (1972:265) cites a Hittite text (c. 1300 BCE) that states:

They cover the wooden beams with plates of silver and gold, the gold they bring from the city of Bi..., the silver from Kuzza... black iron from heaven from the sky.

The Egyptian term for meteoric iron, *bia' n pet* 'iron from heaven', does not occur before the nineteenth dynasty (c. 1320 BCE) and refers to all iron. The earlier term used, simply *bia'*, also seems to refer to both meteoric and smelted iron, in addition to meteoric material in general (Bjorkman, 1973:114). The *Book of the Dead* refers to a wall of heaven made of *bia'* and a chain of *bia'* placed around the neck of the serpent Apep. The dead person is said to conquer heaven and to split its *bia'* Other Egyptian religious texts also say the sky is made of *bia'* (Forbes, 1972:238). Such references point clearly to the celestial connection of iron.

In addition to texts that point to an association between iron and the heavens, there are a number of texts that refer directly to meteors and meteorites. Most of these date to the first millennium BCE, but, according to Bjorkman (1973:91), they often represent copies of materials that originated during the second millennium BCE. Many are of a type known as celestial omens (Bjorkman, 1973:92). Two of the oldest preserved omen texts (not later than 1200 BCE, although they represent copies of even older Akkadian originals) mention stars falling from heaven and are written in Hittite (Bjorkman, 1973:91). Celestial omens, including those that deal with meteorites, are scattered throughout various omen collections, the largest of which is the *Enuma Anu Enlil*, consisting of about seven thousand omens (Bjorkman, 1973:92). Some omens also occur in the *namburû* texts that describe magical procedures for avoiding potential evil, particularly evil indicated by ominous signs. Eighth-and seventh-century BCE references to meteors also occur in letters written by court astromancers to various kings that contain commentaries, prayers, and omens from dreams.

The omens are frequently indicated by either 'falling' or 'flashing' stars. In Mesopotamia, the 'falling' stars seem to have been considered bad omens and 'flashing' stars of either good or bad portent. For example, one text states:

3. The Development of Iron Technology

> If a shooting star flashes (as bright) as a light or as a torch from east to west and disappears (on the horizon) the army of the enemy will be slain in its onslaught. (Bjorkman, 1973:92)

The basic theme running through these texts is of gods speaking to humankind through shooting stars and meteors.

A dream omen in the first tablet of the Gilgamesh Epic refers to a meteorite that falls on Gilgamesh (see Bjorkman, 1973:115-16; cf. Pritchard, 1955:76; the material of which the meteorite is made is not specified). In the story, Gilgamesh relates the dream to his mother, the goddess Ninsun:

> My mother, I saw a dream last night:
> There were stars in the sky.
> Like the *kiṣru* of Anu it descends upon me.
> I sought to lift it; it was too stout for me.
> I sought to drive it off, but I could not remove it.
> Uruk-land was standing about [it],
> [The land was gathered round it],
> The populace jos[tled toward it],
> [The nobles] thronged about it
> [...] my companions were kissing its feet,
> [I] was drawn to it as though to a woman.
> And I placed it at [thy] feet,
> For thou didst make it vie with me.

Ninsun then interprets the dream and explains to Gilgamesh that the *kiṣru* of Anu represents a mighty comrade (Enkidu) who would come to Uruk to befriend Gilgamesh. Ninsun mentions the *kiṣru* of Anu twice more:

> Thy [rival]—the star of heaven,
> which descended upon thee like [the *kiṣru* of Anu...]

and:

> [He is the mightiest in the land]; strength he has.
> [Like the *kiṣru* of Anu], so mighty is his strength.
> [That thou wert] drawn to him [as to a woman],
> [means that he will never] forsake [th]ee.

It is interesting to note here the mediating role of Enkidu, here symbolized by the *kiṣru*, who is sent to Gilgamesh by the gods for the purpose of distracting him from his oppressive policies.

Overall, the texts that refer to shooting stars, meteors, and meteorites indicate that they were regarded as messages from the gods, and as such served as symbols of mediation, although their symbolic quality derived from quite a different understanding than that indicated in Chapter 2 for smelted iron among African societies. But this mediating function of meteorites may have contributed to the development of mediating symbols associated with smelted iron once that technology was developed (see Chapter 5).

To summarize, the combined textual and archaeological information predating the Iron Age strongly suggests that iron was rare and precious. The desire to possess iron, as indicated clearly in the Hittite letter from Hattusilis to Shalmanesar, was not for a strong and technologically superior metal. Rather, it was a desire for a metal with symbolic significance, whether it be in the realm of prestige, wealth, magic, ritual, or ceremonial use. Iron was buried with the dead, stored with other treasures in palaces, and used (or stored?) in temples. It was a metal of cosmic origin, and its cosmic form (meteors) was consulted in times of emergency. Iron was also traded on a small scale, but only during the first millennium BCE did it surpass bronze in the manufacture of utilitarian objects. Iron's usefulness as a utilitarian metal was dependent upon, and was the product of, the discovery of a new technological process in its manufacture. This discovery, the process of carburization, was first made and recognized sometime between 1200 and 1000 BCE, and ushered in a new age of metal technology.

The Search for the Origins of Iron Technology

Early studies on the development of iron technology were concerned in large part with the origins of the technology, particularly with the location and the peoples responsible for introducing the technological breakthrough. These studies operated with the assumption that the innovation could have occurred initially only in one location from which it was subsequently diffused. Of the more recent major studies, only R. J. Forbes takes a strong stance in support of this position. Diffusion from one center, he claims, is the best explanation when

3. The Development of Iron Technology 139

considered in light of the special set of techniques required for working iron, combined with the technical knowledge of working other metals that ironworking presumes (1972:226; cf., e.g., Wright, 1938:5). This center he believes to have been located in the area of Cappadocia in Anatolia (1972:213, 228). In further support of the diffusionist theory, Forbes points to the superstitions and religious taboos attached to the use of iron as evidence of importation (1972:226).

Although many contemporary scholars would agree that Anatolia may have been one of the earliest areas in which experimentation with iron took place, and that ideas originating in Anatolia 'may have played a crucial role in stimulating the desire to produce iron in other areas' (e.g., Stech-Wheeler et al., 1981:263-64), the question of a precise location has receded into the background. There is general agreement that the earliest experimentation with iron took place in the Near East, perhaps even the Levant (e.g., Muhly, 1980:51). But there is more caution about assigning precedence to any particular geographical area. The general consensus is that the development of iron technology took hundreds of years and that it probably took place simultaneously in various areas as the result of general experimentation throughout the ancient Near East. It is necessary to repeat the caution noted earlier in this chapter against proposing simplistic explanations for a complex process of development that certainly incorporated both local innovations and a complex web of the exchange and diffusion of ideas and techniques. Early iron finds and texts have not proven that Anatolia was more advanced than any other areas in any stage in the development of iron technology. Rather, it is more likely that its evolution in Anatolia in general ran a course parallel to those of the neighboring regions (e.g., Coghlan, 1956:70).

Related to the claims that iron technology had its origins in Anatolia is the assertion that during the Bronze Age the Hittites had a 'monopoly' on the 'secret' of producing and distributing iron and iron objects. According to this view, the Hittites discovered the 'steeling' of iron c. 1400 BCE, thus giving them a monopoly on the manufacture of 'true iron' or steel for the ensuing two hundred years (e.g., Forbes, 1972:229). The 'evidence' cited most often is the Hattusilis letter that contains the only Late Bronze Age reference to the manufacture of iron. But this mid-thirteenth-century letter falls short of demonstrating anything like a monopoly. What it does indicate is the Hittite king's striking concern with iron (Snodgrass, 1980:357) and that some smiths in the Hittite empire during the thirteenth century BCE possessed more than a superficial understanding of iron production (Stech-Wheeler et al., 1981:263). It may suggest a certain degree of Hittite control over the production of smelted iron shipped out as a raw material, presumably to the king of Assyria, but gives no indication of Hittite control in relation to other regions (Waldbaum, 1980:81). And it indicates that iron weapons were rare, greatly prized, and fit for royal gifts (Coghlan, 1956:69). But the assertion of a monopoly cannot be upheld for a number of reasons. The most convincing counter-evidence is that of the combined Late Bronze Age textual information and the local nature of many of the finds from regions other than Anatolia (Waldbaum, 1978:68; 1980:81). Furthermore, the Hittite king's failure to oblige his correspondent could be explained in other ways. For example, ironworking may have been a seasonal occupation, or there could have been some religious reasons preventing the work (Coghlan, 1956:69). Even as early as 1940, the flaws in the claims of a Hittite monopoly were recognized:

> There is no reason whatever for the belief that the Hittites wished to monopolise the precious metal for themselves. Nothing indicates that sending the weapons would have involved military secrets. The contemporary Amarna letters are full of such requests. (Goetze, 1940:33 [quoted in Coghlan, 1956:69])

More recently, in an analysis of the Hittite iron industry, J. D. Muhly, R. Maddin, T. Stech, and E. Özgen conclude:

> ... it would seem that the Hittites made iron and were known among their neighbors for doing so, but that they did not have sufficient knowledge of ores to produce good iron on a regular schedule... we do have clear evidence that the Hittites practiced smelting, although we cannot regard them as monopolists or possessors of secrets about effective ironworking. (1985:79-80)

3. The Development of Iron Technology 141

The major problem with the theory is that it relies on many unfounded assumptions, grounded in part in the acceptance of a diffusionist approach. It assumes *a priori* the existence of a Bronze Age Hittite monopoly on iron that in turn presupposes a well-developed iron technology, an advantage to keeping the knowledge secret, and the rapid adoption of iron elsewhere once the 'secret' got out. It also depends on the presupposition that iron was a superior and desirable commodity from the beginning. One might ask why with such an important monopoly the Hittites did not become the absolute overlords of the Eastern Mediterranean when their supposedly superior weaponry was tested against the bronze weapons of others, or why it was possible for the Sea Peoples to conquer them (Waldbaum, 1978:67).

The use of iron in Hittite Anatolia is somewhat better documented than for other areas, but the documentation does not differ essentially from that for other regions during the Bronze Age. Furthermore, there is no evidence either in the texts or the archaeological material that the Hittites made substantial military or agricultural use of iron or that their knowledge of ironworking techniques was any more advanced than that of neighboring peoples. They seem to have treated it the same, as a precious metal, 'superior' only in its worthiness to grace the temple stores. Arguments that attempt to account for the paucity of iron implements recovered from Hittite sites by attributing it to plunder break down when the relatively large number of untouched contemporary bronze artifacts is considered. Neither is corrosion an adequate explanation, since some traces would always remain (Waldbaum, 1980:81-82).

Other questions are raised when the rather wide distribution of both meteoric and smelted iron in a variety of forms and the widespread knowledge of manufacturing techniques throughout the Bronze Age Near East are considered. For example, why did the Bronze Age smiths go no further? Why were the capabilities of iron not more fully explored? Why, following the destruction of the Hittite empire, was there not a more rapid adoption of the advantages of iron technology instead of a process that took two to three hundred years? Why was iron almost always confined to use in manufacturing ceremonial, funerary, or ornamental objects of non-utilitarian function? (Waldbaum, 1978:68). It is clear from such questions that to propose an early entry into a full Iron Age on the part of the Hittites is an oversimplification, as is the dependent theory that the Philistines took over the monopoly (see Chapter 4). In fact, following the advent of the Iron Age, the pattern of iron usage in Anatolia, as in Egypt, is significantly less than in other areas (Stech-Wheeler et al., 1981:263). And the Anatolian 'Early Iron Age', that is, the transitional stage in the introduction of iron technology, lags behind that of other regions, as does the definitive shift to an iron-based technology (c. 1100–850 BCE and 850–600 BCE respectively; Snodgrass, 1980:357).

It is possible to infer from the archaeological and textual information, however, that experimentation with ironworking was carried out in Anatolia and that it may have been a source of technological information. The textual information may also reflect a significant, though largely ceremonial, interest in producing and consuming iron. Unfortunately, none of the textual and archaeological information for Anatolian ironworking has been confirmed by metallographic examinations of the iron artifacts.[1] An 'informed speculation' might postulate a strong interest in iron in areas controlled by the Hittite empire, so much so that smelters could regularly produce desirable products (Stech-Wheeler et al., 1981:264).

---

[1] A recent study (Muhly et al., 1985) has included metallographic examination of several artifacts from Late Bronze Age Anatolia. The conclusions of these analyses indicate that Hittite smiths were successful in some cases in smelting iron.

Chapter 4

THE EARLY IRON AGE

Introduction

The preceding chapter painted a broad picture of the beginnings of iron technology in the ancient Near East in the periods before the advent of the 'Iron Age'. The scope of this chapter narrows to focus on developments in Iron Age I Palestine, with some reference to general trends in Anatolia, Syria, Mesopotamia, Egypt, and Greece. Iron Age I is a transitional period in the history of the ancient Near East during which bronze technology gradually gave way to iron technology as the dominant mode of producing functional tools and weapons. It is this transition which is of primary concern. However, since major shifts are also evident in the economic, sociopolitical, and religious spheres of ancient Near Eastern societies, we cannot divorce the technological shift from the radical shifts that occurred in these other spheres.

Elucidating this enigmatic period is difficult. To recognize this, one need only glance through the archaeological and historical literature, which reveals a general lack of consensus. The social disruptions of the close of the Late Bronze Age were so extensive that literary documentation is scarce and the archaeological information difficult to decipher. In the past, archaeologists and historians have depended heavily on the Hebrew Bible for interpreting the complex puzzles that Late Bronze and Early Iron Age peoples left behind in the archaeological record. This approach, however, has created more questions than it has supplied answers. The biblical descriptions contradict the archaeological information as much as they support it, and vice versa. For example, W. F. Albright's attempts to substantiate biblical claims of a wholesale 'conquest' of Canaan by appealing to archaeological evidence became less persuasive as more and more unearthed information contradicted them. The resulting array of radically differing settlement theories (see, e.g., Ramsey, 1981; Mendenhall, 1973; Gottwald, 1979; Weippert, 1971; Alt, 1968; Miller, 1977) attests to the difficulties of discovering just what exactly did happen in this 'dark age' of ancient Near Eastern history.

The history of the introduction of iron technology is no better understood. There are no literary documents, biblical or extra-biblical, that outline the steps by which the process of ironworking was invented and adopted, so it is necessary to depend entirely on archaeological information as 'evidence'. Attempts to explain the introduction of the technology into Israel on the basis of biblical texts are not only unconvincing, but tend to be based on reading information into the text that is not even there (e.g., the claim, based on 1 Sam. 13.19-23, that the Philistines were responsible for introducing the knowledge of iron technology to the Israelites). The literature on the origins and development of iron technology reveals as little consensus as is the case for the Iron Age I period in general. Was the crucial process of carburization discovered in one locale and subsequently diffused to other areas of the ancient Near East? If so, was this primary center of diffusion located in Anatolia? Was it located in Greece? Were the Philistines, as a result of contact with Anatolia or Greece, responsible for introducing iron technology to the Israelites? Is it possible to refute diffusionist theories and propose reasonable arguments for local innovations that grew out of experimentation in a number of areas? There is no general agreement among metallurgists on the answers to these questions. In part, this lack of consensus is due to the nature of the archaeological evidence (see Chapter 3). But it also arises from such factors as inconsistencies and vagueness in the archaeological reports, variations in archaeological research design, paucity of metallurgical analyses of iron artifacts, and lack of archaeological information for the actual production of iron in Iron Age I. Also of significance are the different theoretical orientations of the interpreters; for example, diffusionist orientations vs. multiple innovations orientations.

4. The Early Iron Age

The primary aim in this chapter, as in Chapter 3, is to set the stage for evaluating the symbolic representation of ironworking in the Hebrew Bible (Chapter 5). Toward this end several topics are considered. First, the general Late Bronze-Early Iron Age historical context and the various theories on the origin and development of ironworking are reviewed. Second, the discussion of the technological processes of ironworking in Chapter 3 is supplemented with a description of the crucial discovery—carburization. Third, a catalogue of the known iron artifacts from Iron Age I contexts in Palestine is presented. Spatial and contextual distribution and the question of 'ethnic' associations are considered. Finally, the relationship of the development of ironworking to the history of ancient Israel and the evolution of the Israelite state is considered.

The Transition from the Bronze Age to the Iron Age

The advent of the Iron Age (c. 1200 BCE) can be linked more directly with social, political, and economic changes than with a shift from a bronze- to an iron-based technology (see Waldbaum, 1978:11). The Late Bronze Age was a time of prosperity and extensive international trade, evidenced in part by the substantial amount of 'imported', painted, and decorated pottery uncovered in excavations. But the end of this prosperous age presents quite a different picture. The Late Bronze Age drew to a close with a series of social, political, and economic upheavals that have defied explanation. Migrations, dislocations, and movements of diverse populations are referred to in Late Bronze Age texts and inscriptions from Ugarit, Alalakh, and Egypt. Mass destruction of Late Bronze Age cities and towns is documented by the archaeological record. This tumultuous period of decline is characterized by destruction, disruption of international trade routes, invasions, shifting populations, and the redistribution of power throughout the Eastern Mediterranean and Near East. Major Bronze Age civilizations in New Kingdom Egypt, Hittite Anatolia, Mycenaean Greece, and Syria collapsed. Troy was destroyed; the Dorians moved into Greece from the northwest; Mycenaean sea power collapsed; the Phrygians migrated to Anatolia; the Sea Peoples attacked Egypt and finally settled the southern coastal region of Palestine; new settlements were established in the previously sparsely populated hill country of Canaan; the Hittite empire collapsed; the great city-states of Ugarit and Alalakh were destroyed; Arameans migrated into Mesopotamia and Syria. Whether these contemporaneous crises were related to one another is unknown, but the Eastern Mediterranean world was plunged into a Dark Age characterized by material poverty and isolation. Even historical records are temporarily deficient for the ensuing several centuries. These crises marked the end of the great Late Bronze Age empires and of the palace economies that had developed around their urban centers (see, e.g., Waldbaum, 1978:10, 67; 1980:83; Muhly, 1982:44; Dever, 1977).

This picture of events and their aftermath at the end of the Late Bronze Age is reflected in the metallurgical finds. There is a decrease in metal luxury goods, and in some areas a deterioration of craftmanship. In addition, iron appears with increasing regularity in the form of functional tools and weapons (Waldbaum, 1978:67).

It was subsequent to these major cultural shifts that iron, specifically 'steeled' or carburized iron, was introduced, and the use of bronze began to diminish in most areas. The relative number of iron objects to bronze objects recovered from excavations, combined with the results of metallurgical analysis, suggests that by the late tenth century BCE smiths in Palestine were able to produce carburized iron on a fairly consistent basis, and that iron was adopted as the primary material for manufacturing utilitarian metal objects (see Waldbaum, 1978; 1980; Stech-Wheeler et al., 1981). It is difficult to ascertain for many areas exactly when this transition from bronze to iron was complete. Adoption of the new technology appears to have been somewhat inconsistent. It is fairly safe to assume that iron technology was adopted in both Palestine and Greece by the end of the tenth century BCE.

For Greece, there is a significant increase of iron artifacts from the twelfth to the tenth centuries, but in contrast to the situation in Palestine jewelry remains the dominant form. Furthermore, most of the finds come from tombs, which makes it difficult to judge the actual utility of iron (Waldbaum,

1978:33). In Crete, on the other hand, the number of iron weapons recovered far outweighs that of tools and jewelry. Again, this can probably be attributed to the contexts from which the objects were recovered, that is, the discovery of more warriors' tombs than tombs of women, which might have yielded more jewelry (Waldbaum, 1978:34).

Information from Syria is sparse, and the only conclusive evidence for the adoption of an iron-based technology comes from a series of burials from the Hama cemetery. The adoption of a completely iron-based economy has been established as dating to some time between 925 and 800 BCE (Period III) (see Waldbaum, 1978:27-29; Snodgrass, 1980:356-57). It is difficult to draw definitive conclusions on the basis of the Hama material, however, because all of the iron artifacts were found in tombs. Furthermore, although there is an increase in the number of iron weapons over time, the predominant form throughout the sequence is jewelry, that is, non-utilitarian.

For Anatolia, it is also difficult to establish when the utilization of iron began to increase significantly. There are virtually no iron objects from a securely dated twelfth-century BCE context in Anatolia, and only four widely scattered sites have yielded iron artifacts (a total of sixteen) that can even be dated tentatively to the tenth and eleventh centuries BCE (Waldbaum, 1978:35). This is surprising given the comparative wealth of textual and artifactual information suggesting experimentation with iron from earlier periods (see Chapter 3). Anthony Snodgrass (1980:57) tentatively dates the adoption of an iron-based economy in Anatolia to c. 850–600 BCE, somewhat later than in Greece and Syro-Palestine.

Mesopotamia also appears to have been a late-comer in the adoption of an iron-based technology (see Pleiner and Bjorkman, 1974; Waldbaum, 1980:82; Curtis et al., 1979). As for other areas, the paucity of iron objects from securely dated Iron Age I contexts contributes to an uncertainty about the date of adoption. Textual information indicates that iron was being worked (although rarely) from at least the thirteenth century BCE on. By the twelfth century, an ironsmith was present at the court of Ninurta-Tukulti-Assur. By the ninth century iron appears to have been widely used but not to have replaced bronze as the material used to manufacture most tools and weapons. It is not until the eighth to seventh centuries that it can be established that ironworking was clearly well developed.

Egypt, where some of the earliest experimentation with iron apparently took place (see Chapter 3), is the area for which there appears to have been the longest delay in accepting the benefits of iron technology (see, e.g., Snodgrass, 1980:364-65; van der Merwe, 1980:465-66). Egyptian axes and other implements dating from c. 900 BCE onward were found to have been carburized, quenched, and perhaps tempered. But the first clear evidence for the acceptance of iron technology comes from a much later period, the seventh century BCE and later. The apparently late adoption of iron technology in Egypt probably attests to the general conservatism of Pharaonic Egypt and to the differing attitudes toward accepting technological innovations.

The Production of Steeled Iron

The crucial technological breakthrough that allowed for the adoption of iron technology for producing utilitarian implements was the discovery and application of carburization.[1] How carburization was discovered is not known, although it is likely that it was accidental. As was demonstrated in Chapter 3, iron objects were produced by Bronze Age smiths in the ancient Near East, but carburization was not consistently applied, nor was it apparently understood. Iron was smelted as a direct process in which a sponge iron was produced in a single operation. The resulting product was wrought iron, a substance that contains little carbon (less than 0.2 percent) and is functionally inferior to bronze. It is the extra carbon content of steel that gives it the property necessary to allow it to be hardened when it is reheated and quenched.

---

1 For descriptions of the technological process of carburizing iron, see, e.g., Forbes, 1972:196-225; Coghlan, 1956:55-60; Maddin et al., 1977:123-30; Wheeler and Maddin, 1980; Waldbaum, 1978:69-70; Tylecote, 1980:209-11.

4. The Early Iron Age

Carburization is achieved by heating iron at a high temperature in contact with carbon. It was necessary either to pack the iron in charcoal and heat it to a high temperature for several days, or to heat and reheat the iron frequently in a charcoal fire. When the smith reheated the bloom following smelting, he would have done so with a charcoal fire in the forge. When the bloom was heated to about 1200 degrees C., it was in direct contact with white-hot charcoal and with the hot carbon monoxide emitted by its combustion. A small amount of carbon from both sources would have slowly diffused into the iron, converting it into carbon steel. The amount and depth of carbon absorption depend on the length of time the iron is in contact with the carbon, and on the temperature of the fire. The solubility of carbon in iron increases significantly above 910 degrees C., temperatures that could be achieved if the smith was using good charcoal and bellows. Carbon content is also considerably increased with repeated forging. Absorption is greatest at the surface of the object and gradually decreases toward the center. Sometimes the hardening is no more than a thin casing. It is not until 0.2 to 0.7 percent carbon is present that iron is fully in the domain of steeled iron. This is the essential difference between the wrought iron produced in the Bronze Age and the steel that was increasingly produced after the tenth century BCE.

Producing low-carbon steel in the early smelting furnaces required no change in furnace construction but necessitated a different method of operation and the use of a suitable ore. The furnace had to be preheated in order to obtain the highest possible temperature, and more charcoal, but less ore, than usual had to be charged. The oxidizing effect of the air draft was significantly reduced by suitable inclination of the air passages for natural draft, or by setting the tuyères a little higher than usual for a forced draft.

Quenching and tempering are the processes most critical to the quality of the finished product of ironworking, but are the least likely to be applied by accident. Quenching involves immersing the highly heated iron into a cold liquid. It has no effect on bronze, nor does it have any effect on iron if it is not carburized. When carburized iron is quenched, a material called martensite is formed. This material is the earth's second hardest substance, next to a diamond. But in addition to being hard, martensite is very brittle, so brittle that an object of pure martensite will shatter upon impact. When carburized iron is quenched, however, only the outer layers are converted to martensite (Muhly, 1982:45; Wheeler and Maddin, 1980:81).

It is more difficult to obtain clear evidence of deliberate quenching than for carburization, so estimating when the quenching process was invented and first applied by ancient metalsmiths is problematic (Wheeler and Maddin, 1980:124; Maddin et al., 1977:129). Recent studies, however, suggest that quenching was practiced by the tenth century BCE, and perhaps as early as the twelfth century BCE (Davis et al., 1985:44). It is also difficult to determine whether the ancient smith initially was aware of the consequences of quenching, which could have been carried out simply to cool the object quickly. The earliest and clearest indication that the smith recognized the improvement wrought by quenching carburized iron is in Homer's eighth- or seventh-century BCE description of the blinding of Cyclops (Polyphemus) in the *Odyssey* (9.389-94). Homer wrote about the Late Bronze Age, and bronze is the metal used by his heroes. But he frequently drew on material from his own historical milieu. In such passages iron suddenly appears as the metal in common use.

> The blast and scorch of the burning ball singed all his eyebrows and eyelids, and the fire made the roots of his eye crackle. As when a man who works as a blacksmith plunges into water a great axe or adze which hisses aloud, 'doctoring' it, since this is the way that steel is made strong, even so Cyclops' eye sizzled about the beam of the olive. (Trans. after that by Richard Lattimore; quoted in Muhly, 1982:49)

Homer seems to have viewed quenching as a kind of 'magical' transformation. The Greek word translated here as 'doctoring' (*pharmassō*) is etymologically related to the English word pharmacy and indicates some magical effect produced by the act. It is this 'doctoring', in Homer's view, that made carburized iron strong (Wheeler and Maddin, 1980:124; Maddin et al., 1977:129; Muhly, 1982:49).

4. The Early Iron Age

Once an iron object has been carburized and quenched, it is very hard but also very brittle and thus not very durable. In order to reduce the brittleness, tempering is necessary. Tempering involves heating the carburized iron to a relatively low temperature (up to but not above 727 degrees C.) and then quenching it again. Tempering reduces some of the martensite, altering the structure of the metal so that its brittleness is reduced, while still retaining adequate strength and hardness for implemental use. The lower the temperature at which the tempering is carried out, the less the hardness of the steel will be reduced.

Since the ancient smith had no means of measuring temperature, he would have had to use what is called the 'tint' method for controlling it. If the surface of the steel object is polished and the steel then heated over a smokeless fire, changes in its color will occur, each color representing a definite temperature or state of hardness. When the metal is quenched, it will retain the hardness appropriate to the color it had attained when heated. Metallurgists who have studied this process generally agree that tempering was probably not applied intentionally until the Roman period, because there is no obvious way of gauging the correct temperature in the forge.

Information from analyses of ancient iron artifacts suggests that down to the Middle Ages the production of iron was something of a hit-or-miss affair, resulting sometimes in tools and weapons of a high quality and other times in implements that were decidedly mediocre. It is probable that the full potential of iron was only occasionally realized (Waldbaum, 1978:70).

The Adoption of Iron Technology

The severe recession and political fragmentation of the Late Bronze/Early Iron Age Mediterranean and Near Eastern worlds may have resulted in a need to develop new resources and local industries based on exploitation of local raw materials (Waldbaum, 1980:83; Stech-Wheeler et al., 1981:245). In other words, 'necessity became the mother of invention' (Muhly, 1982:44).[1]

Although iron was increasingly employed for the manufacture of utilitarian implements from the twelfth century BCE forward, 1200 to 900 BCE was a transitional period during which iron eventually replaced bronze as the predominant working metal. The gradual ascendency of iron can be traced in the archaeological record through the partial conversion of tools and weapons from bronze to iron until a time when iron implements equal or surpass their bronze counterparts. A clear example of this partial conversion is a transition from bronze knives or daggers with iron rivets in the Late Bronze Age to iron knives and daggers with bronze rivets in Iron Age I (see Waldbaum, 1978). Bronze continued to be used during this period, especially for purposes for which iron was not satisfactory.

A number of theories have been proposed to explain the shift from a predominantly bronze-based to an iron-based metal technology. In 1956, H. H. Coghlan noted that the discovery of iron

> opened up an entirely new field in that it led to the availability of a vast quantity of relatively cheap metal which was of a nature much more suitable to the manufacture of tools and weapons than the non-ferrous alloys could be. Also iron is, of course, well suited to a wide range of domestic and general use. (p. 13)

Questions asked today concerning the introduction of ironworking are whether this 'discovery' in itself was sufficient to stimulate the adoption of a new technology. Scholars agree that the discovery of carburization was an important factor in the rise of iron technology, but question the validity of assuming that it was the prime mover.

As indicated in Chapter 3, the notion that ironworking was introduced by the Hittites has now been largely rejected, although some still accept the possibility that ideas originating

---

1 Cf. Forbes (1971:11), who asserts that it is not *need* but *prosperity* that is the mother of invention. This assertion contradicts the material evidence for the introduction of iron technology into the ancient Near East.

4. The Early Iron Age

in Anatolia 'may have played a crucial role in stimulating the desire to produce iron in other areas' (Stech-Wheeler et al., 1981:264; cf. Wertime, 1973:885; Muhly et al., 1985). The Philistines also have been designated as the peoples who introduced ironworking into the Near East, particularly Palestine.

> It would seem that the Philistines had learned to use iron in the north (Anatolia), were holding a 'corner' on the iron market in Palestine, and were closely guarding the trade secrets of its production. (Wright, 1938:6)

Those who accept the theory of a Philistine introduction today suggest that iron technology was originally developed in the Eastern Mediterranean, with Greece and Cyprus playing major roles, and that it was introduced subsequently into the Near East through the migration of the Philistines and other Sea Peoples who had had contact with these centers (Snodgrass, 1980:356; Muhly, 1982:48-49; cf. Muhly, 1980:51). This proposal is disputed by others. Trude Dothan, for example, states:

> the assumption that the Philistines introduced iron production into Canaan, which was generally accepted in the past, can now be refuted by the widespread dispersal of iron technology throughout the Eastern Mediterranean. (1982:91)[1]

The answer is by no means clear. Because textual documentation is lacking, the task of clarification necessarily falls upon archaeologists and upon historians who rely upon their findings. We will return to this issue below.

Lack of, or decreased access to tin, a necessary raw material in the manufacture of bronze, is the most recent and most widely accepted explanation for the increased use of iron after 1200 BCE.

> Since bronze had been satisfactory... for several thousand years and iron did not appear to be useful, it must be inferred that iron was not suddenly adopted as a result of technical innovation, but rather that bronze became scarce. The further inferrence is that the scarcity resulted from an

---

1 Although Dothan refutes the theory that the Philistines were responsible for introducing iron technology, she does allow for the possibility that they had control over the metal industry (1982:91).

interruption in the supply of tin and even of copper to the bronze smelters of the Eastern Mediterranean. (Maddin et al., 1977:122)

A shortage of tin and/or copper, then, probably caused by the disruption of trade at the end of the Late Bronze Age, made it impossible to continue to produce bronze (Muhly, 1980:47). The proposal is that new resources needed to be developed, and because almost every region had some deposits of iron ore, iron could have been utilized at a lower cost than bronze, which was growing scarce. More recently, fuel efficiency has been proposed as a factor in the adoption of iron (see Stager, 1985) since iron production is more fuel-efficient than copper smelting and processing.

Some scholars agree with the former proposal but reject the idea that a shortage of tin was a factor operating outside of Cyprus and the Aegean (e.g., Snodgrass, 1980:367). Their conclusions are based on the fact that the development of ironworking in Syro-Palestine began at approximately the same time as in Cyprus and Greece but thereafter progressed more slowly toward an iron-based economy. The implication is that Palestine did not suffer the same constraints in acquiring copper and tin.

Regardless of the historical factors involved, it is fairly safe to assume that technological factors played a crucial role in determining the development and increased use of iron. Anthony Snodgrass (1980) has postulated a three-stage process for the development of iron technology in antiquity, using criteria that single out steps of real industrial and economic significance. The basic criterion for identifying his stages is the presence of 'working iron', that is,

> iron used to make the functional parts of the real cutting and piercing implements that form the basis of early technology ... The functional parts may be defined as those parts which came into direct contact with the material to be cut or pierced, whether inanimate or (as in the case of weapons) animate. (p. 336)

In stage 1 of this scheme, iron began to be used but was not employed as 'real' working iron. The inventory of iron objects from this stage consists primarily of ornamental objects and objects that have the form of real tools or weapons but whose contexts suggest no practical function. Stage 2 was a transitional stage during which 'working iron' was present but not predominant. In stage 3 iron became the predominant material used for manufacturing utilitarian, functional implements. The transition from stage 1 to stage 2, Snodgrass suggests, reflects a technological change, and from stage 2 to stage 3 an economic one.

> To understand the spread of early ironworking one must distinguish between the essentially *technological* factors, such as those that brought about the initiation of our stage 1 and the transition to stage 2, and the essentially *economic* factors that must lie behind the change from stage 2 to stage 3. The conditions which generated the former may have been unconnected with the latter. (Snodgrass, 1980:368)

Metallurgical analysis is also useful for distinguishing stages. As has already been emphasized, technologically, iron only became a medium superior to bronze for manufacturing utilitarian tools and weapons when it was carburized. Uncarburized iron would have been an unacceptable substitute for bronze.

It is likely that the process of carburization was beginning to be understood by the twelfth to eleventh centuries BCE (see Pigott et al., 1982; Stech-Wheeler et al., 1981). However, it can only be considered a meaningful technical achievement when it is a deliberate process that reflects an awareness that it is responsible for transforming soft wrought iron into steel. This does not mean, of course, that ancient smiths realized that the absorption of carbon from the fuel was responsible for transforming iron into a product superior to bronze. It is more likely that they believed that the correct procedures and the fire purified or altered the material in some other way. Deliberate treatment to produce this effect can only be assumed if an object is fairly uniformly carburized on all sides and if a group of contemporaneous objects reveals similar patterns of carburization (Stech-Wheeler et al., 1981:264). Isolated examples such as the fourteenth-century BCE battle-axe from Ras Shamra, therefore, do not constitute evidence for deliberate carburization. Consistent application of the techniques of carburization in the manufacture of iron objects in Palestine cannot be demonstrated for any period prior to the tenth century BCE (see Stech-Wheeler et al., 1981).

Furthermore, it is necessary to distinguish between *invention*, that is, the discovery or achievement of a new process or form, and *innovation*, that is, the widespread *adoption* of a new process or form (see Renfrew, 1984; cf. Heskel and Lamberg-Karlovsky, 1980). Diffusionist theories often blur this important distinction. Colin Renfrew (1984:393-94) outlines two assumptions that underlie diffusionist arguments. The first assumption is that the fundamental inventions (for example, metallurgy) can only occur once in human history (see, e.g., Wertime, 1964:1257) and that change is exogenous to the location in question. The second assumption is that widespread adoption of a new process follows rapidly and in a regular manner after exposure to 'infection' (i.e., knowledge of the invention). These assumptions, in Renfrew's estimation, fail to take into account the fact that the basic technology required for the adoption of many new processes is often available in many locations, whether through local development or as a result of contact with neighboring societies, decades or centuries before it is in fact utilized on a large scale. Furthermore, the opportunity for invention is present wherever specialist crafts are practiced. The point is that, in contrast to diffusionist assertions, there are many potential primary centers in which the discovery of a technological process may occur (p. 395). The second diffusionist assumption, that adoption of the invention follows rapidly upon exposure, denies what Renfrew considers to be the crucial mechanism in the adoption of a new technological process—human choice. Adoption, or innovation, requires a conscious decision on the part of an individual or individuals to adopt one mode of undertaking a particular activity rather than another. Inventions become innovations only when entrepreneurs adopt them in industry. The process requires not only production and the distribution of knowledge, but entrepreneurial decisions.

On the basis of these observations, Renfrew proposes an 'innovation choice' model in place of the 'infection' model. He suggests replacing the two diffusionist assumptions with two others: 1. any functional invention or innovation in human

4. The Early Iron Age

technology or culture will ultimately occur again, and recurrently, irrespective of time, space, or ethnic group, given the appropriate conditions; and 2. widespread adoption of a new process does not follow automatically upon the inception (whether locally or through outside contact) of the new process or form but depends in a complicated way upon individual choice governed by social and other factors. The availability of the technical know-how and means of production are crucial but not sufficient stimuli for the adoption of a new invention or discovery.

In proposing that we alter our assumptions, Renfrew does not deny that inventions may be introduced from elsewhere or that contact ('diffusion') may impart some general knowledge of a process or form. He merely emphasizes the fact that diffusionist theories do not account for social complexity or the roles of individuals in making decisions. Diffusion may be the source of the invention, but the general knowledge of a process or form may be introduced without precise details and potentially can be reinvented as a result of the stimulus of the contact. The circumstances favorable to the adoption of a new process may also be prompted by continuing contacts with another society, which may or may not be the source of the initial invention. On the other hand, favorable circumstances may develop entirely on a local level. Essentially, Renfrew warns against making simplistic assumptions on the basis of the rapid and widespread appearance of an innovation in the archaeological record, which need not indicate the operation of some external agency upon a culture system.

Heskel and Lamberg-Karlovsky's (1980) proposals, based on an analysis of metallurgical development in Iran, are closely akin to those of Renfrew. The social milieu into which technological innovation is introduced plays a primary role in both the acceptance of the innovation and the kinds of social changes that result from the innovation. Since any kind of technological change must be accepted by the members of a society, especially the leaders and/or those whose status renders their decisions legitimate, it cannot have any kind of social impact until the members of a society indicate approval.

If we apply these proposals to the situation in Iron Age I Palestine, we might characterize it broadly as follows: The archaeological record suggests that the 'invention' of ironworking, that is, the discovery of carburization and intentional application of the process, may have occurred sometime in the twelfth and eleventh centuries BCE. However, an environment conducive to the innovation and adoption of the new discovery evidently did not exist prior to the late tenth century BCE. This conclusion is supported both by the absolute numbers of artifacts revealed through excavations and by metallurgical analyses. In other words, there was a delay of one to two centuries before the discovery of ironworking was implemented in the economic activities of ancient Palestine. Unfortunately, the archaeological record does not supply us with conclusive evidence concerning why the peoples of Palestine were so slow in taking advantage of the discovery. Was it because the Philistines held a 'monopoly' on the production of iron as has so often been argued on the basis of the vague passage in 1 Sam. 13.19-23? Was it because the 'secret' of carburization was closely guarded by these neighbors of the tribes dwelling in the hill country? Was it because the Israelites lacked the know-how and the means to begin producing iron implements on their own?

The following pages in this chapter assess these questions in light of: first the archaeological information on the development of iron technology; and second what we can infer from archaeological material about the parallel sociopolitical development of Israel. The significance of the Philistines in both processes will be considered. The simplistic notions about the invention and adoption of iron technology underlying the assumption that diffusion is the only possible catalyst are in need of reassessment. We need to cease viewing the tribal 'Israelite' peoples as dolts with no technological know-how and consider the possibility that conscious human choice may have contributed to an initial conservatism in adopting iron technology, and ultimately to adopting it in spite of the ambivalent feelings that continued to be expressed for centuries afterward (see Chapter 5).

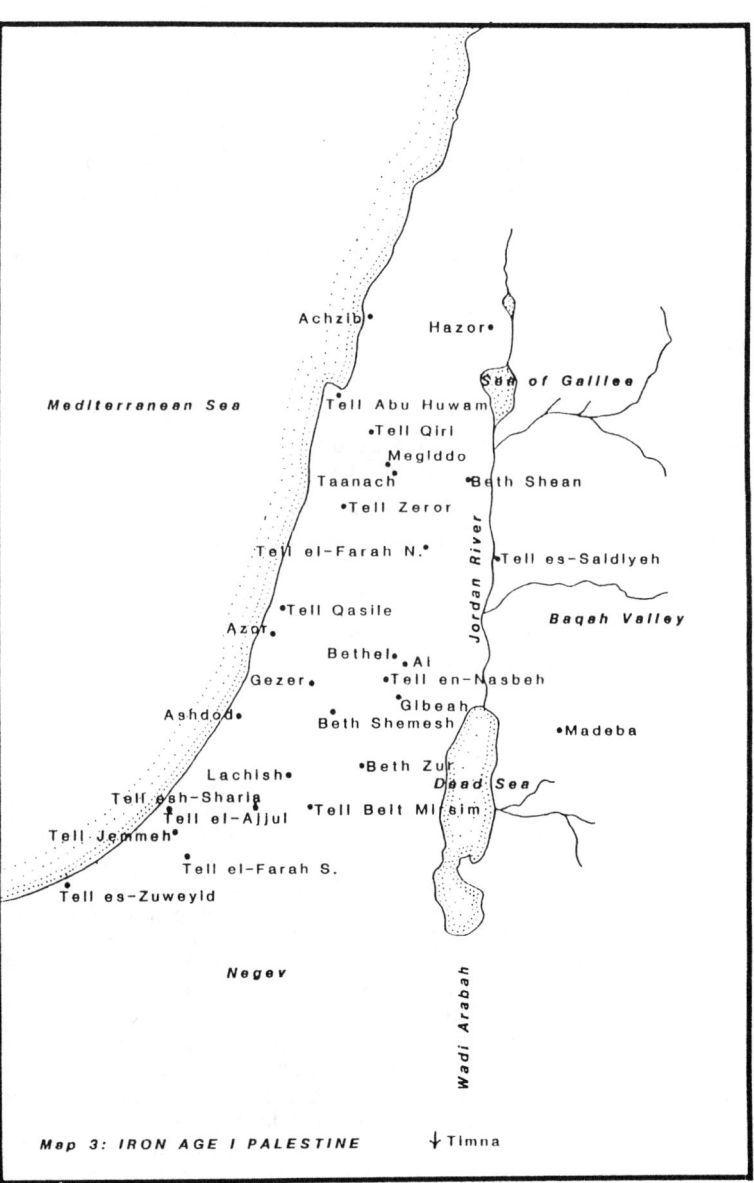

Map 3: IRON AGE I PALESTINE

The Artifactual Information

The following inventory of iron objects from Iron Age I levels in Palestine depends heavily upon Jane Waldbaum's exhaustive 1978 catalogue of iron artifacts from Iron Age I archaeological levels in Palestine. I go beyond Waldbaum's study in including information that has been published since the publication of her catalogue and in providing a brief sketch of each of the sites that yielded iron artifacts. The latter is included primarily for purposes of identifying the types of sites from which iron was recovered and the possible ethnic associations of each site over the three centuries encompassed by the designation Iron Age I. Sites and artifacts added to Waldbaum's catalogue are noted.[1] For each site, brief descriptions of Iron Age I levels are included.[2] Where possible, the material remains in the Iron Age I levels are designated Iron IA, IB, and IC according to the chronology developed by Paul Lapp (see Nancy L. Lapp, 1975:48-49). Iron IA (1200–1000 BCE) and Iron IB (1150–1000) overlap temporally but are distinguished on the basis of presumed cultural differences thought to be represented in the material culture. Iron IB remains are usually attributed to the Philistines on the basis of a new pottery type that appeared in the coastal plains at about the same time the Philistines are known to have settled there. The identification of Iron IB remains with the Philistines is based

---

1 The extensive list of site reports that contain this information can be found in Waldbaum's 1978 study. This list is supplemented in my 1983 Master's thesis. Not included in the inventory and analysis is a twelfth-century curved piece of iron from a Jebel al-Nuzha tomb (Jordan) (Dornemann, 1983:149; Pigott et al., 1982:35). Also not included in the inventory are at least twelve iron objects from tomb 240 at Tell el-Far'ah South (Maxwell-Hyslop et al., 1978) and four iron knives with ivory handles and a large iron ingot recovered from twelfth- to eleventh-century cultic contexts at Tel Miqne, a Philistine site (Dothan, 1989; Dothan and Gitin, 1990). The details of the Tell el-Far'ah tomb have not been published and the century within the Early Iron Age not firmly established, although the tenth century is probable. One of the objects, an iron dagger, has been analyzed and appears to have been fairly heavily carburized.

2 In addition to the sources listed for each site, excellent summaries can be found in Avi-Yonah 1975 and 1976; Avi-Yonah and Stern, 1977 and 1978.

on the geographical and stratigraphic distribution of a unique type of pottery introduced into Palestine during the twelfth century BCE (see, e.g., Mazar, 1985a; Dothan, 1982). The pottery type tends to be concentrated in the coastal plains and borders of the hill country although it has also been found in hill country sites and in Transjordan. Clay analysis has shown that it was manufactured in the coastal regions.

Metopes enclosing stylized birds, friezes of spirals, and groups of interlocking semi-circles are the most characteristic elements of classical Philistine pottery. It is a homogeneous group of locally made ware painted in black and red, usually on a white-slipped background. The pottery is eclectic, and four sources of influence have been identified: Mycenaean, Cypriot, Egyptian, and local Canaanite. The dominant source of influence is Mycenaean. It appears that it developed after the collapse of the Mycenaean IIIb pottery *koine* style of the Late Bronze Age and that it was a product not of a people carrying with them a homogeneous tradition from their country of origin but rather of the cultural influences incorporated along the way in the process of migration.

> Typologically, Philistine pottery reflects the Sea Peoples' Aegean background, plus certain Cypriot, Egyptian, and local Canaanite elements. Geographically, it is found in the major Philistine cities, follows the spread of Philistine influence through Canaan, and diminishes as one moves away from Philistia... Stratigraphically, Philistine vessels appear in strata dated to the first half of the twelfth and eleventh centuries BC. (Dothan, 1982:94)

Philistine burial customs are also considered to be distinctive (see Dothan, 1982:252-88). Particularly characteristic of what has been identified as 'Philistine' is burial in anthropoid clay coffins, a practice believed to have been borrowed from the Egyptians. Some of the coffins (for example, at Tell el-Far'ah and Beth Shean) exhibit the distinctive headgear of the Sea Peoples, as depicted in Ramses III's temple at Medinet Habu.

Iron IA remains, evaluated on the basis of pottery and architectural types, are concentrated in the hill country west of the Jordan river. The Early Iron Age pottery type normally associated with Iron IA material culture is the 'collared-rim' storage jar.

> The jar is typically ovoid rounded, but sometimes with cut-off base. The two handles are attached vertically above the middle of the body, joining the shoulder. The neck is very short and ends with a folded thickened rim... The shoulder is wide and slightly convex... most examples are covered with a flakey white or greenish slip on a reddish to dark brown ware. The core is grey or blackened in most cases. (Ibrahim, 1978:117)

W. F. Albright proposed that these jars were the work of the early Israelite settlers in Palestine, a view that has been widely adopted by biblical historians. The largest concentration of examples of the collared-rim jar comes from the hill country of Palestine, but its distribution also extends into the northern plains area, normally identified with the Canaanites, and east into Jordan. A few examples have been recovered from coastal and southern sites (Ibrahim, 1978).

Iron Age IA material culture has also been distinguished on the basis of the so-called 'Israelite' four-room house, an architectural type that is typical of Iron Age II but begins to appear in Palestine in Iron Age I levels (see, e.g., Shiloh, 1970; Wright, 1978). Examples of the four-room house are concentrated in the northern hill country, but as is the case with the collared-rim jar it has a wider geographical distribution. For example, structures similar in form have been uncovered in eleventh-century strata at Tell Qasile, Tell esh-Shari'a, and Tell Jemmeh, all judged to be Philistine sites, and at sites such as Ta'anach in the northern plains.

Some elements of the Late Bronze Age Canaanite culture also continue into Iron IA and B. Iron IC (1000–918 BCE) remains are characterized by a fusion of cultures and are found throughout Palestine.[1]

The iron artifacts in the following inventory are listed according to their chronological distribution by century (twelfth, eleventh, and tenth) and are further divided into four functional categories: tools, weapons, jewelry, and a miscella-

---

1 For a good description of the problems involved in assigning chronological and ethnic significance to Iron IA, IB, and IC, see Flanagan, 1988.

neous category inclusive of all other types (cf. Waldbaum, 1978).

Achzib

Ancient Achzib was a harbor city located on the northern coastal plain of Acco. It was originally settled in the Middle Bronze Age and was destroyed several times in the Late Bronze Age. It was refortified sometime in the Early Iron Age and reached its greatest expansion between the tenth and sixth centuries BCE. Two cemeteries, one south and one east of the city, have been uncovered. They contained Late Bronze Age burials and Iron Age rock-cut tombs (Prausnitz, 1975). Biblical references assert that Achzib remained a Canaanite city following the 'Israelite settlement' (Josh. 19.29; Judg. 1.31).

Tenth Century
Tools. An iron knife was found in a 'warrior's tomb'.[1]

'Ai (et-Tell)

'Ai or et-Tell is located on the south side of the Wadi el-Jaya in the central part of the hill region in Palestine. The Early Bronze Age settlement at 'Ai was abandoned in EB IIIB (c. 2400 BCE). At about 1250 BCE a 2.5-acre unwalled village was established on the acropolis of the site. The Early Iron Age settlement was abandoned in about 1050 BCE and was never resettled. Two phases in the Iron Age I settlement can be distinguished in the architecture and pottery of the site. The first phase is characterized by a long collared-rim jar (Iron IA) and the second by a low profile collared-rim jar and one with a beveled rim and no collar. The remains at the site suggest that the Iron Age villagers were farmers and shepherds (see, e.g., Callaway, 1976). Conquest of the site is, evidently erroneously, attributed in the Bible to Joshua (Josh. 8.1-29).

Eleventh Century
All of the iron objects recovered at 'Ai have been dated to the eleventh century, and all come from occupation levels.

---

1 Waldbaum (1978:25) includes this artifact in the eleventh-century materials while noting the possibility of a later date (tenth century).

Tools. A single piece of iron bent into a shape identified as tweezers; three knives; a nail; and a tool fragment.
Weapons. Two lanceheads and a conical spearbutt.
Jewelry. Two bracelets.
Other. One unidentified fragment and a 'rod' whose identification and date are doubtful.

Ashdod

Ashdod, one of the five cities of the Philistine pentapolis, is located in the southern coastal plains of Palestine. The site is repeatedly referred to in the biblical text in association with the Philistines (e.g., Josh. 11.22; 13.3; 1 Sam. 5).

The transition from the Late Bronze Age city is clearly represented stratigraphically by a thick layer of ash. The next phase of settlement is characterized by the introduction of Iron IB material remains. The city was fortified in the twelfth century BCE, and the fortifications were subsequently destroyed in the first half of the tenth century BCE.

The earliest phase of Iron IB is characterized by a continuation of the Late Bronze Age 'Canaanite' pottery tradition and locally manufactured Mycenaean and Iron IB wares. The eleventh-century remains include an abundance of Iron IB pottery, as well as 'plain Iron Age I pottery'. Iron IB pottery begins to disappear in the late eleventh-century levels and is not found in tenth-century levels (see, e.g., M. Dothan, 1971a; 1971b; 1979; T. Dothan, 1982:36-43).

Tenth Century
A total of five iron artifacts have been recovered from Ashdod, all from tenth-century contexts.
Tools. One 'Aegean-type' iron knife was found in a stratum X burial (Dothan, 1982:42; Stech-Wheeler et al., 1981:257); one large blade/pick; and one axe (Stech-Wheeler et al., 1981:257).
Jewelry. One ring, location and context unidentified.
Other. One fragment.

Azor

Azor is located on the northern edge of the southern coastal plain. Surveys and salvage excavations have uncovered traces of Iron Age occupation. The finds include a complete range of

Iron IB pottery, from the earliest types to the later debased, assimilated types (see T. Dothan, 1982:54-57).

Twelfth Century
Jewelry. One iron bracelet was found in a child's burial (burial 56) at Azor. On the child's throat a unique scarab from the Nineteenth or Twentieth Dynasty was found. Also found in the burial were a bronze mirror and Iron IB pottery. Dothan identifies the burial as a 'plain burial,' the most common type found at the site.

Baq'ah Valley (Jordan)

The Baq'ah Valley is located on the central Transjordanian plateau about 20 km. northwest of Amman. A series of Late Bronze Age II and Iron Age IA burials have been uncovered in the Ummad-Dananir region of the valley. Two major sources of iron ore in the Wadi Zarqa and Ajlun regions are located ten to eighty km. north of the burial site (see McGovern, 1981; 1982a; 1982b; Pigott et al., 1982).

Twelfth Century
A total of eleven intact iron objects and forty fragments of another twenty-four such artifacts come from burial cave A4, dated to the earliest part of the Iron Age (c. 1200-1040 BCE) (Pigott et al., 1982).
Jewelry. All of the objects are jewelry. The intact objects consist of eight iron bracelets and three iron rings. Five of the bracelets were tested for carbon content, and the results proved that four of these were carburized, verifying the earliest instances of mild steel from Jordan.

The burial cave contained the remains of 220 individuals. Males, females, and children were represented. Associated artifacts included: a unique assembly of seventy-eight Iron Age IA whole vessels; bronze anklets and bracelets, earrings, and rings; beads of a wide assortment of types and materials; toggle pins; buttons; one pendant; one scarab; one stamp seal; and one cylinder seal.

Bethel

Bethel is mentioned in the Hebrew Bible more frequently than any other town except Jerusalem. The site is located near the Wadi et-Tahuneh in the southern part of the high hill region of Mount Ephraim. A definite cultural break between the Late

Bronze and Early Iron Ages is indicated by a thick layer of ash and rubble and a decline in material culture. The Iron Age I material culture is characterized by the use of piers in masonry, 'ramshackle huts', and poorly made pottery. The ceramic inventory from this period consists primarily of collared-rim storage jars and Iron IA cooking pots. Two phases are evident in the construction of the collared-rim storage jars. The earlier jars have high collars, and the later jars have heavy rolled rims. A very small amount of Iron IB pottery has been found at Bethel (see Kelso, 1968).

> *Tenth Century*
> A total of eleven iron objects from definite Iron Age I levels has been found at Bethel (Kelso, 1968). All eleven artifacts have been assigned to the tenth century here since the reports do not indicate what levels they came from aside from 'Iron Age I'. All artifacts were listed in the report without regard to context.
> *Tools.* Three narrow iron pieces, each about 6 cm. in length, described by the excavator as possible tool points (Kelso, 1968:85); and an iron hammer.
> *Weapons.* Four iron arrowheads; and an iron javelin point.
> *Jewelry.* An iron fragment 'probably from an iron ring' (Kelso, 1968:90).
> *Other.* An iron fragment 6 cm. in length.

Beth Shean
Beth Shean is situated between the Jezreel and Jordan Valleys. The biblical texts indicate that Beth Shean was one of the Canaanite towns that resisted Israelite attack (Josh. 17.11 and Judg. 1.27). The exposure of the bodies of Saul and his sons on the wall of Beth Shean by the Philistines is referred to in 1 Sam. 31.12.

Beth Shean has been recognized as an important Egyptian stronghold during the Late Bronze and Early Iron Ages. Many vessels of Egyptian shape come from these levels, but local types that are a continuation of the Late Bronze Age 'Canaanite' culture and Mycenaean pottery types are also present. There are a few examples of the collared-rim jar (Iron IA) and a very small amount of Iron IB pottery of the debased type dated to the late eleventh century BCE. The exception is one elaborately decorated sherd that was not 'well stratified' (Dothan, 1982:82).

The extent of Philistine influence at the site remains unclear. A Philistine presence, probably as part of an Egyptian garrison, has been claimed by some interpreters on the basis of a number of Early Iron Age burials with associated clay coffins assigned to the Sea Peoples (e.g., Dothan, 1982:81). Several problems are inherent in this interpretation: first, the lack of associated Iron IB pottery, and second, the fact that many of these 'burials' consist of groups of objects that had been thrown out of their original rock-hewn chambers. These problems have prompted other interpreters to deny Philistine control of the site.

> If we follow the archaeological criteria, we must conclude, then, that the 'Philistines' of the Pentapolis—defined as the users of a certain type of pottery found in southern Palestine—do not seem to have held Beisan. (James, 1966:137)

It is generally agreed that Beth Shean was under Israelite influence by the tenth century BCE (see, e.g., James, 1966; Dothan, 1982:81-82).

Twelfth Century
Tools. Three iron nails come from Level VI.
Weapons. Five fragments of an iron dagger were recovered from Level VI.
Jewelry. One ring was found in a tomb in the northern cemetery. The clay coffins from Beth Shean are associated with this cemetery.
Other. From Level VI are: a round knob pierced with a hole (possibly intrusive); a fragment (of a tool or weapon?); and fragments of iron adhering to a mass of bronze (sealed below late Level VI walls).

Tenth Century
All tenth-century iron objects come from lower Level V at Beth Shean.
Tools. Four knives.
Weapons. A fragment of a weapon (unidentified).
Other. Four unidentified fragments.

Beth Shemesh ('Ain Shems)

Beth Shemesh is situated in the northeastern Shephelah lowlands. Its location is mentioned in Josh. 19.41; 21.16; and 1 Kgs 4.9. Beth Shemesh is also identified as the city to which the Ark was returned by the Philistines (1 Sam. 6.9ff.).

The site was fortified from c. 1700 to 900 BCE. Of the four main strata, Stratum III and parts of Stratum II have been dated to Iron Age I. Stratum III is characterized by an abundance of Iron IB pottery, typical of the twelfth and first part of the eleventh centuries BCE, and a thick destruction layer. Also present in this stratum were Egyptian wares, collared-rim jars typical of Iron IA material culture, and evidence of copper-smelting furnaces. Although it is difficult to determine the date of the end of Stratum III, a date of c. 1000 BCE is probable.

Strata IIa and IIb are dated to the early and late tenth century BCE and are characterized by pottery similar to much of the Stratum III destruction layer, including the collared-rim jar. Iron IB wares are absent (see, e.g., MacKenzie, 1912-13; Grant, 1929; Dothan, 1982:50-51).

Eleventh Century
Iron artifacts from Stratum III at Beth Shemesh include:
Tools. A chisel; a curved knife; a tool fragment; and a sickle.
Other. A fragment with bronze rivets.

Tenth Century
Iron objects from tenth-century contexts come from Strata IIa and IIb, and Tomb 1. Tomb 1 is a natural burial cave located in a cemetery north of the city and was evidently used for many generations (MacKenzie, 1912-1913:53).
Tools. One ploughshare from Stratum IIa and one from Stratum IIb.
Weapons. Three arrowheads from Tomb 1.
Jewelry. Two bracelets, rusted together, from Stratum IIa; and one bracelet from Tomb 1.

Beth Zur

Beth Zur is located on the eastern edge of the Judean hill country. The Bronze Age city was destroyed c. 1560 BCE and abandoned for approximately three centuries. It was resettled in Iron Age I, abandoned again c. 1000 BCE, and not resettled

4. The Early Iron Age

until the seventh century BCE. Reference is made to the Iron Age city in Josh. 15.58; 1 Chron. 2.45; and 2 Chron. 11.17.

Iron Age I architecture at Beth Zur is characterized by poor masonry and the reuse of earlier structures. An abundance of collared-rim jars (Iron IA) come from eleventh-century contexts. Iron IB ceramic finds from Beth Zur are 'quite meagre and atypical and belong to a debased version' (Dothan, 1982:44; on Beth Zur, see, e.g., Dothan, 1982:44-48; Sellers et al., 1968).

Eleventh Century
Jewelry. One iron toggle pin.

Gezer (Tell Jezer)
The site of ancient Gezer is a thirty-acre mound situated in the foothills of the Judean range where it slopes down into the Shephelah region. Gezer is mentioned in a variety of Late Bronze Age texts from Egypt and Mesopotamia, as well as in the biblical text. Those from Egypt are an inscription of Thutmose III (c. 1490-1436 BCE) at Karnak; an inscription of Thutmose IV (c. 1410-1401 BCE) in his mortuary temple at Thebes; the Amarna letters; and Merneptah's 'Israel' stela (c. 1220 BCE). A number of references occur in the biblical text. These include Josh. 10.33; 12.12; 16.3, 10; 21.21; Judg. 1.29; 1 Chron. 6.67; 7.28; 14.16; 20.4; 2 Sam. 5.25; 1 Kgs 9.15-17. Together these texts confirm that there was no Israelite occupation of Gezer until the time of Solomon (mid-tenth century BCE).

Although dating materials from the early excavations (MacAlister, 1912) is difficult, later excavations did control for stratigraphy and chronology. The combined evidence suggests a partial break in material culture at the very end of the thirteenth century BCE and the beginning of the twelfth century BCE (Stratum XIV). The ceramic assemblage from this level is made up mostly of local traditions of a degenerate Late Bronze Age type. There is no evidence that the destruction accompanied the Sea Peoples' arrival in the early twelfth century BCE.

An abundance of Iron IB pottery, of almost every known type, in Strata XIII-XI (twelfth and first half of the eleventh centuries BCE) has been interpreted as indicating that Gezer was under the influence of the Philistines at this time. It is difficult, however, to determine whether the city was actually controlled by them. The biblical text usually refers to Gezer as a sort of buffer zone between Philistia and Israel, and other passages imply that it was the farthest outpost of Philistine influence (2 Sam. 5.25; 1 Chron. 14.6; 20.4).

Strata X to IX (late eleventh century to early tenth century) are usually identified as post-Philistine or pre-Solomonic. Stratum IX ended in destruction. (1 Kgs 9.16 states that Gezer was captured and burned in the campaigns of an Egyptian pharaoh.)

The first level attributed to Israelite occupation is Stratum VIII (mid-tenth century BCE). The domestic architecture of this level is described as unimpressive. To this stratum is assigned a typical Solomonic four-entryway gate (see, e.g., MacAlister, 1912; Dever et al., 1970; 1974; Dothan, 1982:51-54).

Eleventh Century
Tools. From Tomb 58 come one iron knife with three bronze rivets and one iron rivet from a bronze bucket handle. A meagre assemblage of Phase II Iron IB pottery (eleventh century) belongs to the Iron I phase of the tomb's use (Dothan, 1982:52-53).
Other. From Tomb 59 comes an iron bar of uncertain purpose. A diverse collection of Iron IB pottery, mostly phase II (eleventh century) but a few examples of phase I, were recovered from this tomb (Dothan, 1982:53).

Tenth Century
A total of twenty-one iron objects have been assigned a tenth-century date.
Tools. Six knives were found, one in Tomb 31, one in Tomb 85 (possibly a cleaver), two in Tomb 96, and two in Field II. 'Several' nail fragments come from Tomb 84-85, which contained a small amount of Iron IB pottery lacking clear context, and a group of cultic vessels datable by a cartouch of Rameses III (Dothan, 1982:53). Two iron tool fragments and another tool fragment come from Fields III and II respectively.
Weapons. Five iron arrowheads come from Fields II and III, three from Field III and two from Field II.
Jewelry. Two iron bracelets were found in Tomb 96 and one ring in Field III.

Other. Miscellaneous iron objects from tenth-century Gezer include an iron fragment, possibly from a vessel, a cylindrical iron rod with fragments of a bronze sheet wrapped around it, and a 'disc' from Field III.

Gibeah (Tell el-Fûl)

The ancient fortress of Gibeah is located in the Mount Ephraim region. The town was founded at the beginning of the twelfth century BCE. Textual references to Gibeah include Judges 14 and 19-20; 1 Sam. 10.26; 11.4; and 15.34ff.; 2 Sam. 23.29; 1 Chron. 11.31 and 12.3; and 2 Chron. 13.2. It is reported in 1 Sam. 10.26, 11.4, and 15.34ff to have been Saul's residence.

Five periods have been distinguished in the archaeological strata at Gibeah, two of which fall in Iron Age I. Period I of the Iron I stratum is dated to the twelfth century BCE and Period II to the eleventh century BCE (IIA the first half of the eleventh century BCE, and IIB the second half). The collared-rim storage jar (Iron IA) is the distinguishing feature of Period I. In Period II the fortress was established. Pottery types characteristic of this period are the transitional form of the collared-rim jar with a heavier rim (c. mid-eleventh century BCE) and cooking pots typical of eleventh-century BCE contexts (see, e.g., Sinclair, 1960; 1964).

Eleventh Century
Tools. A single iron plough point comes from the fortress at Gibeah.

Har Adir

The material culture of Har Adir is similar to that of neighboring sites in the upper Galilee in Northern Israel, but differs in its being a large fortified citadel of a form foreign to the 'Israelite' pattern of settlement. The ethnic identity of the Har Adir population remains enigmatic (see Mazar, 1985a; 1985c).

Twelfth Century
Tools. An iron pick was found during salvage excavations of a fortified casemate wall at Har Adir near Sasa. The location of the pick suggests that it may have been used for excavating foundation trenches observed in the bedrock. Associated

with the pick was twelfth-century pottery reflecting a connection with Cyprus. Tests have proven that it is made of quench-hardened steel with a hardness similar to modern steel. It is also one of the earliest known iron artifacts to have been subjected to tempering after steeling (Davis et al., 1985).

Hazor

Hazor is a northern site situated in the Huleh Valley near the Jordan Rift Valley in Upper Galilee. Frequent reference to Hazor in Egyptian texts and its mention in the eighteenth-century BCE Mari texts indicate that Hazor was a flourishing commercial center in the Bronze Age. Biblical references to the city include a description of its destruction and burning by Joshua during the Israelite 'conquest' (Josh. 11.10-13) and its reconstruction during the reign of Solomon (1 Kgs 9.15).

Twenty-one strata of occupation have been identified at the site, three of which (XII-X) have been assigned Iron Age I dates. The stratum directly below these Iron I strata (XIII) indicates that the city was at its peak of prosperity in Late Bronze Age II. Before the close of the thirteenth century, the city was destroyed by conflagration and evidently abandoned for a short period of time. The twelfth century stratum (XII) indicates that a small settlement was established at this time. This settlement's material remains consist primarily of deep silos, hearths, and foundations for tents and huts, all of which suggest it was not permanent. The typical pottery of this period is similar to the collared-rim jar generally found at twelfth-century Iron IA sites. The typical Iron I cooking pots found throughout Palestine are also present. Traces of permanent settlements have been found in the next stratum (XI), dated to the eleventh century BCE. This stratum's most distinctive feature is a *bamah*, or 'high place'. In the tenth century (Stratum X) Hazor was rebuilt as a fortified city. On the basis of stratigraphy, pottery, and biblical references, this project has been attributed to Solomon (see, e.g., Yadin, 1972).

Tenth Century
Tools. One small riveted knife comes from Stratum X at Hazor.

4. The Early Iron Age

Khirbet Raddana

Salvage excavations at Khirbet Raddana, located near 'Ai (et-Tell) in the central hill region of Ephraim, uncovered an Early Iron Age settlement. Two building phases were evident. Houses exposed during the excavations indicate that the small, apparently unfortified, site was contemporary with Iron Age I 'Ai. The collared-rim jar (Iron IA) was present in both phases at Raddana. The site was evidently destroyed and abandoned before the use of this pottery type terminated in Palestine. The mid-eleventh century has been established as the latest possible date for the destruction (Aharoni, 1971:134).

> *Eleventh Century*
> *Tools.* Two iron tools come from eleventh century contexts at Khirbet Raddana, a tool point and a knife.
> *Other.* One iron 'rod' comes from an eleventh-century context.

Lachish (Tell ed-Duweir)

Lachish was a prominent city in Palestine's Shepelah region. Its peak of development was during the Late Bronze Age. This Late Bronze Age settlement was burned and destroyed c. 1150 BCE.[1] An apparent gap in habitation between the Late Bronze Age city (Level VI) and the Iron IC city (Level V) indicates that the site was deserted and was not resettled until the tenth century BCE. A poor habitation level marks the renewal of settlement during the early phase of Level V, preceding construction of the Iron Age palace fort. Characteristic of this phase are a paucity of ceramic objects, flimsy walls, and a number of pits.

The Canaanite city of Lachish is first mentioned in the fourteenth-century BCE Amarna letters. It is further mentioned in a contemporary letter found at Tell el-Hesi. The biblical references include a description of the city's defeat by Joshua and its subsequent inclusion in the territory of Judah (Josh. 10.15; 10.26; 15.39 and 32-33).

---

1 David Ussishkin (1987:34) raises the date from the earlier estimate of 1234 BCE on the basis of the discovery of a cartouche bearing the name of Ramses III (1182–1151 BCE).

The absence of biblical references to Lachish between the times of Joshua and Rehoboam are in accord with the lack of building activity represented in the Iron Age I strata of the site (see, e.g., Tufnell, 1953; Ussishkin, 1978; 1987).

> *Tenth Century*
> All of the Iron Age I iron objects recovered at Lachish have been assigned to the tenth century BCE (Level V).
> *Tools.* A total of six iron tools come from Lachish: a knife with iron rivets from Level V; a knife from Tomb 16; three knives—two with iron rivets—from Tomb 521; and one trident or pitchfork, also from Tomb 521.
> *Weapons.* Two armor scales come from Level V.
> *Jewelry.* A fragment of an iron bracelet and a plain arched fibula were recovered from Tombs 218 and 283 respectively.

Madeba

The ancient town of Madeba, located in the plains of Transjordan, is first mentioned in Num. 21.30 as a town taken over by the Ammonites. Joshua's conquest of the town during the Israelite 'conquest' is also mentioned. Further references are in 2 Sam. 10 and 1 Chron. 19. The only area that has been excavated is a tomb in a large natural cave east of the ancient tell. The tomb is Late Bronze Age/Early Iron Age (with a latest possible date of c. 1150 BCE) and was apparently used for several generations. It is similar to some of the fosse tombs found at Tell el-Far'ah South. There are further connections with Lachish, Beth Shean, and Tell Beit Mirsim. No Iron IB ware was found in the tomb, but some Mycenaean pottery—indicating some foreign influence—was present (Harding, 1955).

> *Twelfth Century*
> *Jewelry.* A total of four pieces of iron jewelry was recovered from the tomb at Madeba: a bracelet with a plain closed band, a plain bracelet with open ends, and two rings, one with open ends and one with closed ends.

Megiddo

The ancient fortified city of Megiddo is located in the Jezreel Valley. The name of the city appears in a fifteenth-century BCE inscription of Thutmose III, in one of the Ta'anach letters, one of the Amarna letters, in the city lists of Thutmose III and

4. The Early Iron Age 175

Seti I, and in the Papyrus Anastasi (dated to the reign of Ramses II). All of these texts indicate that Megiddo was an important Canaanite city during the Bronze Age. Biblical references in Judg. 5.19 and Josh. 12.21 refer to a battle fought near Megiddo. Josh. 17.11-13, Judg. 1.27-28, and 1 Chron. 7.29 list it among the Canaanite cities unconquered by the tribe of Manasseh. It is further cited in 1 Kgs 4.12 and 9.15 as being among the cities fortified by Solomon.

Although in some cases the stratigraphic evidence is unclear, the following strata have been attributed to Iron Age I occupation (Rast, 1978:4):

> Stratum VIIB: late thirteenth century BCE to c. 1175 BCE
> Stratum VIIA: c. 1175–1125 BCE
> Stratum VIB: c. 1075–1050 BCE
> Stratum VIA: latter half of eleventh century BCE
> Stratum VB: early tenth century BCE
> Stratum VA-IVB: late tenth century BCE

The Late Bronze Age strata yield evidence of a flourishing city influenced by the Egyptians. Stratum VIIA follows the Late Bronze Age strata and is the earliest level that can be ascribed with any certainty to the Iron Age. A layer of debris and clear signs of destruction separate Strata VIIB and VIIA, especially in the structure designated as a palace. Most of the public buildings of Stratum VIIB, including the palace that was rebuilt on a smaller scale, were reused in this period, and the Late Bronze Age culture seems to have continued. This level's date has been determined by the presence of Ramses III and Ramses IV cartouches. Both Iron IB ware and the collared-rim jar (Iron IA) were present in Stratum VIIA. Some Iron IB sherds were found in association with the Ramses III cartouche. Trude Dothan has interpreted the presence of Iron IB pottery as evidence of a Philistine garrison stationed at Megiddo (1982:76).

The city of Stratum VIIA was totally destroyed. The succeeding occupation of Stratum VIB is characterized by buildings of very poor construction and absence of fortifications and cultic structures. A poor assemblage of Iron IB ware[1] and some jars of the collared-rim type were found (Albright, 1940:548).

New and extensive building activities are evident in Stratum VIA. The newly planned and well-built city included public buildings and some fortifications. An abundance of metal tools and ceramic finds came from this level, including Iron IB ware[2] and ceramic remains 'typical of the eleventh century BC' (Yadin, 1977:851). W. F. Albright claims that 'the dominant ceramic type (of VI) is the collared store-jar' (1940:548). This level was destroyed by conflagration.

The buildings of the succeeding level, Stratum VB, are poorly built and indicate a period of decline. The city of this level appears to have been completely unfortified and is perhaps a product of the 'first Israelite occupation of Megiddo' (Yadin, 1977:851).

Stratum VA and succeeding strata evidence another period of renewed building activity, probably during the reign of Solomon (see, e.g., Aharoni, 1972; Albright, 1940; T. Dothan, 1982:70-80; Engberg, 1941; Loud, 1948; Yadin, 1977; Davies, 1986).

Twelfth Century
Tools. One iron hook comes from Stratum VIIA.
Jewelry. One iron ring comes from Stratum VIIA.

Eleventh Century
Tools. A total of seven iron tools comes from eleventh-century contexts at Megiddo: five knives, four from Stratum VI and one from Tomb 39; a needle from Stratum VI; and a staple, also from VI.
Weapons. One iron dagger that had been 'killed' (twisted out of shape) comes from Tomb 1101B.

---

1 Cf. T. Dothan, 1982:70-76. Dothan suggests that some of the Iron IIB ware originally attributed to VIA actually belongs with the assemblage from VIB.
2 Several explanations have been offered for the presence of Iron IB pottery in this level. B. Mazar suggests that the large structure in which the pottery was found may have been used by a Philistine ruler during the last half of the eleventh century BCE (Yadin, 1977). Engberg (1941), on the other hand, claims that the presence of this pottery type is the product of normal commerce.

4. The Early Iron Age

Jewelry. Four pieces of iron jewelry come from eleventh-century contexts: one ring with an iron core covered with gold from Tomb 39; and three bracelets, one from Tomb 221b and two from a hoard found in Level VIA.

Tenth Century[1]

Tools. Nine tools come from tenth-century Megiddo: three knives, one with bronze rivets in the haft, one with iron rivets, and one with no rivets, all from Stratum V; a borer (awl) with a bone handle from Stratum V; a tool fragment in a bone handle from Stratum V; two socketed axes from Stratum VA-IVB; a sickle from Stratum VA-IVB; and a tool fragment, also from VA-IVB.

Weapons. A total of twenty-two iron weapons are dated to the tenth century: twenty-one arrowheads, fourteen from Stratum V and seven from VA-IVB; and one armor scale from Stratum V.

Jewelry. Two iron bracelets were found, one in Stratum VA-IVB, and one on the arm of an infant in Tomb 37B.

Ta'anach

Tell Ta'anach is a forty-five dunam mound located forty-five meters above the Jezreel Plain. A significant gap in occupation seems to have occurred between the mid-fifteenth and late thirteenth centuries BCE. The site was reoccupied in the late thirteenth century and was finally destroyed c. 918 BCE. It was protected by city walls in all major periods and was probably a satellite of Megiddo.

The earliest textual reference to Ta'anach is in a fifteenth century BCE inscription of Thutmose III at Karnak. Both Thutmose III in 1468 BCE and Shishak I in 918 BCE list Ta'anach as a city captured by their forces. In Judg. 5.19 ('The Song of Deborah'), Ta'anach is mentioned as the site of a battle between the Israelites and Canaanites.

In Judg. 1.27 it is stated that the Israelites failed to occupy Ta'anach because of the Canaanites' strength. A number of

---

1 A number of the tenth-century BCE iron artifacts from Megiddo come from a small room abutting the court wall of the palace. The room also contained materials identified as iron ore, ash, and slag. The inventory of the room is similar to that of the 'Cultic Structure' at Ta'anach. Both are conjectured to be metallurgic workshops (Stech-Wheeler et al., 1981:256).

other references to the city are scattered throughout the books of Joshua, Judges, 1 Kings, and 1 Chronicles.

Four phases of occupation are evident in the Iron Age I strata of Ta'anach as follows (Rast, 1978:6):

IA c. 1200–1150 BCE
IB c. 1150–1125 BCE (destruction c. 1125 BCE)
IIA c. 1020–960 BCE
IIB c. 960–918 BCE

A twelfth-century house attributed to IA consisted of rooms surrounding a courtyard. A later structure dated to IB was built over it. This is indicative of the interruption in building activities between IA and IB that were resumed in IB. The IB city was destroyed c. 1125 BCE, and the site was apparently not resettled until c. 1020 BCE, at which time construction of a substantial number of structures and installations began.

The collared-rim type of storage jar (Iron IA) was present in all Iron Age I levels. The ethnic identity of the population of twelfth-century Ta'anach remains enigmatic in light of the apparently contradictory nature of the biblical and archaeological information. On the basis of the close resemblance of the twelfth-century material culture to 'Israelite' sites in the central hill country, A. Mazar suggests that the town was 'Israelite at the time' (1985a; 1985c).

The site was probably incorporated into the Israelite kingdom during the time of David and destroyed by Shishak in 918 BCE. It was never associated with the Philistines.

Ta'anach is the only site at which a substantial study of Iron Age I iron artifacts has been made (Stech-Wheeler et al., 1981). The iron artifacts from this site are recognized as one of the largest groups of closely datable artifacts from Palestine because many of them come from well-stratified contexts (p. 247). The largest group of iron artifacts was recovered from the two rooms that comprise the 'Cultic Structure' (period II) and the associated courtyard area containing a plastered basin. The inventory of artifacts from this structure includes a mixture of cultic and secular material. A cult stand was found in a nearby cistern. Also found in this structure was material associated with metalworking: tuyères, a broken copper tool, copper spillage and 'corroded amorphous bits' that may have resulted from casting operations (Stech-Wheeler et al., 1981:249), and two unfinished iron objects. The evidence suggests that some kind of metallurgic activities may have taken place here, perhaps under religious auspices (p. 256), and that the metal objects were a collection of broken or damaged items set aside for later repair (p. 248). A similar collection of iron artifacts was recovered from Megiddo.

Eleven of the iron artifacts from tenth-century contexts at Ta'anach were tested for carbon content. Of these eleven objects, six showed detectable carburization. It was inferred from the test's results that tools made for constant heavy use were carburized (see Lapp, 1964; 1969; Rast, 1978; Stech-Wheeler et al., 1981).

Eleventh Century
Tools. One chisel dated to approximately the eleventh century comes from the Cultic Structure. Tests showed no evidence of carburization.

Tenth Century
Tools. Eight iron tools come from tenth century contexts: two ploughshares, one from the cultic basin that was deliberately carburized (Stech-Wheeler et al., 1981:253), a sickle or scythe fragment for which there is good evidence for carburization (p. 253);[1] a sickle; a ploughpoint; a carburized blade, probably from a goad, and two unfinished, carburized objects, one a blade and one perhaps an incipient axehead (p. 252).
Weapons. Four iron weapons have been found in tenth-century contexts: an arrowhead for which there is no evidence of carburization; fragments of a sword blade (slightly carburized);[2] and two armor scales, one carburized and one for which there is no evidence of carburization (Stech-Wheeler et al., 1981:251, 253).
Jewelry. One piece of iron jewelry, a toggle pin, comes from the Cultic Structure (Stech-Wheeler et al., 1981:249).

Tell Abu Huwam

Tell Abu Huwam is the site of a small ancient harbor city located on the Plain of Acco near Megiddo and Ta'anach. The settlement was founded c. 1400 BCE, possibly by the Egyptians

---

1 Called a 'pointed tool' by Waldbaum (1978:27).
2 Called a 'knife' by Waldbaum (1978:27).

during the time of Sethos I, to serve as an Egyptian navy base and port (Maisler [Mazar], 1951:22).

The Late Bronze Age/Early Iron Age Stratum V revealed fortifications and contained Mycenaean and Cypriot pottery. The site was destroyed in the first quarter of the twelfth century BCE.[1] There is evidence of another destruction and a subsequent abandonment about the mid-twelfth century BCE (Stratum IVA). The site was resettled in the late eleventh century BCE (Stratum IVB) on a smaller scale. Several small residential units were found in this stratum, each consisting of two rooms and a closed court. New fortifications were built in the Stratum III settlement (late tenth century BCE). No Iron IB ware was found in any of the Iron Age I levels (see Hamilton, 1934).

> *Tenth Century*
> Tools. One iron sickle was found in Level III.
> Weapons. One iron arrowhead was found, also in Level III.

Tell 'Aitun
Tell 'Aitun is a Bronze Age/Iron Age site located in the Shephelah region of Palestine. A number of Bronze and Iron Age tombs were uncovered in the extensive cemetery associated with the site. Among these were a row of Late Bronze Age/Early Iron Age tombs hewn into the slope several hundred meters from the mound. One tomb contained Iron IB pottery as well as pottery that was typical of the twelfth century. The artifact inventory included bronze jewelry, bronze arrowheads, and beads. One of the deceased had a bronze necklace with three stone seals on his chest, which T. Dothan ascribes to the Philistine culture (1982:44). Another tomb (twelfth century) contained a rich assemblage of bronze knives and other utensils, iron bracelets, and an abundance of pottery (see Department of Antiquities, 1968; Dothan, 1982:44).

> *Twelfth Century*
> Jewelry. 'Iron bracelets' were found in an early Iron Age tomb dated to the twelfth century BCE (Dothan, 1982:44).

---

1 The chronology used here is that of Rast (1978).

4. The Early Iron Age   181

Tell Amal
I found no information on this site.[1]

Tenth Century
Tools. One axe or adze blade was recovered from Level 3 at Tell Amal.

Tell el-'Ajjul
Tell el-'Ajjul, located in the Philistine coastal plains, was a major city in the Bronze Age. The site has been identified as both Beth Eglayim and Sharuhen (Kempinski, 1974). Because most of the mound proper is still unexcavated, the bulk of the material evidence for the site comes from the extensive cemeteries to the east and west of the mound. No strata on the mound can be dated to Iron Age I, but Iron I remains in the cemetery suggest that it was still in use at the time. A small amount of Iron IB pottery, mainly from the last phase, was found in tombs 1139 and 1112 (see Dothan, 1982:35).

Tenth Century
Jewelry. One iron fragment, probably from a bracelet, comes from Tomb 1023 at Tell el-'Ajjul.

Tell Beit Mirsim
Tell Beit Mirsim is an eight-acre mound located at the edge of Palestine's high hill country where it merges with the Shephelah. The Iron Age settlement was sparsely populated and was destroyed c. 918 BCE. It was resettled following the destruction and was destroyed c. 587 BCE.

The Iron Age I stratum at Tell Beit Mirsim has been divided into three phases by the excavator, W. F. Albright: B1 (pre-Philistine), B2 (Philistine), and B3 (post-Philistine). Raphael Greenberg (1987) raises doubts about Albright's reconstruction. His sequence, according to Greenberg, depended largely on the identification of Tell Beit Mirsim with biblical Debir/Kirjath-sepher. Since Albright's reconstruction, Debir has been identified with Khirbet Rabud, and the character of 'Israelite' and 'Philistine' settlement patterns and material culture has been redefined. Viewed independently of historical

---

1 This information was a personal communication to Waldbaum by G. Edelstein (1978:84 n. 148).

considerations related to Debir, Greenberg suggests, Tell Beit Mirsim rather exemplifies an indigenous 'Canaanite cultural sequence'.

Iron Age I Tell Beit Mirsim was unwalled and sparsely settled. Most of the pottery finds come from grain pits. B1 (twelfth century BCE) is poor in architectural and pottery remains and contains some pottery of the collared-rim storejar type (Iron IA).[1] The characteristic pottery of this phase is a decadent Late Bronze Age type. No Mycenaean, Cypriot, or Iron IB ware was found. B2 (late twelfth to eleventh century) is characterized by the presence of some Iron IB pottery. Both Phase 1 and Phase 2 are represented, and one sherd of the debased type of the last phase was found. The B2 pottery indicates both continuing 'Canaanite' traditions and some coastal influence ('Philistine' or Phoenician) (Greenberg, 1987:69). Greenberg (1987:76) notes that the amount of Iron IB pottery is negligible and that the urbanism characteristic of Iron IB settlements is entirely absent.

No Iron IB ware is represented in Phase B3. Phase B3 pottery is the characteristic Iron IC type typical of other regions of Judah (see Albright, 1932; 1943; Dothan, 1982:43-44; Greenberg, 1987).

Tenth Century
Tools. A total of six objects identified as tools come from Tell Beit Mirsim: a riveted knife; two fragments of one 'tool'; three sickles; and one ploughshare.

Tell el-Far'ah North

Tell el-Far'ah North, generally identified as the biblical site of Tirzah, is located in the northern part of the Mount Ephraim region in Palestine's central hill country. Tirzah is mentioned in Num. 26.33 and 36.10-11 and in Josh. 17.3. The Late Bronze Age stratum of the site is not well preserved, so it is difficult to determine the extent of its occupation. In the Iron Age I Stratum III (1200–1000 BCE) a number of the four-room type of house were uncovered. The culture of this stratum, judging from cultic installations, appears to have

---

1 Greenberg (1987:70) indicates that there is only one certain occurrence of this form.

4. The Early Iron Age

been 'Canaanite'. The city was destroyed toward the end of the tenth century BCE but was not completely abandoned until c. 600 BCE (see de Vaux, 1976).

Tenth Century
All of the iron artifacts from Tell el-Far'ah North come from Stratum III.
Tools. One axehead, one sickle, a knife blade, two needles, a ploughshare, and a socketed pick.
Weapons. Four iron arrowheads.
Other. Two unidentified iron fragments.

Tell el-Far'ah South (Tell Sharuḥen)

Tell el-Far'ah South, normally identified with ancient Sharuḥen, is located in the western Negev along the southern boundary of Philistia. The city is mentioned in the descriptions of the Egyptian military expeditions of Ahmose, Thutmose III, and Shishak, and in Josh. 19.6. The archaeological evidence suggests that the city was a rich and densely populated settlement. There is evidence of an Egyptian presence starting at the beginning of the Late Bronze Age and abundant evidence of Iron IB material culture in tombs and occupation levels dating from the twelfth and eleventh centuries BCE. Iron IB remains include tomb architecture, anthropoid clay coffins (see Waldbaum, 1966), pottery, weapons, and seals. Also recovered were a few examples of Midianite pottery. The stratigraphy is relatively clear in parts of the site and supports the division of Iron IB pottery into three phases that can be dated fairly accurately (cf. McClellan, 1979). The tombs at Tell el-Far'ah South seem to reflect Mycenaean influence (see Petrie, 1930; Starkey and Harding, 1932; Dothan, 1982:27-33).

Twelfth Century
Weapons. The remains of one dagger with an iron blade, a caste bronze handle, and a curved bronze pommel were found in Tomb 542, dating from approximately 1150 to 1100 BCE. The dagger was 'killed' (snapped in two) (Dothan, 1982:32). Three small iron rings were found that were apparently part of the dagger's fittings. A bronze dagger was also found in this tomb.
Jewelry. 'Several' iron bracelets also came from Tomb 542. 'Several' iron rings come from Tomb 552, dating from

slightly later than Tomb 542. Phase I Iron IB pottery and an anthropoid clay coffin were part of the tomb's remains (Waldbaum, 1966:332).

Eleventh Century
Tools. Four iron tools come from eleventh-century contexts at Tell el-Far'ah South. Two knives come from Tombs 227 and 615 (the latter containing Iron IB pottery). A riveted knife was recovered from Tomb 562 that also contained an anthropoid clay coffin, Egyptian types of pottery characteristic of anthropoid coffin burials, Iron IB pottery representing a fusion of Iron IB and local decorative traditions, and 'more typical' pottery (Dothan, 1982:32). A hafted axehead comes from Level 376.
Weapons. Three arrowheads come from Levels 376 and 378.
Jewelry. One iron ring was found in Tomb 615 containing Iron IB pottery, and five bracelets come from Tombs 625, 617, 506, 859, and 839. Tombs 675, 839, and 859 contained Iron IB pottery.

Tell en-Nasbeh

Tell en-Nasbeh is located north of Jerusalem in the Judean hill country. It is normally identified with biblical Mizpah which is mentioned as a place where the Israelites prepared for battle against Gibeah (Judg. 20.1ff.), as one of the places where Samuel was active (1 Sam. 7.16-17), and as a city that was fortified by Asa after the end of the divided monarchy (1 Kgs 15.17-22).

The site was excavated in its entirety. The conclusions of the excavators were based almost entirely upon typological considerations because the stratigraphy of the site was poorly preserved. A wall was constructed around the eleventh-century BCE city, but the 'Great Wall' was built some centuries later, probably in the ninth century BCE. Most of the Early Iron Age houses were poorly constructed. Three examples of the four-room type of house were found. The Early Iron Age pottery inventory includes both Iron IB pottery (forty-seven sherds) and one of the richest and most complete collections of Iron IA, especially in some of the tombs that contained iron objects (see below, tombs 32 and 54). Included in the Iron IA pottery collection from Tell en-Nasbeh were some jars of the collared-rim type (see, e.g., McCown, 1947; Ibrahim, 1978:121; Dothan, 1982:54).

Tenth Century
Weapons. Two iron arrowheads come from Tomb 54 containing Iron IA pottery.
Jewelry. An iron fibula and two iron rings come from Tomb 32, also containing Iron IA pottery, and twenty-five iron ring fragments come from Tomb 54.
Other. One unidentified iron fragment was recovered from Tomb 54.

Tell es-Sa'idiyeh

Tell es-Sa'idiyeh is located in Transjordan, 1.8 km. east of the Jordan River on the south bank of the Wadi Kufrinjeh. Forty-five burials from a cemetery situated above Early Bronze Age remains were excavated. The ceramic evidence indicates that these burials were in use from the last half of the thirteenth century BCE through the first half of the twelfth century BCE. Four Iron Age levels of occupation were distinguished (see Pritchard, 1980; 1985).

Twelfth Century
Tools. One iron knife comes from Tomb 113 at Tell es-Sa'idiyeh (Pigott et al., 1982:35).

Tell esh-Shari'a (Tel Sera')

Tell esh-Shari'a is situated in the northwestern Negev and has been identified by some scholars as ancient Ziklag. Ziklag is mentioned as a city of Judah (Josh. 15.31) and as a city in the territory of Simeon (1 Chron. 4.30). It is also referred to as being in the 'country of the Philistines' (1 Sam. 27.6-7) and 'south of the Cherethites' (1 Sam. 30). As a Philistine stronghold, the King of Gath is said to have given it to David for refuge during his flight from Saul (1 Sam. 27.6). The Iron Age I stratum of the site (VIII) is situated directly above the Late Bronze Age destruction level but has not revealed any remains from the second half of the twelfth century BCE. A number of houses of the four-room type were found in this stratum. Because of the presence of typical late phase Iron IB pottery in the earliest of these houses (eleventh century), it has been suggested that the four-room house was originally a

Philistine architectural tradition that was later adopted by the Israelites (Oren, 1978:1059-69; Dothan, 1982:87).

Eleventh Century
Tools. One iron knife from Tell esh-Shari'a has been dated to the eleventh century (Dothan, 1982:92).

Tell es-Zuweyid

Tell es-Zuweyid was a frontier town on the Egyptian border of the Northern Sinai coast. It is the southernmost site at which Iron IB pottery has been found. The meagre assemblage comes from Levels N and M (Dothan, 1982:26; cf. Waldbaum, 1978:24). The dates of the Iron Age levels at Tell es-Zuweyid are not clear. Level N may span a period from the second half of the twelfth century BCE to the tenth century BCE. The approximate date of the beginning of Level M is the second half of the eleventh century BCE (Dothan, 1982:25-27). Level L is dated to the tenth century. Level N appears to have been completely destroyed by fire. In regard to the presence of Iron IB pottery at Tell es-Zuweyid, Dothan claims that, 'although meagre, these finds indicate a Philistine presence at Tell es-Zuweyid, or at least its influence...' (1982:27) (see Petrie, 1937).

Twelfth Century (Level N)
Tools. One iron tool fragment, possibly from a chisel, is dated to the twelfth century BCE.
Weapons. One iron arrowhead.

Eleventh Century (Level M)
Weapons. One iron spearhead.
Other. Two unidentifiable fragments.

Tenth Century. (Level L)
Tools. One iron awl.
Weapons. Two daggers, one with a 'rat-tail' tang, and three arrowheads, one possibly a lancehead.

Tell Jemmeh

Tell Jemmeh, located in the western Negev on the southern bank of the Wadi Gaza, was the site of a flourishing city from the Middle Bronze Age II through the Hellenistic period. Level JK has been assigned to a period covering the twelfth to

4. The Early Iron Age

eleventh centuries BCE, and GH to the tenth century BCE. An abundance of Iron IB pottery spanning all three phases was found in these two levels. A pottery kiln found at the site was clearly associated with twelfth- or eleventh-century BCE Iron IB pottery. There is evidence of conflagration between the periods of the Phase 1 and 2 Iron IB pottery and that of the Phase 3 pottery.

Among the finds recovered from Level GH were two buildings that are probably of the four-room type and an oven associated with a large quantity of slag. Petrie originally identified this as an oven used for iron smelting. The slag seems to have been produced at temperatures above 1100 degrees C., but analysis failed to yield any traces of iron, so there is no sure proof of iron smelting at the site (see Petrie, 1928; Dothan, 1982:33-35).

Eleventh Century
Tools. One riveted iron knife.
Weapons. One tanged arrowhead and one dagger.
Other. An unidentified curved iron fragment.

Tenth Century
Tools. One iron adze or axehead; two awls, a socketed axe or pick; four hoes with broad, flat blades and hammered open sockets; two ploughshares; a razor, called a 'knife' by the excavator; a sickle; a broad edged chisel; and five knives, one from a four-room structure, were assigned to the tenth century.
Weapons. Two spearheads, one with a midrib and tang and one with a tang and no rib; and five arrowheads, one called a 'borer' by the excavator, come also from levels assigned to the tenth century.
Jewelry. Three rings, a bracelet, and two straight loop headed pins.
Other. A piece of iron wire with cylinders of bone and wood strung on it.

Tell Qasile

Tell Qasile was a Philistine coastal town that covered an area of about fifteen to sixteen dunams. The city is unique because it was evidently founded and developed by the Philistines during the first half of the twelfth century BCE. Other known Philistine cities were Canaanite before this time (Dothan, 1982:57).

The site is located in a fertile region on a ridge above the northern bank of the Yarkon River. The success of agriculture in the region is attested by grain pits, silos, presses, store rooms, storage jars, and agricultural implements. The city also appears to have been a flourishing port during the eleventh century. The archaeological finds include remains of a bronze metal industry and several workshops.

Twelve strata of occupation have been identified, dating from the twelfth century BCE to Arab and Mameluk times. Strata XII to X (twelfth century BCE to the beginning of the tenth century BCE) yielded abundant Iron IB materials and clear stratigraphic divisions. The earliest stratum (XII) revealed the presence of a relatively small population. Phase I Iron IB pottery was present, and the local Late Bronze Age tradition continued in plain household wares. The remains of Stratum XI indicate a significant increase in building activity, including fortifications, the presence of a metal industry, and a ceramic assemblage that is a continuation of Stratum XII. Stratum X is a post- or late-Philistine level characterized by the presence of Iron IA cultural elements and evidence of trade (attested by foreign elements in some of the pottery). The presence of Iron IA material culture in this stratum is attested in both architecture and pottery. Iron IB pottery is less abundant than in previous strata and is of the degenerative Phase 3 type typical of the period. Stratum X was destroyed by fire at the beginning of the tenth century BCE. Stratum IX reveals changes in the organization of the new city (tenth century) and is poor in ceramic and small finds. There are several examples of the four-room house.

Three superimposed temples were found in Strata XII through X. The series of temples is the only known one of its kind that can be attributed to the Philistine culture (see Mazar, 1980; 1985b; Dothan, 1982:57-67).

Twelfth Century
Tools. The single example of iron from twelfth-century Tell Qasile is the remains of an iron knife blade with three bronze rivets attaching it to an ivory knife handle. The knife comes from the Stratum XII courtyard east of the temple. It is one of the earliest examples of an iron knife in Palestine and has been considered to be an important indicator of

connections between Palestine and Cyprus (Mazar, 1975: 78).[1] Analysis indicates that it was probably not carburized (Stech-Wheeler et al., 1981:257).

Eleventh Century
Tools. Two iron knives come from Stratum X.
Weapons. One iron sword blade comes also from Stratum X.
Jewelry. One iron bracelet was found in the Stratum X temple. Associated artifacts included cult vessels and pottery, and a socketed bronze double-axe indicative of connections with the Aegean (Dothan, 1982:67).
Other. One piece of unworked iron comes from Stratum XII or XI.

Tenth Century
Tools. A knife with two bronze rivets and a sickle were found in Stratum IX.
Jewelry. One iron bracelet was also found in Stratum IX.

Tell Qiri (Ha-Zore'a)

Tell Qiri is located between Megiddo and Yokneam on the eastern slopes of the Carmel ridge leading to the Jezreel Valley. There is evidence of continuous occupation at the site from the twelfth or eleventh century through the eighth and seventh centuries BCE. A small amount of Iron IB pottery has been recovered from late twelfth-century/early eleventh-century contexts, but the main material culture seems to be an extension of the Late Bronze Age II traditions also found at Megiddo (see Ben-Tor, 1975; 1976; Dothan, 1982:90).

Twelfth Century
Tools. A single iron axe of twelfth-century date has been recovered from Tell Qiri (Dothan, 1982:92 n.2).

Tell Zeror

Tell Zeror is the westernmost of the ancient sites in the Sharon Valley region. Occupation at the site extended from Middle Bronze Age IIA to the Roman period. It was not fortified in the Late Bronze Age (Stratum XII), but a metalworking industry is attested by the presence of smelting furnaces, crucibles, clay bellows' pipes, and copper slag. Two Iron Age I occupation

---

1 Similar knives have been discovered recently in excavations at Tel Miqne. See Dothan, 1989 and Dothan and Gitin, 1990.

phases follow the Late Bronze Age II destruction. The only signs of occupation discovered in the twelfth- to early eleventh-century stratum were a number of storage pits containing refuse such as animal bones, pithoi (storage jars), and typical 'Israelite' cooking pots.

Stratum X (the 'Philistine' phases—second half of the eleventh century BCE to the early tenth century BCE) revealed a well-built brick fortress and pottery typical of the eleventh century BCE. It has been suggested that this was a settlement of Sea Peoples, possibly the T-K-R (Dothan, 1982:70).

In the cemetery northwest of the mound a number of multiple burials in stone cist tombs were uncovered. The rich funerary offerings in the burials included pottery (some of the Iron IB type) and bronze vessels, bronze and iron weapons and jewelry, beads, and figurines.

Stratum IX (post-Philistine phase) yielded one example of a collared-rim jar and a number of the four-room type house (see Ohata, 1967; 1970; Dothan, 1982:69-70).

Eleventh Century
All of the iron artifacts recovered from Tell Zeror came from tombs.
Tools. Five iron knives, one with iron rivets from Tomb I, one with a curved blade from Tomb III, one from Tomb V, and one from Tomb VII with one bronze rivet preserved, and a haft with iron rivets from Tomb V come from Tell Zeror.
Weapons. Three iron daggers have been found, two from Tomb V and one from Tomb VIII.
Jewelry. Six pieces of iron jewelry come from three different tombs; two bracelets from Tomb III, a bracelet from Tomb V, and two bracelets and a ring from Tomb V.

Timna'

A total of eleven Late Bronze Age/Iron Age I camps with clear signs of metalworking were discovered in the Timna' Valley (thirty km. north of the Gulf of Elath-Aqabah) along the Wadi Arabah. The valley was a major source of copper, mined as far back as the Chalcolithic period. Iron Age I pottery found in the mined areas indicates that copper was exploited during that period.

4. The Early Iron Age

In all of the areas excavated in the valley, three essentially different kinds of pottery are predominant: ordinary wheel-made pottery, Negev-type pottery, and 'Midianite' pottery that is identical to pottery found in the Hedjaz in northwest Arabia.[1]

One of the campsites typical of those found is Site 2, a smelting camp dated to the Ramesside period. Smelting activity is indicated by the presence of slag heaps, furnaces, workshops, copper ore, and stone-crushing tools. A large building complex at the site contained workshops, storage areas, and a large number of clay tuyères. Layers of windblown sand indicate that it may have been occupied seasonally rather than year-round.

A cultic structure was uncovered near the industrial complex. Its remains included broken animal bones, ashes, pottery, and a row of five maṣṣeboth with a large stone bowl, perhaps for libations, in front of them.

Seventy meters west of the actual smelting area, an oval-shaped tumulus with a floor of carefully laid flat stones on solid rock was found. A large number of sherds, some from Midianite ware, beads, several very small copper spatulas and needles, numerous perforated Red Sea shells and ostrich-egg shells, and the remains of metallurgical activities were found in association with the tumulus. On the 'floor' itself were several goat horns, copper rings, two iron bracelets, and a large quantity of beads. Rothenberg has suggested that this area is probably a *bamah*. He further proposes that the metallurgical operations at Timna' were an integral part of worship and that the Midianites were the worshipers.

Another cultic area, the Hathor sanctuary, is centrally located in the ancient mining and smelting area of Timna'. Finds from the Hathor Temple (numbering about 10,000) include copper and iron jewelry, a copper snake, and a faience face of Hathor. The final phase of the temple (dated no later than the mid-twelfth century BCE) has been attributed by the

---

1 'Midianite' Sherds have also been identified at Lachish, Tell Jurdur, Tell el-Far'ah, Tell Masos, and other sites, i.e., it is present in sites extending from the Arabah and the Red Sea to the Mediterranean coast (Dornemann, 1983:46). On Midianite pottery, see also Rothenberg and Glass, 1983.

excavator to a revival of the use of the temple by the Midianites. The main phases of the original temple (Strata III and IV) are dated to the XIX and XX Dynasties of Egypt (the end of the fourteenth century BCE to the mid-twelfth century BCE).

The Midianite phase of the temple yielded evidence (large quantities of cloth and pole-holes) that a large tent had been erected over the temple court. This tent shrine, which also contained a row of maṣṣeboth and round incense altars, is the first of its kind ever discovered. Beautifully decorated Midianite pottery and a copper serpent with a guilded head, found *in situ* in the naos, were also recovered.

Rothenberg (1972:183-84) suggests that the Kenites may have had some role in metalworking at Timna', although there is no way of confirming this with archaeological evidence. The presence of a tent shrine and a copper serpent are suggested as being of possible significance for clarifying the relationship between Moses and the Midianites. The tent suggests some connection with the biblical Ohel Mo'ed, and the copper serpent supports the suggestion that Jethro was responsible for teaching Moses how to fashion the Nehushtan, the magic copper serpent (Rothenberg, 1972).

Twelfth Century
Jewelry. Two iron bracelets come from the tumulus west of Site 2.
Other. One unidentified iron fragment (Dothan, 1982:92).

Distributional Analysis: 'Philistine' vs 'Non-Philistine'

The Problem of Ethnicity
Identifying the relationship between ethnicity and material culture requires consideration of a complex web of interrelationships both within and between societies. It has become increasingly apparent to Syro-Palestinian archaeologists that differentiating among Philistine, Israelite, and Canaanite peoples on the basis of Iron Age I material remains is not as simple as it was once thought to be (see, e.g., Amitai, 1985; Flanagan, 1988).

Until recently, there has been a tendency among Palestinian archaeologists to assign ethnic identity or dominance on the basis of the presence of a few sherds or architectural types.

4. The Early Iron Age

Labels were often also assigned on the basis of biblical references. Recent studies, however, have made it clear that neither occasional literary references nor isolated archaeological discoveries are conclusive evidence for economic or political dominance or for identifying the ethnicity of populations. 'Canaanite', 'Philistine', and 'Israelite' are distinguished in the biblical literature but are not so easily distinguished in the archaeological remains. 'Canaanite' and 'Israelite' are especially difficult to separate and may in fact be two distinctive social organizations within the same culture, a point that G. E. Mendenhall's studies have made so clear (1973). Ta'anach, for example, reveals a material culture that closely resembles that typical of 'Israelite' sites in the central hill country, although it is listed in Judg. 1.27 as one of the unconquered cities in the north along with Megiddo, Beth Shean, and Dor (Mazar, 1985c:62).

Two recent studies of ancient Palestinian pottery suggest that caution should be used in assigning ethnicity on the basis of pottery in a given area. The first is Moawiyah Ibrahim's study of the distribution of the collared-rim jar (1978); the second is Peter Parr's study on the distribution of Nabataean pottery (1978). Ibrahim's survey indicates that the collared-rim jar has been found in a number of sites outside the region usually associated with the Israelites. On the basis of his distributional analysis he concludes:

> The presence of the collared-rim jar during the late 13th-12th centuries cannot be attributed to one single ethnic group. The origin and the long use of the type under discussion, whenever and wherever, ought to be considered in connection with a social-economic tradition. (1978:124; cf. Mazar, 1985c:69)

In the opening comments of his study of Nabataean pottery, Parr states:

> [It is] perhaps the single most important assumption in archaeological methodology that the movements and activities of specific groups of people can be distinguished in the archaeological record most readily and certainly from a study of ceramic typology. The assumption is undoubtedly correct in many instances; but at a time when archaeologists, both 'new' and 'old,' are looking more closely than

ever before into their methodology, and when improved laboratory techniques are making it possible to extract more physical data than ever before from potsherds, it will not come amiss to subject the assumption to scrutiny. (1978:203)

Parr's study suggests that the distribution of Nabataean pottery is not co-terminous with the Nabataean cultural province in either time or space (1978:204). Temporally, the Nabataeans existed as a tribe for as much as 250 years before Nabataean pottery appeared, and the pottery type continued to be popular well after the Nabataean Kingdom was extinct and thus is 'quite irrelevant to a study of the Nabataean polity' (p. 204). The pottery's geographical distribution, on the other hand, did not even extend to the boundaries of Nabataean influence but was confined to the central region of Nabataean control.

A similar argument has been made for the distribution of the 'Israelite' four-room house (e.g., Mazar, 1985c). This architectural type is not limited to Israelite settlements but is found in various regions of Palestine, including sites assigned to the Philistines and Canaanites and sites in Transjordan. Amihai Mazar suggests that this house type should be regarded as a common feature of Iron Age I that is not limited to any single ethnic group (1985c:68).

The socioeconomic, as opposed to ethnic, significance of the material culture of Iron Age I Palestine is beginning to be taken more seriously, a position that is made very clear in a statement by Lawrence E. Stager:

> Without clear indications from texts, I seriously doubt whether any archaeologist can determine the ethnic identification of Iron Age I villagers through material culture remains alone. For example, were the twelfth-century BCE inhabitants of Taanach 'Israelites' or 'Canaanites'? Even in contexts where collared-rim pithoi, storage pits, and three- or four-room pillared houses appear together..., these items do not in themselves provide an adequate indication of ethnos. The contrast between a twelfth-century city, such as Megiddo VII A, and a village, such as Taanach, during the same period reveals differences that derive more from socioeconomic than from ethnic factors. They reflect different settlement types of the same period. (1985:86)

4. The Early Iron Age

In addition to the exclusively archaeological studies cited above, ethnoarchaeological studies of material culture have illuminated the complexity of identifying ethnicity on the basis of the presence or absence of particular artifactual forms. In a study of the material culture of several African societies, Ian Hodder (1982b) has demonstrated that more is reflected in the distribution of material culture and cultural and stylistic variation than ethnicity, domination, degrees of interaction and communication, and 'reflections' of social behavior. One of his primary assertions is that cultural artifacts are symbols that not only 'reflect' but play an active part in giving meaning to social behavior (1982b:8-12).

Among Hodder's conclusion are: 1. We cannot assume that material culture 'reflects' the degrees of interaction among social or ethnic groups because the *nature* of the interaction and the degree or intensity of competition among groups also play a significant role. On the one hand, material culture does reflect and express competition among groups, but, on the other hand, it also actively *justifies* the actions and intentions of human groups (pp. 35-36). Material culture has the potential of transforming the relationships in other non-material spheres, and it does so within a particular frame of beliefs, concepts, and attitudes (p. 207). 2. Pottery types that serve as symbolic markers of group identity form distinct spatial patterns and tend to be especially marked in border areas where the greatest tension and competition exist, but many artifact types do in fact cross tribal boundaries (pp. 48, 56-57). 3. It is not possible to predict the relationship among resources, competition, and ethnic distinctions in material culture without also considering social organization and subgroups within society. Social organization is particularly relevant to the tension between the maintenance and disruption of boundaries. For example, material symbols that disrupt and cross boundaries may be actively employed in distinguishing subgroups based on, for example, age, sex, or social status, rather than degree of communication or ethnic dominance (pp. 73, 120-21). 4. Material symbols play an active role in the social strategies and intentions of subgroups within a particular society. Material symbols are manipulated in particular ways that depend on local social context and on the specific meanings assigned to them in that context (p. 75). 5. In some situations, group distinctions that are asserted verbally on the part of two or more distinctive groups participating in a non-competitive symbiotic relationship are not reflected in the material culture. Rather, evaluation of the material culture alone would suggest a single group. In such cases, social context, economic strategies, the history of socio-economic relations between the groups, and the history of cultural traits must be considered in identifying the nature of the relationship between the groups (pp. 103-104).

As indicated by Hodder's ethnographic study of material culture and the archaeological studies cited above, assumptions that the presence of particular items of material culture in a particular area are necessarily indicators of dominance, or even of interaction and communication, cannot be validated without also taking into consideration a number of other significant factors. Unless we account for the possible significance of these other important variables, we do not do justice to the complexity of the human situation in our analyses.

The conclusions of the studies cited here suggest that the assignment of ethnicity based on Iron Age I archaeological remains must be embraced cautiously. The Iron Age I archaeological information suggests the same. The distribution of Iron IB pottery, for example, does seem to correspond somewhat to temporal and geographical limits described in the biblical text for the Philistines. Thus, there is evidence that a particular group of people in a particular geographical area of Palestine (the southern coastal region) manufactured pottery based on Mycenaean prototypes. A problem arises, however, when small amounts of Iron IB pottery are found outside of the Philistine region, or when this pottery is found in combination with pottery or architectural types attributed to other 'ethnic' groups. A Philistine presence, or dominance, for example, has often been asserted on the basis of a few sherds (see, e.g., Dothan, 1982:81, on Beth Shean). Some sites, for example Megiddo, yielded both Iron IA and Iron IB pottery, in addition to pottery types that continue Late Bronze Age traditions. The questions that arise are, on the one hand, what amount of pottery must be present at a given site in order to

4. The Early Iron Age

conclude the dominance of one group over another, and, on the other, what significance can be attributed to the presence of a pottery type. In other words, is the question of dominance even the right question?

The 'Israelite' four-room house presents us with a similar dilemma. Its features are typical of Iron Age II architecture in Palestine, but the type begins to appear in Iron Age I levels at some sites. If the house is an Israelite innovation, then we must consider why it also occurs in association with Iron IB pottery in the geographical region associated with the Philistines.

Obviously, there is a need to subject assumptions of ethnicity to further scrutiny and seriously consider such proposals as that of G. E. Mendenhall that the Philistines, Israelites, and Canaanites were not ethnically distinct peoples but new social organizations of existing population groups with differing value systems (1973:153).

In the following distributional analysis of iron in Iron Age I Palestine, I distinguish only between 'Philistine' and 'non-Philistine' cultures. 'Non-Philistine' encompasses sites that in the past have been assigned ethnic labels as either Israelite or Canaanite. My decision to collapse these into a single category is based on recent research that has called into question the assertion that two distinctive ethnic groups can be identified in the material remains. My assignment of these labels is not definitive and is admittedly based on criteria similar to those I have called into question.

Furthermore, the statistics incorporated in the distributional analysis are by no means definitive, and I am aware that they are subject to question and revision. I am also aware that this type of simplistic statistical analysis is open to criticism. A truly valid statistical analysis would consider not only absolute numbers of artifacts, but also such variables as the total number of sites excavated in the region, the size of each site, and the area that has been excavated at each site.

My primary aim in what follows is to raise questions regarding the past tendency on the part of biblical scholars and archaeologists to assign to the Philistines a monopoly on the knowledge and practice of ironworking in Iron Age I Palestine. Those who support this claim tend to point to the relative abundance of iron artifacts from 'Philistine' sites without supplying either absolute numbers or conclusive evidence that particular sites were in fact 'Philistine'. In addition to considering the relative absolute numbers of artifacts recovered from 'Philistine' sites and 'non-Philistine' ('Israelite'/'Canaanite') sites, I also consider the significance of the acceptance of the technological innovation during Iron Age I and the meanings (symbolic, economic, political, etc.) that can be discerned from an evaluation of artifactual types and contexts. My primary assertion, when all is considered, is that the question of technological dominance on the part of any one ethnic group is the wrong question to be asking in evaluating the Iron Age I archaeological information on ironworking.

Twelfth Century

The predominant metal found in twelfth-century BCE levels of excavated sites in Palestine is bronze (Waldbaum, 1978:39). The total number of iron artifacts from twelfth-century BCE levels is sixty-six (Table 13). From four Philistine sites (Table 6) come 13.6 percent of this total, and from nine non-Philistine sites (Table 7) come 86.4 percent, that is, the number of iron artifacts from non-Philistine sites is six times that of artifacts from Philistine sites. The predominant type represented in both cultures is jewelry and ornamental objects (Tables 14 and 15). The average number of iron artifacts per site from non-Philistine sites is approximately three times that of artifacts from Philistine sites (Table 12).

It may be significant that in Philistine finds 100 percent of the iron artifacts occurred in burials and temples as opposed to 75 percent of non-Philistine finds (Tables 18 and 19).[1] In other words, iron has been recovered from occupation levels only in non-Philistine sites.

---

1 The statistics here are far from reliable, because 35 of the 57 iron objects from non-Philistine sites are from one site (the Baq'ah Valley in Jordan), and because the number of artifacts from Philistine sites is so low that the figures must be considered random.

4. The Early Iron Age

Table 6: *Twelfth Century: 'Philistine'*

Site	Tools	Weapons	Jewelry	Other	Total
Azor	–	–	*1	–	1
Tell 'Aitun	–	–	*2	–	2
Tell el-Far'ah S.	–	*1	*4	–	5
Tell Qasile	**1	–	–	–	1
Total	1	1	7	0	9

* tomb or burial
** temple or cultic structure

Table 7: *Twelfth Century: 'Non-Philistine'*

Site	Tools	Weapons	Jewelry	Other	Total
Baq'ah Valley	–	–	*35	–	35
Beth Shean	3	1	*1	3	8
Har Adir	1	–	–	–	1
Madeba	–	–	*4	–	4
Megiddo	1	–	1	–	2
Tell es-Sa'idiyeh	*1	–	–	–	1
Tell es-Zuweyid	1	1	–	–	2
Tell Qiri	1	–	–	–	1
Timna	–	–	**2	1	3
Total	8	2	43	4	57

* tomb or burial
** temple or cultic structure

A greater variety of types within the four categories of tools, weapons, jewelry, and miscellaneous types also indicates the predominance of bronze in the twelfth century BCE (Waldbaum, 1978:40). Fourteen known types of bronze tools come from this period. Only one iron tool type has been found with Philistine remains. Six types made of iron have been found with non-Philistine remains (Table 16). Weapon types are also more numerous in bronze, with one type made of iron represented from Philistine sites and two from non-Philistine sites (Table 17).

If the Philistines had brought with them to Palestine the knowledge and practice of working iron, it would presumably be reflected in the material remains of their culture. The paucity of artifacts from twelfth-century Philistine sites does not indicate that the Philistines were experienced workers of iron.

It may be concluded on the basis of this material that archaeology does not attest to a possession of the 'secrets' of ironworking by the Philistines. First, the raw count of iron artifacts and their distribution indicate that non-Philistine peoples of twelfth-century BCE Palestine used iron more extensively than the Philistines. Second, non-Philistine sites have yielded a greater variety of potentially functional types of iron in the form of tools and weapons. And finally, the contexts of finds from Philistine sites point to a ceremonial or ritual function for iron objects, whereas there is at least a suggestion of utilitarian use by the 'Canaanites' and 'Israelites'.

Eleventh Century

In the eleventh-century levels there is an increase in iron artifacts throughout Palestine and in the number of sites in which they are found. There is also evidence of more emphasis on manufacturing utilitarian objects (Tables 14 and 15). Bronze, however, remains the predominant material, again in all categories (Waldbaum, 1978:39). The number of Philistine iron artifacts outnumbers that of non-Philistine artifacts (Tables 8 and 9), but not as much as might be expected if the Philistines did indeed have a monopoly on iron during the eleventh century. Philistine sites yielded 57.5 percent of the total, and non-Philistine sites yielded 42.5 percent (Table 13). The average number of artifacts per site for Philistine and non-Philistine is 6.57 and 4.86 respectively (Table 12). From Philistine sites, 58.7 percent of the total come from tombs and temples, as opposed to 11.8 percent from non-Philistine sites (Tables 18 and 19). There is also an increase in the ratio of tools and weapons, that is, utilitarian objects, to jewelry and ornamental objects in both types of sites (Tables 14 and 15). The number of subtypes represented in the categories of tools and weapons increases as well. Eight iron tool types are represented in non-Philistine sites and seven in Philistine sites (Table 16), compared to fourteen bronze tool types found in eleventh-century BCE strata (Waldbaum, 1978:40). Bronze weapon types total seven. Three iron weapon types were found in Philistine sites and four were present in non-Philistine sites (Table 17).

Table 8: *Eleventh Century: 'Philistine'*

Site	Tools	Weapons	Jewelry	Other	Total
Beth Shemesh	4	–	–	1	5
Gezer	*2	–	–	1	3
Tell el-Far'ah S.	*3+1(4)	3	*6	–	13
Tell esh-Shari'a	1	–	–	–	1
Tell Jemmeh	1	2	–	1	4
Tell Qasile	2	1	**1	1	5
Tell Zeror	*6	*3	*6	–	15
Total	20	9	13	4	46

* tomb or burial
** temple or cultic structure

Table 9: *Eleventh Century: 'Non-Philistine'*

Site	Tools	Weapons	Jewelry	Other	Total
'Ai	6	3	2	2	13
Beth Zur	–	–	1	–	1
Gibeah	1	–	–	–	1
Khirbet Raddana	2	–	–	1	3
Megiddo	*1+6(7)	*1	*2+2(4)	–	12
Ta'anach	**1	–	–	–	1
Tell es-Zuweyid	–	1	–	2	3
Total	17	5	7	5	34

* tomb or burial
** temple or cultic structure

In summary, the eleventh-century material indicates an increase in the absolute number of iron artifacts over the twelfth century BCE. Iron from Philistine sites outnumbers that from non-Philistine sites, but the non-Philistine sites, as in the twelfth century BCE, have yielded a greater variety of both tools and weapons. In addition, we may assume from the contextual evidence that iron maintained a more ritualistic or ceremonial function for the Philistines, perhaps symbolizing status, than it did for those groups composed of non-Philistine elements. Overall, the eleventh-century archaeological evidence does not support a claim of a technological monopoly of iron by the Philistines.

Tenth Century
From the eleventh century BCE to the tenth century BCE the number of iron artifacts increases more than twofold (Tables 10 and 11; Table 13), and it is in this period that the number of utilitarian iron objects surpasses that of bronze (Waldbaum, 1978:39). There is a greater variety of weapon types, six types of iron vs four types of bronze (Table 17), and the variety of iron tool types comes close to that of bronze (Table 16) with thirteen iron tool types and fifteen bronze (Waldbaum, 1978:40). By this time the advent of the 'Iron Age' can be documented in the archaeological record.

Table 10: *Tenth Century: 'Philistine'*

Site	Tools	Weapons	Jewelry	Other	Total
Ashdod	*1+2(3)	–	1	1	5
Tell el-'Ajjul	–	–	1	–	1
Tell Jemmeh	18	7	6	1	32
Tell Qasile	2	–	1	–	3
Total	23	7	9	2	41

* tomb or burial

Table 11: *Tenth Century: 'Non-Philistine'*

Site	Tools	Weapons	Jewelry	Other	Total
Achzib	*1	–	–	–	1
Bethel	4	5	1	1	11
Beth Shean	4	1	–	4	9
Beth Shemesh	2	*3	*1+2(3)	–	8
Gezer	*6+5(11)	5	*2+1(3)	3	22
Hazor	1	–	–	–	1
Lachish	*5+1(6)	2	2	–	10
Megiddo	9	22	*1+1(2)	–	33
Ta'anach	**1+7(8)	4	**1	–	13
Tell Abu Huwam	1	1	–	–	2
Tell Amal	1	–	–	–	1
Tell Beit Mirsim	6	–	–	–	6
Tell el-Far'ah N.	7	4	–	2	13
Tell en-Nasbeh	–	*2	*28	*1	31
Tell es-Zuweyid	1	5	–	–	6
Total	65	54	40	11	167

* tomb or burial
** temple or cultic structure

4. The Early Iron Age

Iron objects from non-Philistine sites far outnumber those from Philistine sites (Table 13), but the average numbers of artifacts per site are almost equivalent (Table 12). Although the number of objects from Philistine sites decreases from the eleventh century BCE to the tenth century BCE, this may be explained in part by Israelite occupation of areas previously under control of the Philistines. The substantial increase in both numbers of iron artifacts and the number of sites in which they are found indicates that it is not just a shift in political dominance that affected the increased use of iron for producing utilitarian objects throughout Palestine. Iron resources and the necessary technology for producing iron must have been available to both the Israelites and the Philistines in the tenth century BCE. This claim is supported by the analysis of iron objects from Ta'anach (Stech-Wheeler et al., 1981), which determined that a technological advancement in their manufacture, that is, carburization, was evident. The study's results suggest that carburized iron was consistently produced in Northern Palestine by the end of the tenth century BCE. Complementary studies of eleventh-century iron objects from Philistine sites did not impart the same technological consistency. Technically and statistically, the Iron Age began when the Philistines were not in power.

Table 12: *Average Number of Artifacts per Site*

	'Philistine'	'Non-Philistine'
12th Century	2.25	6.33
11th Century	6.57	4.86
10th Century	10.25	11.33

Table 13: *Total Numbers and Percentages of Iron Artifacts in 'Philistine' and 'Non-Philistine' Sites*

	'Philistine'		'Non-Philistine'		Total	
	No.	%	No.	%	No.	%
12th Century	9	13.6	57	86.4	66	100
11th Century	46	57.5	34	42.5	80	100
10th Century	41	19.4	170	81.6	211	100

Table 14: 'Philistine': Types of Iron Artifacts

	Tools		Weapons		Jewelry		Other	
	No.	%	No.	%	No.	%	No.	%
12th Century	1	11.1	1	11.1	7	77.8	–	–
11th Century	20	43.5	9	19.6	13	28.3	4	8.7
10th Century	23	56.1	7	17.1	9	22.0	2	4.9

Table 15: 'Non-Philistine': Types of Iron Artifacts

	Tools		Weapons		Jewelry		Other	
	No.	%	No.	%	No.	%	No.	%
12th Century	8	14.0	2	3.5	43	75.4	4	7.0
11th Century	17	50.0	5	14.7	7	20.6	5	14.7
10th Century	65	38.2	54	31.8	40	23.5	11	6.5

Table 16: Tool Subtypes

	Bronze	'Philistine' (iron)	'Non-Philistine' (iron)
12th Century	14	1	6
11th Century	14	7	8
10th Century	15	10	13

Table 17: Weapon Subtypes

	Bronze	'Philistine' (iron)	'Non-Philistine' (iron)
12th Century	7	1	2
11th Century	7	3	4
10th Century	4	2	6

Table 18: 'Philistine': Context of Iron Artifacts

	Occupation		Burial		Temple	
	No.	%	No.	%	No.	%
12th Century	–	–	8	88.9	1	11.1
11th Century	18	39.1	27	58.7	1	2.2
10th Century	39	95.1	2	4.9	–	–

Table 19: 'Non-Philistine': Context of Iron Artifacts

	Occupation		Burial		Temple	
	No.	%	No.	%	No.	%
12th Century	14	24.6	41	71.9	2	3.5
11th Century	29	85.3	4	11.8	1	2.9
10th Century	116	68.2	52	30.6	2	1.2

4. The Early Iron Age

The overall distribution patterns of iron artifacts from the twelfth through the tenth centuries BCE indicate a shift from technological superiority, if it can be called that at all in the twelfth century BCE, by the non-Philistine groups in Palestine to a slight edge in terms of quantity, but not variety, of iron objects by the Philistines in the eleventh century. The tenth century is characterized by a vast increase in iron throughout Palestine.

The fact that bronze was the predominant metal for manufacturing utilitarian objects, and the evident ceremonial and ritual use of iron by the Philistines, suggests that during the period of conflict between the Philistines and Israelites iron was not relied upon as a necessary material for promoting military or political advantages. It was not until the tenth century BCE, when iron's use surpassed that of bronze, that iron played a significant role in the political, military, and economic spheres of Iron Age Palestine. An iron monopoly on the part of the Philistines could not have been a factor in the threat they posed to the Israelites.

It seems that we must look further than the isolated passage in 1 Sam. 13.19-23 to discover the true role of the Philistines and iron in the biblical text. It is suggested here that the art of iron metalcraft and the traditions and symbols connected with it add further insight into the role that iron played in the emerging Age of Iron.

Metallurgy and Symbols

The symbolic significance of iron in ancient Israelite traditions will be elaborated in Chapter 5, but it is appropriate to consider here what information the Iron Age I archaeological material contributes to evaluating the symbolic significance of iron. Hodder's study (1982b; cited above) is relevant to this issue. The fact, for example, that iron in 'Philistine' sites is often associated with cultic or ritual contexts (e.g., burials) may tell us more about the symbolic significance of iron *internal* to Philistine society than about the technological relationship of the Philistines to other peoples. The presence of iron in Philistine tombs perhaps reflects and legitimates concepts of prestige or status, concepts that would have more social significance in a centralized, socially stratified society than in one based on more egalitarian social values. In contrast, the relative non-occurrence of iron objects in hill country burials might suggest that legitimation of social status through such material symbols was not of great concern among the tribal peoples of that region, for whom status markers would have been less important. The more pronounced the social and political stratification is in a society, the more emphasis there is on expressing social differentiation through the manipulation of material symbols to preserve, reinforce, and legitimate the distance between upper and lower status groups (Hodder, 1982b:121). It is probable that the presence of iron weapons in Philistine burials does not say anything about the *functional* use of iron in the twelfth and eleventh centuries BCE and therefore cannot be appealed to as evidence of technological dominance.

As was indicated in Chapter 2, iron is a particularly appropriate material for use in ritual contexts because of its inherently mysterious nature and the transformative quality of the ironworking process itself. Robert Drennan (1976:357) notes that we can expect artifacts used in religious ritual to be objects that are considered helpful in inducing religious experience.

> Two categories of physical objects that might help to induce such experience suggest themselves. The first kind include objects inherently mysterious, different, and foreign to the experience of their observers... The second kind includes objects that, although not necessarily inherently mysterious, are given the required characteristics during their manufacture. They are made into symbolic shapes or decorated with symbols, and thereby take on the mysterious and esoteric properties of the referents of these symbols. (p. 357)

The characteristics of iron make it a substance that fits either of Drennan's categories. In twelfth- and eleventh-century BCE Palestine, the technological potential of iron was just beginning to be discovered and mastered. It was a substance with apparent symbolic value in the previous two millennia, probably connected with an understanding that in meteoric form it somehow functioned as a mediator between the heavenly and earthly realms. But once carburization was discovered, and the mysterious occasional transformation of iron recognized, it probably took on added symbolic significance. In addition to this new mysterious quality, iron was a substance that could be given shape or decoration to enhance its symbolic value. It is also necessary to bear in mind the ambivalent attitudes that were evidently held toward iron in ancient Israel (see Chapter 5).

Among African peoples, the symbolic significance of iron is expressed in part in the close association between ironworking and sacred space. Unfortunately, there is little, if any, archaeological evidence for the actual working of iron in either Iron Age I Palestine or anywhere in the ancient Near East.[1] However, it is possible to infer from archaeological information on bronzeworking installations something about the relationship between the art of metalcraft in general and the institution of religion. Of particular interest are metalworking sites that have been uncovered at Deir 'Alla and Timna'. Of related interest are a Late Bronze to Early Iron Age (thirteenth to eleventh centuries) metalworking complex at Kition, Cyprus, and evidence of metalworking activities at Ta'anach.

In the twelfth- to eleventh-century BCE levels at Deir 'Alla (Phases A-D) in Transjordan, excavations have uncovered an industrial area containing a number of furnaces, a tuyère, and slag from bronze-casting operations (Franken, 1969:20-21; Dornemann, 1983:39). Also found in association with this Iron Age I metalworking complex was a shrine. Because of

---

1 The 'evidence' that has come to light in archaeological excavations of Iron Age I sites is ambiguous. Many of the assertions about sites identified as containing evidence of smelting or forging operations or of mining operations have since been refuted (see, e.g., Waldbaum, 1978:59-62; Stech-Wheeler et al., 1981:259-61). Since Waldbaum's 1978 study, several other possible ironworking installations have come to light, one at Tell Yin'am (Liebowitz, 1981; 1983) and one at Telul Dhahab in the Zarqa Valley near the Ajlun hills (Gordon, 1984; Gordon and Villiers, 1983), an area known to be a source of iron during later periods. However, the assertion that there are smelting furnaces at Tell Yin'am is debated (e.g., Rothenberg, 1983; Stech-Wheeler et al., 1981:261), and the association of signs of a foundry and iron slag with Iron IC sherds recovered in the survey of Telul Dhahab will not be known until the site is excavated.

the presence of a temple and the apparent absence of a defense system and ordinary dwellings, H. J. Franken suggests that the site functioned in the Late Bronze Age as a cultic center. During the early Iron Age, the function of the site as a cultic center apparently continued, although it seems to have been used by a different cultural group. The architectural remains for this period are scanty, and aside from the shrine and the evidence of metalworking the only evidence of occupation are courtyards, pits, occasional holes for wooden posts, and ovens. Because of the nature of the Iron Age I remains at Deir 'Alla, Franken suggests that semi-nomadic itinerant smiths occupied the site on a seasonal basis.

The other ancient Palestinian metalworking site with clear religious associations is that discovered at Timna', where the remains of metalworking activities are clearly associated with both an Egyptian Temple of Hathor and several shrines, one possibly associated with the Midianites. The association of metalworking with cultic remains at these sites makes it plausible to suggest that worship was an integral part of the metallurgical operations.

A similar complex was uncovered at Kition on Cyprus (Karageorghis, 1973), where three large copper-smelting workshops with associated slag, crucibles, tuyères, bone ash employed as a flux, kilns for converting bone to ash, and storerooms were uncovered west of two temples. These were possibly dedicated to a male and a female deity of Near Eastern origin who presided over the copperworking industry. The association of the metalworking area with the temple complex is clearly indicated by the doors, corridors, and courtyards that connect the two. Here, as at Deir 'Alla and Timna', religion appears to have played a significant role in the metalworking operations.

Finally, the building identified as a 'cultic structure' at the site of Ta'anach in northern Israel appears to be connected with metalworking activities (Stech-Wheeler et al., 1981). Similar associations between industrial activities and religious installations have been uncovered recently at Tel Miqne (Dothan and Gitin, 1990).

Although the nature of the association of metallurgical activities with cultic sites cannot be clearly defined from the archaeological remains, the suggestions made by the excavators that the activities were carried out under religious auspices are quite plausible, especially when interpreted in light of the ethnographic material from Africa. It is certainly not unusual for metallurgical activities to be carried out under the supervision of religious practitioners nor for the religious practitioners themselves to be involved in the production of metals.

Implications for Reconstructing Israel's Early History

The archaeological information suggests that iron technology was adopted gradually during Iron Age I in Syro-Palestine over a period of several centuries. This period coincides with an important, yet little understood, transitional stage in early Israel's history. It was during this enigmatic period that the disparate peoples of Iron Age I Palestine began to move toward centralization and statehood. The social mechanisms that stimulated the move toward centralization and the nature of the transition itself are debated, but Iron Age IC archaeological materials indicate a clear break between the diversity of material culture represented by continued Late Bronze Age traditions and Iron Age IA and IB, and the more homogeneous material culture of Iron Age IC, the period attributed in the biblical texts to a consolidation of a united Israel under the leadership of Saul, David, and Solomon. What, if any, role the development of this new technology played in this transition cannot be determined definitively on the basis of the available evidence.

It is not likely, as some have asserted, that iron technology played a major role in the threat the Philistines may have posed to the Israelite tribes, nor is it likely that iron played any significant role in the agricultural enterprises of the newly settled twelfth- and eleventh-century BCE populations of the central hill country as, for example, Norman Gottwald has suggested (1979:655-58; cf. Frick, 1985:169-89; Hopkins, 1985:217-23). The archaeological information seems to indicate clearly that the innovation of carburization, probably made sometime before or during the twelfth century BCE, was not adopted for utilitarian purposes until the tenth century.

Although there is certainly evidence of the sporadic use of iron, for both ritualistic and perhaps utilitarian purposes, before the tenth century, it was not sufficient to have had any impact either in the pursuits of warfare or agriculture.

If anything, we must consider the situation of the tenth century BCE as the arena in which the new technology was finally accepted and adopted, and thus as the time during which the impact of the new technology began to play a part in social, political, and economic processes. Because this was a time during which moves toward consolidation and centralization were apparently accelerating, it is plausible that the adoption of iron technology was a significant factor in the strategies employed by individuals who played crucial roles in the transition.

Chiefdom has recently been proposed as a stage of sociopolitical evolution succeeding that of the segmentary tribal organization of Iron Age IA Israel, and preceding the establishment of the Israelite state (Flanagan, 1981, 1988; Frick, 1985). James W. Flanagan (1988) has suggested that the chiefly leaders of the beginning of Iron IC were mediators who used their skills to pacify and reduce fissioning among the disparate peoples of Late Bronze Age, Iron IA, and Iron IB cultures and eventually to unify them in a centralized polity called Israel.

One of the mechanisms by which this unification and the move toward centralization may have been effected was the control and distribution of important resources. We might postulate that the chiefly leaders of Iron Age IC took advantage for the first time of the important technological innovation of ironworking, gained control of the local sources of iron ore, and encouraged the adoption of the new technology for utilitarian use (in spite of the apparent ambivalent attitudes toward the technology that prevailed for many centuries afterward).

The fact that the occurrence of iron in Israelite burials increased during the tenth century BCE suggests that it continued to be a substance of ritual significance, possibly associated with an increased emphasis on status in an increasingly stratified society. But in addition to its ritual function, iron also became the dominant metal used for manufacturing utilitarian tools and weapons.

Whatever the mechanism by which iron technology was ultimately adopted in ancient Syro-Palestine, the coincidence of its acceptance with the rise of the Israelite state was a significant factor in Israel's later portrayal of its development as a people under the guidance of the national God Yahweh. It is to iron's symbolic role in the portrayal of Israel's sacred 'history' that we turn in the following chapter.

Chapter 5

BIBLICAL SYMBOLS

Introduction

Just as the archaeological information provides a window through which to view the ancient Israelite domain of actions, so the biblical material gives some insight into the domain of notions. As has often been noted by anthropologists, the latter domain does not always correspond with the former; what people say they do and what they actually do can be two different things (see, e.g., Flanagan, 1988:88-94). This principle applies to ancient Israelite culture just as it applies to any other human situation. It is clear from the archaeological information that these ancient peoples were fully incorporated into ancient Near Eastern 'civilization' and that they took full advantage of developments in the realm of technology. Yet, it is equally clear that both 'civilization' and technology were accepted with highly ambivalent feelings. God created the world and all living things and gave to humans authority over the things of the earth (Gen. 1.26; Ps. 8.4-8), but was not believed to have been responsible for creating all of the trappings of civilization and technology. This was the responsibility of humans. In the Hebrew Bible, it is Cain, one of the most clearly ambivalent figures in the biblical story, who is ultimately responsible for introducing to humankind some of the primary elements of civilization (cities, musical instruments, metal technology) through the activities of his descendants (Gen. 4.17-22). This paradoxical individual, an agriculturalist according to the tradition, is also responsible for shedding the blood of his pastoral brother, upon whom God, passing Cain over, had bestowed the Divine blessing (Gen. 4.1-16). Agriculture was clearly a necessary means of providing sustenance to the Israelite community, but it is presented as a pursuit that ideally is not as noble as that of the pastoralist. Even after Cain commits this heinous crime against a blood relation, God nevertheless extends to him Divine protection, symbolized by a 'mark' (Gen. 4.15).

The ambivalence with which civilization and technology are portrayed in the ancient Israelite domain of notions is revealed over and over in the sacred tale preserved in the Hebrew Bible. Human corruption, closely identified with civilization, is responsible for so defiling God's creation that God decides to wipe the slate nearly clean and begin anew (Gen. 6–9). But corruption persists in spite of this re-creation (Gen. 9.20-27). Noah preserves agriculture and the cycle begins anew. The human pursuit of further developing civilization is equated in the Tower of Babel story with the human desire to obtain the power that is God's (Gen. 11.1-9). Here again, civilization and the technology that is necessary to build it are presented in a less than desirable light. Throughout the Deuteronomistic History, the dangers of civilization, symbolized most forcefully by the Canaanites, are emphasized repeatedly. In one of the Samuel traditions, the desire for a king, yet one more step in the direction of developing civilization, is interpreted as a threat to the sovereignty of God (1 Sam. 8.4-22). In the so-called 'conquest' narratives in the books of Joshua and Judges, the Israelites suffer from the superior technology of the Canaanites in the form of chariots (e.g., Josh. 17.16, 18; Judg. 1.19; 4.3, 13). Yet, when access to this technology is made available to David, he has most of the chariot horses hamstrung (2 Sam. 8.3-4). However, in spite of the ambivalent attitude toward this military technology, it is again clear that chariots were used widely in Israel once the monarchy was established (see, e.g., James, 1978:107). Even during the monarchic period, when civilization has clearly been physically embraced, those who reject the trappings of civilization and the technology that is so crucial to its survival (e.g., the Rechabites; 2 Kgs 10.15-28; Jer. 35) are considered more spiritually pure than those who do embrace it. Ultimately, it is quite clear that actions and notions, particularly related to what is considered to be the ideal, do not always agree.

Iron Technology

In order to clarify the complex attitudes of the ancient Israelites toward the tenth-century BCE technological innovation that allowed for the production of the strong, durable, and superior metal iron, it is necessary to peruse the biblical literature for clues and to consider them in relation to the 'actions' represented in the archaeological record. Further insight is gained by considering both the biblical and the archaeological information in light of the more comprehensive picture of the interplay between actions and notions in African societies.

As the biblical information on iron technology is reviewed, it is important to bear in mind the fact that, in all probability, most references are from later rather than earlier traditions.[1] In the so-called 'historical' literature, references to iron can be attributed primarily to Deuteronomic and later traditions. Outside this corpus of literature, references to iron occur in both prophetic texts and the Writings. But these clearly date to periods somewhat later than that during which iron was introduced into common use in Palestine. Thus, caution must be used in evaluating those references that imply that iron technology played some significant role in the periods predating the rise of the monarchy in the tenth century BCE. References to 'chariots of iron', for example, as the military technology that kept the Israelites from defeating the Canaanites must be evaluated not for their historical value (in the context of the tribal period), but for their symbolic value (in the context of the monarchic period, during which many older traditions were edited).

The following pages consider: 1. the symbolic value of references to iron in the Hebrew Bible; 2. the mythological, social, and symbolic value of ancient Near Eastern and Israelite artisans and smiths; 3. the symbolic value of the smith's furnace; and 4. the overall symbolic role iron technology plays in the

---

1 The argument that *parzon* in the Song of Deborah (Judg. 5.7, 11) should be translated as 'iron' (Garbini, 1978; Ackroyd, 1979) breaks down when the archaeological information is considered. If this poem predates the tenth century BCE, it is unlikely that the suggested association of power and superiority is a possibility.

ancient Israelite understanding and presentation of its sacred story.

The Symbolic Value of Iron

The Hebrew term for iron, *barzel*, is apparently a word of foreign origin with no identifiable Hebrew or Semitic etymology (see, e.g., Baumgartner, 1976:148-49; Sawyer, 1983:131; Rendsburg, 1982). On the basis of etymological analysis, combined with faulty analysis of archaeological materials, it has been argued that the negative attitudes toward iron portrayed in the Hebrew Bible derive from attitudes toward its foreign origin. But as we have seen in Chapter 4, there is no definitive evidence that iron technology was adopted by the ancient Israelites from external sources. Furthermore, the ambivalent attitudes toward iron technology that have been documented in contemporary societies are associated not with contempt for some external group that may or may not have introduced the technology, but with technological, economic, social, and ideological factors internal to the societies themselves.

In the Hebrew Bible, iron and iron technology belong to the same category of paradox and ambivalence as technology and civilization in general. There is ample evidence, both in the archaeological and literary materials, that the ancient Israelites took advantage of their access to this new technology following its adoption sometime during the tenth century BCE and that it was highly valued. Clearly represented in the archaeological record is a shift to iron as the primary metal used to manufacture the tools and weapons necessary to survival. The increased incidence of iron objects in Israelite burials beginning in the tenth century BCE suggests that iron began to be perceived as a marker of social status and thus a material of some social value. In the Pentateuch and the Deuteronomistic History, iron is included among the precious objects, set aside from the total destruction of the *ḥerem*, that must be dedicated to God at the shrine (Num. 31.22; Josh. 6.19, 24; 22.8). The value of the Promised Land is measured in part by the presence of 'stones of iron' (Deut. 8.9). The iron axehead retrieved miraculously by the prophet Elisha is evidently considered to be an object of no little value (2 Kgs 6.1-7). In Ezekiel's lament over Tyre (Ezek. 27), iron is listed among other metals as part of the wealth that flows from Tyre (vv. 12, 19). And in Trito-Isaiah's salvation oracle describing the imminent transformation of Zion (Isa. 60.15-18), iron, although not as highly valued as silver, is nevertheless listed among the symbolic objects of value in the transformed Zion.

> Instead of bronze I will bring gold,
> and instead of iron I will bring silver;
> instead of wood, bronze,
> instead of stones, iron. (v. 17)

Although iron is considered a substance of some value, it is nevertheless a substance that is also feared (cf. Sawyer, 1983). Again, there are indications of this attitude toward iron in the Deuteronomistic History. Particularly striking are several references in which the use of iron tools for constructing altars (Deut. 27.5; Josh. 8.31) and the Jerusalem temple (1 Kgs 6.7) is prohibited. In Deuteronomy 27, a taboo against using iron tools to construct an altar to Yahweh occurs in the context of Moses' directives concerning Israel's imminent crossing of the Jordan River and entrance into the Promised Land (27.1-8). Moses directs the people to set up stones inscribed with the law at Mt Ebal on the day they cross over the river, and to build an altar of unhewn stones for offering sacrifices to God.[1] Iron is specified as the metal that is not to be used in preparing the stones. In Josh. 8.30-35 the directives in Deuteronomy 27 are carried out. Here again, the warning is given not to lift up iron tools in constructing the altar. Both of these passages are apparently additions of later editors since they appear to interrupt the flow of the narratives. They therefore tell us more about attitudes toward iron in some later period than about how iron was perceived during the tribal period.

1 Kings 6.7 is reminiscent of the passages in Deuteronomy 27 and Joshua 8, although the use of iron is not directly mentioned as taboo. Here it is noted that the stones used to con-

---

1 The Samaritan Pentateuch applies this directive to Mt Gerizim and includes it in the Decalogue as the tenth commandment. The use of iron is prohibited here also (see, e.g., Bowman, 1977:24).

struct Solomon's temple were prepared at the quarry 'so that neither hammer nor axe nor any tool of iron was heard in the temple, while it was being built'. The use of iron tools for preparing the stones is evidently allowed, but it is implied that their use in the immediate environs of the temple would be offensive to God. Aside from this single reference, there is no mention of iron being used in Solomon's building activities in 1 Kings. This is in stark contrast to the parallel account of these activities in Chronicles where iron is mentioned a number of times. In David's preparations for the construction of the temple, he provides 'great stores of iron for nails for the doors of the gates and for clamps' (1 Chron. 22.3; cf. 22.14) as well as artisans, including those skilled in working gold, silver, bronze, and *iron* (1 Chron. 22.15-16). These preparations are reiterated in David's investiture of Solomon (1 Chron. 29) where again David's provision of 'iron for things of iron' (v. 2) is included among others. When Solomon begins his preparations, he requests of Huram king of Tyre that he provide him with skilled artisans, including those skilled in working iron (2 Chron. 2.7). Huram responds by sending 'a skilled man, endued with understanding, Huramabi' (v. 13), who is trained in working iron among other things (v. 14). Finally, the Chronicler also includes workers of iron among those who are paid to repair the temple during the reign of Joash (2 Chron. 24.12).

Clearly, a shift takes place in how iron is perceived between the writing of the earlier traditions portrayed in the Deuteronomistic History and those represented in the postexilic Chronicler's History. The taboos against using iron in the earlier traditions contrast with the apparent acceptance of iron technology by the time of the Chronicler. There is no way of determining why such a shift in attitudes would have taken place. It is possible that over time the technology simply lost some of its mystery over several hundred years of use following its initial adoption. As was indicated in Chapters 3 and 4, it often takes quite a long time, sometimes centuries, for a new technology to be accepted by the general population to which it was initially introduced. A shift in the social status of smiths from marginality to a more integrated social status during the postexilic period, as Max Weber has suggested (1952:29; see

5. Biblical Symbols

below), may be related to a parallel shift in views of iron technology in general.

Although valued for its utilitarian superiority, iron (in at least the preexilic period) was nevertheless considered to be dangerous enough that its use was prohibited for constructing structures dedicated to Yahweh, structures that facilitated communication between God and people. Perhaps involved in the institution of this taboo were several factors: 1. Tools and weapons, particularly those manufactured from iron, represent the civilization created by human beings. 2. Tools and weapons are used both to help sustain life and to bring life to an end. Both temple and altar were believed to be places of peace and refuge where bloodshed was prohibited (e.g., 1 Kgs 1.50-53; 2.28-31; see de Vaux, 1961:276). This is clear, for example, in 1 Chron. 22.8 and 28.3 where it is indicated that David could not carry out his plan to build the temple because he had shed too much blood.

> Underlying this humanism is the assumption that the Temple is above the realm of ordinary politics, with its wars and bloodshed. It was, in fact, a place of asylum, and an old law forbids the altar in any shrine to be made of dressed stone, 'for you have struck your sword against it and thus profaned it' (Exod 20.25). (Levenson, 1985:96)

3. Iron was a substance that was magically transformed by smiths, who themselves were regarded with some ambivalence. Although there is no explicit assertion that smiths were perceived as individuals whose impurity endangered the efficacy of rituals, as is the case for many East African societies, such an attitude may be reflected in taboos against using iron to construct ritualistic structures. 4. Iron technology was often identified with power, power of the kind that humans had attempted to attain against God's wishes since creation.

In the majority of references to iron in the Hebrew Bible, iron symbolizes power, strength, and durability, all properties derived from the transformation that occurs in the ironworking process. The fact that the end product in the process is so much stronger than the soft ore with which the process begins contributes to the efficacy of these symbolic representations. Again, in reviewing these passages, we see the ambivalence with which iron is perceived. Both positive and negative perceptions (sometimes a combination of both) of the strength, power, and durability of iron are represented, although the negative seems to be emphasized (see Sawyer, 1983). Bronze sometimes occurs together with iron in poetic passages in which these properties of iron are emphasized, but the significance of this seems to lie in the fact that bronze, also used to manufacture tools and weapons, is the most appropriate substance to use as a parallel to iron. The use of this type of parallelism is characteristic of Israelite poetry.

On the positive side, iron is *valued* for its strength, power, and durability. For example, according to Moses' blessing in Deuteronomy 33, Asher is to be blessed with strength, prosperity, and longevity:

> And of Asher he said,
> 'Blessed above sons be Asher;
> let him be the favorite of his brothers,
> and let him dip his foot in oil.
> Your bars shall be iron and bronze;
> and as your days, so shall your strength be.' (33.24-25)

The positive characteristic of durability is also emphasized in Job's second reply to Bildad (ch. 19) in which Job wishes that his 'words' were inscribed in a book, which would resist the ravages of time, with an iron pen, graven in the rock forever (vv. 23-24; compare Jer. 17.1: 'The sin of Judah is written with a pen of iron'). Iron represents for Job something that would permit his words to endure until his redeemer avenges his honor after his death (vv. 25-29).

Iron is also associated in several passages with the royal power and ascendancy of the Israelite king. In Moses' blessing of Joseph (Ephraim and Manasseh) in Deut. 33.13-17, the royalty of this tribe is symbolized by the horns of the wild ox:[1]

> His firstling bull has majesty,
> and his horns are the horns of a wild ox;
> with them he shall push the people,
> all of them, to the ends of the earth;

---

[1] Compare Zech. 2.1-4 [1.18-21] and Daniel 7 and 8 where horns symbolize the power of Israel's enemies.

such are the ten thousands of Ephraim,
and such are the thousands of Manasseh (v. 17).

In 1 Kgs 22.11 (cf. 2 Chron. 18.10), the royal symbol is elaborated and becomes identified with 'horns of iron'. In this passage, a prophet by the name of Zedekiah makes 'horns of iron' and relays an oracle to King Ahab concerning a proposed battle with the Syrians: 'Thus says the LORD, "With these [the horns of iron] you shall push the Syrians until they are destroyed"'. Here the iron horns symbolize the power and strength of the Israelite king over his enemies. The same imagery is used in Mic. 4.13 to symbolize the future restoration of the Davidic kingdom and the triumph of the kingdom over its enemies following the judgment:

Arise and thresh,
    O daughter of Zion,
for I will make your horn iron
    and your hoofs bronze;
you shall beat in pieces many peoples,
    and shall devote their gain to the LORD,
    their wealth to the Lord of the whole earth.

Finally, in Ps. 2.9, a 'rod of iron' has a similar symbolic value. Psalm 2 celebrates the universal dominion Yahweh gives to the earthly king. The power of this earthly king against his enemies is symbolized by a rod of iron:

I will tell you of the decree of the LORD;
He said to me, 'You are my son, today I have begotten you.
Ask of me, and I will make the nations your heritage,
    and the ends of the earth your possession.
You shall break them with a rod of iron,
    and dash them in pieces like a potter's vessel.' (vv. 7-9)

In all of these passages, the power symbolized by iron is divinely bestowed upon its recipient.

In one instance, the strength of iron is bestowed by God upon a prophet—Jeremiah. In Jeremiah's call (Jer. 1), God assures Jeremiah of divine support by promising that he will be provided with the strength necessary for him to persevere in the face of the difficult task set before him. A series of metaphors of strength and endurance is used for emphasis:

> And I, behold, I make you this day a fortified city, an iron pillar, and bronze walls, against the whole land, against the kings of Judah, its princes, its priests, and the people of the land. They will fight against you; but they shall not prevail against you, for I am with you, says the LORD, to deliver you. (1.18-19)

Iron is also used as a positive symbol to indicate the power that either the king or God has over enemies.[1] Although corrupt and difficult to interpret (see, e.g., McCarter, 1984:479), the reference to iron in 2 Sam. 23.7, the closing line of the so-called 'last words of David', apparently represents the power of the king to punish those who do not show him loyalty. A similar representation occurs in Isa. 10.34 which uses an image of God cutting down trees in a forest to symbolize how the Assyrians will be cut down. The implement used by God in this image is simply 'the iron' (*habbarzel*). And in Job 20.24, the fate of the wicked and the godless, as interpreted by Zophar, is represented by reference to iron and bronze weapons:

> He will flee from an iron weapon;
> a bronze arrow will strike him through.

In many cases, however, iron symbolizes the power of God's or Israel's adversaries. In the book of Job, the strength of the chaos monsters is represented in part by reference to iron, although ultimately it is God's power over these beasts that is emphasized:

> Behold Behemoth,
>   which I made as I made you;
>   he eats grass like an ox.
> Behold, his strength in his loins,
>   and his power in the muscles of his belly.
> He makes his tail stiff like cedar;
>   the sinews of his thighs are knit together.
> His bones are tubes of bronze,

---

[1] A similar symbolic representation of iron occurs in Assyrian texts where the iron dagger was used not only as a symbol for slaughter and bloodshed, but also for the king's army or military power in general. In decrees dating from the time of Assurbanipal the king's troops were symbolized as the iron dagger of the god Assur (Pleiner and Bjorkman, 1974:287-88).

> his limbs like bars of iron. (40.15-18)
> He [Leviathan] counts iron as straw,
> and bronze as rotten wood. (41.27)

In a number of passages, iron symbolizes the threats of Israel's enemies, enemies who are more powerful than Israel. The giant Goliath wields a massive iron spear against David, the young shepherd (1 Sam. 17.7). The power and strength of this Philistine giant, over against the youth and comparably slight stature of Israel's future king, are emphasized by his massive size (17.4), his impressive bronze armor (17.5-6), and his weapons, particularly his iron spear: 'and the shaft of his spear was like a weaver's beam, and his spear's head weighed six hundred shekels of iron' (17.7).[1]

Og, king of Bashan and the last of the legendary Rephaim whom the people defeat on their journey to the Promised Land, is said to have possessed an iron bed of massive proportions (Deut. 3.11). The significance of this strange reference is not clear, but it presumably symbolizes the overwhelming strength of this particular adversary of Israel, as does Goliath's iron spear. However, it is again the power of God over Israel's enemies that is emphasized in this passage—God gives Og, his people, and his land into the hand of the Israelites (3.2).[2]

The superior strength of iron as representative of the threats of Israel's enemies is also emphasized in Amos' oracles of judgment against the nations (Amos 1.3) and in Jeremiah's reference to 'iron from the north' (Jer. 15.12). In Amos, Damascus is judged for devastating Gilead with 'threshing sledges of iron' in the Syrian conquest of Gilead. Jeremiah's question, 'can one break iron, iron from the north, and bronze?' may be an allusion to the enigmatic and ominous 'foe from the north' mentioned elsewhere in Jeremiah.

Finally, iron is also associated with the threatening military and technological superiority of the Canaanites in the tradi-

---

1 It is probable that the story of David and Goliath is not a part of the oldest naratives about the rise of David. See McCarter, 1980:295.
2 J. F. A. Sawyer suggests that the iron bed's significance is associated with the foreignness and ugliness of iron. The implication, according to this interpretation, is that Og lay on an ugly iron object, as befitted his barbaric foreign origins (1983:133).

tions about the 'conquest' of Canaan by the Israelite tribes. In Josh. 17.16 the people of the tribe of Joseph complain to Joshua that the land allotted to them in the hill country is not sufficient to support their large population and that it is not possible to take possession of the adjacent plains because the Canaanites have 'chariots of iron'. In Josh. 17.18 they are assured that they can take possession of a larger portion of the hill country and that they will be able to drive the Canaanites out in spite of their strength and their 'chariots of iron'. In Judg. 1.19 it is noted that although Yahweh was with Judah, who was able to take possession of the hill country, the tribe could not drive out the inhabitants of the plains (the Canaanites) because they had 'chariots of iron'. And in Judg. 4.3 and 13 'chariots of iron' are again cited as a major threat to the well-being of Israel. Israel has been cruelly oppressed by Jabin king of Hazor, whose power over them lies in the fact that he possesses nine hundred 'chariots of iron'. These are clearly metaphorical references dating to a time somewhat later than the events to which the traditions refer. Iron technology was not adopted in Israel until at least the time of the establishment of the monarchy in the tenth century BCE. Furthermore, even if iron was used in later periods in the construction of chariots, it would only have been used for making chariot fittings, or perhaps for iron tires, which would not have constituted any metallurgical or military advantage over bronze (see Stech-Wheeler et al., 1981:261-62; Drews, 1989). These references retroject into the past the knowledge of iron technology that developed sometime during the monarchic period. Robert Drews (1989:21) suggests that perhaps

> ... when the Old Testament writer attributed 'chariots of iron' to the enemies of Joshua and Deborah, he had in mind either scythed chariots or chariots with iron-tired wheels. Neither type was known before c. 700 BCE.

We may conclude, then, that once iron was adopted in the tenth century BCE, and its superior qualities were recognized, it was used symbolically to speak of the superior military and technological strength of the external powers that continually posed threats to Israel's well-being, from Og's iron bed and the Canaanite 'chariots of iron' in the early period of Israel to the threatening 'iron from the north' toward the closing days of the monarchic period.

One of the most prominent symbolic representations of iron in the Hebrew Bible is oppression. This symbol is related to iron's qualities of strength and durability. Oppression is something not easily broken or worn down, except by the power of God. In most instances in which iron is associated with oppression, Israel is oppressed by some other nation, and God is portrayed as having the power to bring this oppression to an end. But God also uses iron to oppress Israel, and Israel uses iron to oppress others. Furthermore, in those instances in which Israel is the object of oppression, oppression is part of the process whereby a *transformation* is facilitated (see the discussion of Egypt as an 'iron furnace' below). The typical metaphors used to refer to a state of oppression are a yoke or collar of iron or iron fetters.[1] Psalm 105.18, which celebrates God's saving activity on behalf of Israel, uses these images to describe Joseph's state of slavery as he passes into Egypt. Another psalm (107) offers thanksgiving to God for releasing from oppression those who cry out for help in their distress, some of whom sit 'in darkness and in gloom, prisoners in affliction and in irons' (v. 10). God 'shatters the doors of bronze; and cuts in two the bars of iron' (v. 16). Conversely, the symbolic power of iron can refer to oppression imposed upon Israel by God. Among the curses listed in Lev. 26.19 and Deut. 28.23 that would result from breach of the covenant is one that brings oppression in the form of a famine: 'and I will break the pride of your power, and I will make your heavens like iron and your earth like brass' (Lev. 26.19; the association of iron/brass and heaven/earth is reversed in Deut. 28.23). The implication is that the heavens will be closed up and will not yield rain and the earth will not produce food.

Similar metaphors are used to refer to Israel's oppression of its enemies. According to the traditions in 2 Sam. 12.31 and 1 Chron. 20.3, David forced the Ammonites 'to labor with saws

1 In Assyrian documents, iron fetters came to be a political symbol of the king's power. The act of putting conquered kings in iron fetters was an expression of the Assyrian ruler's power, and the phrase 'I threw him into bonds and fetters of iron' developed essentially into a symbol of that power (Pleiner and Bjorkman, 1974:298-300).

and iron picks and iron axes' (2 Sam. 12.31) following his conquest of their territory. Iron fetters are one form of oppression found in Psalm 149, a hymn celebrating the kingship of Yahweh. This hymn extolls the glory of the faithful who bring judgment upon the nations:

> Let the faithful exult in glory;
>   let them sing for joy on their couches.
> Let the high praises of God be in their throats
>   and two-edged swords in their hands,
> to wreak vengeance on the nations
>   and chastisement on the peoples,
> to bind their kings with chains
>   and their nobles with fetters of iron. (vv. 5-8)

Conversely, this type of metaphor is also used to symbolize the oppression of Israel by other nations, nations interpreted as instruments of Divine judgment. Deuteronomy 28.48 apparently alludes to the oppression experienced during the Babylonian exile, as does Jer. 28.13-14. Both passages use the metaphor of an iron yoke. The parallel metaphor used in Jer. 28.13 is 'bars of iron', which is also used by Deutero-Isaiah to represent this exilic experience from which Yahweh will deliver Israel (Isa. 45.2). Here again, there is reference to God's ultimate power over the strength of the oppressor.

That iron continued to be associated with power and the oppression of Israel by other nations as late as the second century BCE is clear in Daniel's vision of four beasts in Daniel 7 and his interpretation of Nebuchadnezzar's dream in Dan. 2.31-45. In the former passage, great iron teeth (vv. 7 and 19) and ten horns (symbolizing great power) are cited as characteristics of the dreadful fourth beast that symbolizes the tyranny of Antiochus IV (e.g., Porteous, 1965:97). In the latter passage is described a colossal statue constructed of gold, silver, bronze, iron, and clay.

> The head of this image was of fine gold, its breasts and arms of silver, its belly and thighs of bronze, its legs of iron, its feet partly of iron and partly of clay. As you looked, a stone was cut out by no human hand, and it smote the image on its feet of iron and clay, and broke them in pieces; then the iron, the clay, the bronze, the silver, and the gold, all together were broken in pieces, and became like the chaff of the summer

threshing floors; and the wind carried them away, so that not a trace of them could be found. But the stone that struck the image became a great mountain and filled the whole earth. (vv. 32-35)

This image represents a sequence of metal ages similar to those in Hesiod's *Works and Days* (109-201) and Ovid's *Metamorphoses* (1.89-150). Parallels also occur in the *Avesta* and in Buddhist and Zoroastrian literature. Represented in these metal ages is a degeneration of civilization through time, from an earlier golden age to an oppressive period associated with iron. Daniel interprets the dream as referring to the succession of nations that controlled Palestine from the neo-Babylonian period down to the Ptolemaic/Seleucid period of the writer's own time. Gold is associated with the power and glory of Nebuchadnezzar (vv. 36-38), silver and bronze with the Medes and Persians (v. 39), and iron with the Greeks (vv. 40-41) (see, e.g., Porteous, 1965:44-51). The last of these kingdoms is represented as the strongest and, it is implied, the most oppressive.

> And there shall be a fourth kingdom, strong as iron, because iron breaks to pieces and shatters all things; and like iron which crushes, it shall break and crush all these. (v. 40)

The feet of the image, composed partly of iron and partly of clay, signifies the division of the Greek kingdom, following the death of Alexander the Great, between the Ptolemies and the Seleucids. The mixture implies the instability of the kingdoms—'partly strong and partly brittle' (v. 42). Finally, the stone that strikes the image represents the apocalyptic kingdom established by God that will be even stronger than iron and will endure forever (v. 44). As in other passages, the power of God over the oppressive powers symbolized by iron is emphasized.

The Symbolic Role of Artisan Gods in Ancient Near Eastern Mythology[1]

As was shown in Chapter 2, artisans and artisan gods in African societies tend to function as mediators in various social and cultural realms, although it is the ironsmith who is perceived as the mediator *par excellence*. This role as mediator is closely related to the role of the artisan as one who gives form to substance. Similar roles are also apparent for the artisan gods of the ancient Near East.

Enki/Ea

Particularly relevant to the present discussion is the Mesopotamian artisan god Enki (the god's Sumerian name) or Ea (his Akkadian name). Enki is not a god of iron nor is he directly associated with ironworking. But he is an artisan god and he exemplifies many of the qualities that are associated with smiths in their representation in the Hebrew Bible. Although ultimately he is responsible for more than the handicrafts of the human social world, Enki functions in Mesopotamian myth and religion in much the same way as the ironsmith gods do in West African myths and religions.

Enki is one of the four most powerful gods in Mesopotamian religion and is regarded in cosmic terms as god of the waters. His abode is *apsû*, the abyss of waters or underworld ocean upon which the earth rests. Enki means 'Lord of the soil', a name that reflects the role of water in fertilization (Jacobsen, 1976:111). Enki's association with water may also contribute to his association with artists and artisans (Jacobsen, 1976:111). When water moistens clay, it gives it plasticity so that it can be given many shapes. This power to shape is expressed in one of Enki's names, Nudimmud, which means 'image fashioner' and seems to underlie his function as god of

---

1 Although there are numerous references to smiths and artisans in the ancient Near Eastern literature, I have not included a discussion of the status and roles of smiths outside Israel. This is because the extant references provide little information on how smiths and artisans were regarded. For a comprehensive survey of the Near Eastern literature, see Bjorkman, 1968; see also Pleiner and Bjorkman, 1974:303-304.

artists and artisans—e.g., potters, metalworkers, stone-cutters, and jewelers. From this attribute of Enki also stems his epithet *mummu* (from Sumerian *umun*, 'mold', 'form'). In Akkadian this word means 'original form' or 'archetype'.

Of his many aspects, Enki is regarded first and foremost as the god of wisdom. He is known for his superior intelligence, his skill, and his cunning. He is a god who exerts his will not by force of power, but through diplomacy or guile, that is, through his wisdom. Related to his wisdom are the many other attributes of this multifaceted god. For example, among the roles attributed to him in the opening lines of the 'Enki and World Order' myth are: the one who brought craftsmanship to his 'Apsu of Eridu'; record-keeper of heaven; ear and mind (?) of all the lands; and the one who directs justice (see Kramer, 1963:175). He is regarded as the source of all secret magical knowledge and as instructor of humans in all the arts and crafts necessary for human well-being. It is he who reveals to humans the mysteries of writing, building, and agriculture.

In Sumerian mythology, the role of culture hero is shared by Enki with Enlil, in many respects the principal deity of the pantheon. Enlil is the source of vegetation, cattle, agricultural implements, and the arts of civilization, although indirectly through creating lesser deities who carry out his instructions. Enlil is also responsible for creating the pick-axe and giving it to the 'black-headed people' (i.e., the Sumerians) to assist them in their building activities. But it is Enki who is primarily responsible for organizing the earth in accordance with the decisions and plans of Enlil. The actual details and execution are left to Enki. In one instance, Enki is credited with advising Enlil to create the cattle and grain deities (Lahar and Ashnan) to provide cattle and grain for the earth, and thus food and clothing for the gods (see, e.g., Kramer, 1956:144-46). According to the myth 'Enki and World Order: The Organization of the Earth and Its Cultural Processes' (Kramer, 1963:122, 171-83), Enki is also responsible for providing Sumer with the necessary elements of civilization. This myth provides a detailed account of Enki's creative activities in instituting the natural and cultural phenomena essential to civilization. He does this by travelling through different parts of the world 'fixing the destinies', that is, bringing order into the world.

Enki is also given responsibility in Sumerian myths as keeper of the *mes*, divine forces that exist in all phenomena and determine their essential character and nature. In Samuel Noah Kramer's estimation (1963:160), the *mes* are 'the basis of the culture pattern of Sumerian civilization'. In one myth, over one hundred culture traits and complexes are listed. These relate to political, religious, and social institutions, arts and crafts, music, and an assortment of intellectual, emotional, and social patterns of behavior (Kramer, 1963:160).

In addition to his role as mediator of culture, Enki (Ea) plays a mediating role in the Mesopotamian myths of creation and the deluge. In the Babylonian *Enûma elish* (see Pritchard, 1955:60-72), Ea mediates the process of creation in several ways. First, he formulates a plan to counteract the plot of the older generation of gods against those of the younger generation.

> He of supreme intelligence, skillful, capable,
> Ea, comprehending everything,
>   sought a strategem against them.
> He formed, yea, he fixed against him
>   the configuration of the All,
> skillfully made his overpowering sacred spell.
> He recited it so that he [Apsû] quieted down
>   in the waters,
> poured slumber over him,
> so that he soundly slept. (Jacobsen, 1976:172)

Second, by his actions Ea gained control of 'the original watery form' (Apsû and Mummu), thus creating the potential for the present world with its multiplicity of forms (Jacobsen, 1976:172). Finally, Ea mediates creation by fathering the creator god Marduk. Ea himself is not directly involved in the creative act but acts as a mediator through his initial actions and by fathering the god who is responsible.

Enki (Ea) is regarded in Mesopotamian myth as a god who is especially favorable toward humans. In several Sumerian versions of the creation myth and in the Babylonian *Enûma elish*, he plays an important role in the creation of humanity (sometimes in the context of mediating a conflict among the gods), and in the various Sumerian and Akkadian versions of the flood myth it is through the intervention of Enki (Ea) that humanity escapes total destruction. Enki (Ea) figures prominently as a mediator in these myths—a mediator between the gods and humanity, between the heavenly and earthly realms.

In one variant of the flood myth, the human mediator Atrahasis is portrayed as a wise individual and a servant of Enki who appeals to Enki to intercede on behalf of humanity. W. F. Albright (1983a:24-25) has suggested that there is a connection between Atrahasis and the Canaanite artisan deity Kothar wa-Hasis (also simply Kothar or Hasis), who is identified with Ea in the Ugaritic vocabularies. Hasis, or Atrahasis, he asserts, means 'very intelligent' and Kothar, Hebrew *koshar*, means 'very skillful'. These are both attributes of the Mesopotamian Enki (Ea). If this linguistic connection is correct and Atrahasis was originally identified as an artisan, it adds further support to the assertion that artisans were perceived as mediators in the ancient Near East. In the Israelite literature, artisans are also regarded as persons who are both wise and skillful (e.g., Exod. 31.1-5; 1 Kgs 7.13-14; 2 Chron. 2.13-14; Sir. 38).

An earlier Sumerian version of the deluge, 'The Eridu Genesis' (Jacobsen, 1976:114) or 'The Deluge' (Pritchard, 1955:42-44), combines the flood motif with a prelude describing the introduction of various elements of culture: city life, a redistributional economic system symbolized by measuring cups, irrigation agriculture, and kingship (Jacobsen, 1976:114).

Another variant of the flood myth, embedded in the Babylonian version of the Gilgamesh Epic, gives some indication of the relative importance of both precious metals and artisans. The inventory of what is taken aboard the ship by the hero of the story, Utnapishtim, indicates that in addition to all living creatures, certain elements regarded as essential to cultural continuity are also saved from destruction:

> [Whatever I had] I laded upon her:
> Whatever I had of silver I laded upon her;
> Whatever I [had] of gold I laded upon her;
> Whatever I had of all the living beings I [laded] upon her.
> All my family and kin I made go aboard the ship.

> The beasts of the field, the wild creatures of the field,
> All the craftsmen I made go aboard. (Pritchard, 1955:94)

Several of Enki/Ea's other attributes are relevant to the mediating role of the artisan god: his role as mediator between life and death, his role in the heavenly system of justice, his ritual functions, and his function as mediator of magical spells.

Two myths are relevant to the first of these (Enki's role in mediating between life and death, heaven/earth and the netherworld): 'The Descent of Inanna into the Netherworld' (in the Babylonian version Ishtar; see Pritchard, 1955:52-57, 106-9) and 'Gilgamesh, Enkidu, and the Netherworld' (see Pritchard, 1955:97-99). In 'The Descent of Inanna', Inanna, the goddess of fertility, descends on a whim into the netherworld and is killed by Ereshkigal, the goddess who reigns there. As is typical of Enki's character, it is he who conceives the plan to bring the goddess back to life and spirit her away from the land of the dead. The Gilgamesh myth is similar. In this myth, Enkidu, Gilgamesh's friend, is entrapped in the netherworld, and Gilgamesh appeals to Enki for help. Enki assists him by giving orders to the sun god Utu to open a passageway from the netherworld through which Enkidu's ghost is able to ascend to earth.

Enki also appears in the myths as one of the gods responsible for meting out justice, although this is primarily the responsibility of the sun god Utu. Enki's role in this system is made explicit in a text that speaks of the *bît rimki* purification ritual (see Laessoe, 1955), a ritual enacted when the king is threatened by the evils of an eclipse of the moon. The ritual takes the form of a lawsuit before Utu and the assembly of the gods in which Utu acts as judge and hears the complaint. Enki's role is to guarantee that the verdict is enforced (see Jacobsen, 1976:112). In the related 'Eclipse Myth', Enki allays the impending crisis of the moon's eclipse by sending Marduk to the aid of Nanna, the moon god. Again, it is Enki who deflects the crisis by coming up with a plan.

Finally, Ea plays a prominent role in Babylonian magical texts. In these texts, he and his son Marduk are typically represented as cooperating in the efficacious working of spells and incantations (see, e.g., Hooke, 1953; Thompson, 1908). These magical texts indicate that water, often referred to as 'water of life', is an essential element in incantations for delivering humans from disease and the assault of demons. Thus Ea, as god of waters, is specially invoked in spells and incantations and is known as 'lord of incantations'. He is also the patron god of the various orders of religious specialists trained in the practice of exorcism, in the knowledge of spells and incantations, and in the interpretation of dreams and omens.

Jacobsen (1976:116) sums up Enki's character as follows:

> Enki is the cleverest of the gods, the one who can plan and organize and think of ways out when no one else can. He is the counsellor and adviser, the expert and the troubleshooter, or manipulator, of the ruler; not the ruler himself. He organizes and runs the world, but at the behest of An and Enlil, not for himself; he saves mankind [sic!] and the animals from extinction in the flood, but does not challenge Enlil's continued rule. His aim is a workable compromise, avoiding extremes. Generally friendly to man [sic!], he does not go to extremes for him . . . he is a trimmer, a *moderator* [emphasis mine], but not a wielder of ultimate power.

Enki is not an ironsmith god and his role as god of artisans is only one of many, but his function as mediator is very similar to that identified in Chapter 2 for African gods of iron or ironsmith gods. Many of his attributes are associated with wisdom, knowledge, and skill, all attributes of artisans in general and symbolic of the skills that were eventually necessary for the development of iron technology.

Kothar wa-Hasis

The Canaanite artisan god, Kothar or Kothar wa-Hasis, was introduced briefly above. This god is also portrayed as wise and skillful, as his name suggests (Albright, 1983a:24-25; Gaster, 1950:154-56). His home is in Memphis, the city of his Egyptian counterpart Ptah, with whom he is identified in the Ugaritic texts. He is also associated with *kptr*, possibly biblical Caphtor (Crete?), and is identified in the Ugaritic vocabularies with Ea (Gibson, 1977:3 n. 2). Furthermore, two of his standard epithets are *hyn* ('deft' or 'expert') and *d-ḥrṯ ydm* ('handyman') (Gaster, 1950:155). In the Ugaritic myths (see, e.g., Gibson, 1977), Kothar is responsible for forging the weapons with which Baal defeats Yam, equipping the sanctuaries for the gods, supervising the building of Baal's palace, and making bows for the gods. Under the name 'Sir Fisherman' (Gaster, 1950:154), he is responsible for imprisoning Yam in a net after he has been defeated and for throwing Yam into the sea when he arises to encroach upon the earth. Kothar also plays an important role in mollifying Asherah, the consort of El, when Baal and Anat approach her with the request that she intervene with El on their behalf by encouraging him to allow Baal to have a palace built for himself. Kothar mediates by providing Baal with the gifts that appease Asherah and influence her decision.

According to the tradition handed down by Sanchoniaton (Eusebius, *PE* I, 10.11f.), Chusor, the Phoenician equivalent of Kothar, was the first to discover iron, was associated with music and song, and introduced the arts of 'tricking out words' and composing chants and incantations. A linguistic connection with Kothar of Ugaritic myth is suggested by the Ugaritic term *kôtarât* which is used to refer to chanters (Gaster, 1950:154-55).

As is typical of smiths and artisans in contemporary West African mythology, Enki (Ea) and Kothar are deities whose primary mythological roles are associated not only with providing tools and weapons and introducing and organizing civilization, but also with mediating conflicts (or potential conflicts), advising other deities, and mediating such oppositions as those between heaven and earth, divine and human, and major and minor deities.

In ancient Israel, technology and religion were evidently regarded with more ambivalence than they were by Israel's neighbors and predecessors. Nevertheless, the myths preserved in the Hebrew Bible suggest that the symbolic roles of smiths, particularly as mediators, were essentially similar to those of smiths and artisans in both African and ancient Near Eastern mythology.

The Smith in Ancient Israel

Direct references to smiths in the Hebrew Bible are few, so it is difficult to gain a very clear picture of how the ancient Israelites perceived the smith's status and roles in Israelite society. It is also difficult to distinguish always between ironsmiths and other types of metalsmiths and artisans. Jane Waldbaum (1980:89) suggests the possibility that for some time after the adoption of iron technology in ancient Israel the ironsmith and bronzesmith were not strictly separated; that is, one smith could work both metals. For these reasons, references to both smiths and artisans in general are considered here. In order to bring the picture into sharper focus, it is also necessary to consider the following: 1. the motif of Yahweh as Divine Smith; 2. the mythical origins and ancestors of smiths and artisans—Cain and his descendants; and 3. the literary roles of the various peoples who have been interpreted as having some connection with smiths and play a part in Israel's sacred story—the Kenites, the Midianites, and the Rechabites. The picture may be brought into even sharper focus by considering the fragmentary information from the Hebrew Bible in light of the analysis and interpretation of the roles and statuses of African smiths.

The two Hebrew terms that have been translated as 'smith' are *ḥārāš* and *masgēr*. The former is a general term used for artisans of many kinds: workers in metal, wood, stone, and gems. It is also an inclusive term that designates artisans as a group. In only one instance (Isa. 44.12) is this term used explicitly to denote a worker in iron (*ḥāraš barzel*). In its other usages associated with metalworking (Deut. 27.15; 1 Sam. 13.19; Hos. 8.6; 13.2; Jer. 10.9; Isa. 40.19; 41.7; 44.13; 54.16; 1 Chron. 29.5; 2 Chron. 24.12) the metal is not specified. *Ḥārāš* also occurs in plural form in 1 Chron. 4.14 and Neh. 11.35 where reference is made to *gê haḥărāšîm* ('valley of the craftsmen'). The significance and location of this valley are unknown (see Har-El, 1977). The second term, *masgēr*, is found only in texts that refer to the deportation of smiths with other important persons in the exile to Babylonia (2 Kgs 24.14, 16; Jer. 24.1; 29.2).

In Gen. 4.22, the term *lōṭēš* ('forger'/'hammerer') is used in reference to Tubal-Cain, the metalworking descendant of Cain. In Gen. 25.3, the Letushim are identified as the descendants of the union of Abraham and Keturah, as is Midian (see below). In Isa. 41.7 *maḥălîq paṭṭîš* ('one who smooths with the hammer') and *hôlem pa'am* ('one who strikes the anvil') refer to metalworkers. One other direct reference to a worker of iron occurs in Sir. 38.28.

There is little information that can be gleaned from these sparse references to smiths in the Hebrew Bible. Several passages point to the important contribution smiths make to society. The fact that smiths and artisans are numbered among the king, princes, and 'mighty men of valor' who were carried off into captivity by the Babylonians (2 Kgs 24.14, 16; Jer. 24.1; 29.2) suggests that by the sixth century BCE they were highly regarded for their social contributions. In a later, second century BCE reference (Sir. 38.24-34), the status and role of the ironsmith are clearer. Sirach compares the social contributions of scribes with those of artisans, among whom are counted ironsmiths:

> All these rely upon their hands,
>   and each is skilful in his own work.
> Without them a city cannot be established,
>   and men can neither sojourn nor live there.
> Yet they are not sought out for the council of the people,
>   nor do they attain eminence in the public assembly.
> They do not sit in the judge's seat,
>   nor do they understand the sentence of judgment;
> they cannot expound discipline or judgment,
>   and they are not found using proverbs.
> But they keep stable the fabric of the world,
>   and their prayer is in the practice of their trade. (38.31-34)

Although not as wise as the counselor or judge, according to Sirach, the artisan's skills are necessary not only for the maintenance of social stability (v. 32) but also for the stability of the 'fabric of the world' (v. 34). The characteristics and significance of artisans in this description are reminiscent of those applied to Enki (Ea) in Mesopotamian myths and Kothar wa-Hasis in Canaanite myths.

5. Biblical Symbols

It is interesting to note that an earlier verse in this same chapter (v. 28) has been singled out as evidence of the 'hostility and scorn with which the smith was popularly regarded' (Sawyer, 1983:132). This argument hinges on the partial description of the ironsmith's working conditions:

> So too is the smith sitting by the anvil,
>   intent upon his handiwork in iron;
> the breath of the fire melts his flesh,
>   and he wastes away in the heat of the furnace;
> he inclines his ear to the sound of the hammer,
>   and his eyes are on the pattern of the object.
> He sets his heart on finishing his handiwork,
>   and he is careful to complete its decoration.

According to J. F. A. Sawyer, this passage supports his assertion that:

> His [the ironsmith's] dirty, frightening and often, one might add, unsuccessful work, and the soot, smoke, sparks, heat, bellows and hammering in his smithy frequently attracted suspicion and hatred. It seems likely that the comparison of Israel's house of bondage in Egypt to an 'iron furnace' (Deut. 4.20; I Kgs 8.51; Jer. 11.4) owed something to this popular impression of the working conditions of the blacksmith. (1983:132)

Sawyer further suggests that the foreign origin, inferior quality, and ugly appearance of iron, combined with this attitude of fear and hostility toward the smith, probably contributed to the 'ugly overtones' of the word *barzel* in the Hebrew Bible (p. 133).

Although there is certainly an ambivalent attitude toward smiths expressed in the texts of the Hebrew Bible, this attitude carries with it, as in African societies, both positive and negative overtones. Sawyer is certainly correct in pointing to the suspicion and fear with which the ancient Israelite smith was regarded, but he neglects the flip side of the coin—the respect and awe accorded the smith for the skills and social contributions emphasized in Sirach 38 and other biblical passages. In several other biblical traditions, it is clear that artisans, including those who work metals, are accorded great respect. In Exod. 31.1-5, Bezalel, the artisan commissioned by God to construct the ark and the tent of meeting, is credited not only with skill, intelligence, and knowledge, but with having been filled with the Spirit of God, that is, he becomes a charismatic individual of sorts (cf. Weber, 1952:28). Wisdom and skill are also attributed to Hiram of Tyre, a bronzeworker (*ḥōrēš nĕḥōšet*) commissioned by Solomon to assist in building the temple (1 Kgs 7.13-14). In 2 Chron. 2.13-14, the same artisan (here identified as Huram-abi) is said to be 'endued with understanding'. In this tradition, Huram-abi's skills are expanded to include the ability to work gold, silver, *iron*, stone, wood, and dyes, in addition to bronze.

Beyond the references to smiths in Genesis, Exodus, 1 and 2 Kings, 2 Chronicles, Jeremiah, and Sirach, we gain very little overtly-stated information about the ancient Israelite perceptions of the social statuses and roles of smiths. Isaiah 54.16 asserts that God is ultimately responsible for the smith's products, because it is God who created the smith. A number of passages indicate that smiths and artisans are responsible for the manufacture of idols (e.g., Deut. 27.15; Isa. 40.19; 41.7; 44.12; Jer. 10.9; Hos. 8.6; 13.2). Emphasized in these references is the mere humanness of these fashioners of graven images.

Finally, reference is made to smiths in 1 Sam. 13.19. Traditionally, this passage has been interpreted as evidence of a Philistine monopoly on ironworking during the early days of the Israelite monarchy. However, as was indicated in Chapter 4, this is unlikely. In the first place, iron is not even mentioned in the passage, and the Hebrew term for 'smith' used here (*ḥārāš*) can refer to all kinds of metalsmiths as well as other types of artisans. And in the second place, it is unlikely that iron technology had been adopted yet anywhere in Palestine by this time. A more likely interpretation of the passage is that the reference is to smiths in general and that 1 Sam. 13.19-22 reflects the interpretation of a later editor or editors who were aware of the tradition that the Early Iron Age Israelites were forced to confront powers (Philistine and Canaanite) that were socially, militarily, and technologically superior (cf. Stech-Wheeler et al., 1981:261-62; Waldbaum, 1978:42).

God as Divine Smith

More light is shed on the ancient Israelite perception of smiths in those passages in which the image of God as Divine Smith occurs (Ps. 12.7 [6]; Prov. 17.3; Isa. 1.25; 31.9; 48.10; Ezek. 22.17-22; Mal. 3.1-4; Zech. 13.9). Emphasized in these passages is God as purifier and transformer of Israel. For example, in Isa. 48.10, Deutero-Isaiah contrasts the 'former things' with the 'new things' that Israel has not yet heard. God as Divine Smith has refined *(ṣārap)* Israel and tried its people in the 'furnace of affliction'. The 'furnace' *(kûr)* is not directly identified, but certainly refers to the exile in Babylonia. In light of Deutero-Isaiah's emphasis on a New Exodus, the ambiguity in this reference may express an identification of the Babylonian exile with the 'exile' in Egypt (see the discussion of Egypt as 'iron furnace' below).

The transformative quality of the metalsmith's work is emphasized in the image of Yahweh as Divine Smith in Ezek. 22.17-22. Here Ezekiel proclaims that God will gather the house of Israel in Jerusalem as the smith gathers metals (silver, brass, iron, lead, and tin) into a furnace *(kûr)* to smelt *(nātak)* them (cf. Isa. 31.9; here the Hebrew term for furnace is *tannûr*). The image of the smelting process is used here as a means of communicating to the people that they are in need of purification by means of the fire of the Divine wrath. Ezekiel draws an analogy between the coming judgment and a smelting furnace in which slag *(sigîm)*, the impurity, is removed.

Transformation in the form of purification is also stressed in Mal. 3.1-4 where it is indicated that the messenger of God, likened to a 'refiner's furnace' *('ēš měṣārēp)*, will refine *(zāqaq)* and purify the Levites as gold and silver are purified (cf. Zech. 13.9; Ps. 12.7 [6]; Isa. 1.25).[1] The image of God as Divine Smith, then, is used in portrayals of God as one who transforms the people Israel, whether through judgment or purification, or a combination of both. I will return below to the significance of the furnace in these passages.

Cain
Also important for determining the roles and status of the smith in ancient Israel are references to the Kenites, the

---

[1] The purifying power of fire is also represented in other passages. See, e.g., Num. 31.23.

Midianites, and the Rechabites, and to the eponymous ancestor of the Kenites, Cain.

As in West African mythology, the culture hero in Israelite myth (Cain) is the eponymous ancestor of smiths (i.e., the Kenites). In the genealogy of Genesis 4, Cain is identified as the ancestor of Tubal-Cain, the first 'forger of all instruments of bronze and iron' (Gen. 4.22). Cain is a marginal and ambivalent figure in Israelite mythology. He is a murderer, yet marked by God in order that none should kill him (Gen. 4.15), an agriculturalist for whom the earth will not bear fruit (Gen. 4.12-13), a marginal wanderer who dwells in the land of Nod ('wandering') (Gen. 4.16). As the ancestor of both city-dwellers (Enoch) and tent-dwellers (Jabal) (Gen. 4.17, 20), he is socially marginal. His descendants, metalworkers and musicians, introduce to human society both arts and technology (Gen. 4.17-22). As metalworker and musician, Tubal-Cain and Jubal represent categories of persons who would be equally welcome among nomads and settled agriculturalists. As such, they function in the genealogy as mediators of the opposition between the tent-dwelling and city-dwelling descendants of Cain (cf. Leach, 1969:60).

Cain's mark (Gen. 4.15) is a symbol of his ambivalent and marginal character. The mark is a 'stigma' that identifies him as a person not quite human (one who is not to be slain although he is a murderer), an anti-social mediator who is neither human nor divine (Aycock, 1983).[1] The characterization of the stigmatized as anti-social is essential to Cain's role as a mediator who can communicate in both the human and divine realms. He represents the margins of oppositions—purity/pollution, life/death, limitation/creativity, this world/the other world (cf. Leach, 1969:60).

According to D. Alan Aycock, stigmata, as applied to mythical individuals such as Cain,

---

[1] Note Isaac Schapera's interpretation of Cain's fratricide and his escape from the traditional punishment for murder based on ethnographic parallels (1985 [1955]). Clearly, there is also a theological message in the story that concerns family and ethical issues. However, my concern here is more with literary structures of meaning.

may... be regarded metaphorically, as visual clues to the moral status of a particular actor, where it is important that the moral status of that actor be *multivalent*, according to the level of interpretation which the audience evokes. This multivalence is diagnostic of mythological contexts, producing in the audience an intuition simultaneously of emotional involvement and of interpretive complexity... there are four distinguishable, but interrelated levels subsumed by the metaphor of stigma: (1) stigma as an existential paradox expressing contradiction between physical mortality and spiritual immortality; (2) stigma as a sort of brand, a mark of 'ownership' by a particular deity who sets apart the stigmatized person from his [sic!] society and thus from conventional morality; (3) stigma as an element of sacrifice, mediating the realms of the human and divine; (4) stigma as a mythic paradox of creation and destruction akin to the worldwide theme of the 'trickster'. (1983:120-21)

Cain's character as represented in the biblical myth incorporates all of these levels of stigmatization. Furthermore, his characteristics are closely parallel to those identified in Chapter 2 for African smiths. In the African myths, smiths are often portrayed as both human and divine, as individuals set apart from conventional morality, as sacrificing something of themselves for the good of humankind, and as creators/destroyers. A similar stigmatization can be seen, for example, in the Dogon characterization of smiths as individuals who possess a diminished life force that removes them from the category of the 'living' (i.e., other Dogon). This diminished life force derives from the sacrifice of energy by the first smith for the common good of humanity, and contributes to the belief that as a result smiths are impure. The Bambara belief that smiths possess and manipulate *nyama* is similar. *Nyama* connotes both the impersonal power that animates the universe and filth, which is rich in *nyama*. The stigma of East African smiths is often identified with the potency of their blood which causes them to be ritually impure and induces fear in those who do not belong to smith 'castes'. Some of the characteristics of Cain and African smiths can also be seen in the literary portrayals of related groups.

The Kenites

On the basis of linguistic analyses, Cain (*qayin*) has been claimed as the eponymous ancestor of the Kenites (*haqqênî*). The Kenites are one of those enigmatic peoples in the Hebrew Bible for whom information is sparse and difficult to interpret. They are portrayed in biblical tradition as staunch supporters of both Israel and Yahwism. In Judg. 5.24-27 Jael, a Kenite woman, is praised for her bravery in the war with Sisera (cf. 4.17-22). The positive relationship between the Israelites and the Kenites is affirmed again in 1 Sam. 15.6 where it is acknowledged that the Kenites showed loyalty to Israel during the exodus experience. And in 1 Sam. 30.29 they are included among the peoples to whom David sends gifts of tribute.[1] They are not mentioned again in the traditions concerning the later history of Israel, but many scholars believe that they are closely related to the Rechabites, who are referred to in 2 Kings and Jeremiah. Some interpreters have gone so far as to hypothesize that the southern tribes had been familiar with the Kenites for generations before the exodus and that the Kenites were responsible for introducing Yahwism into the ancient Near East (see, e.g., Budde, 1899; Gressmann, 1913; Morgenstern, 1920-21; Rowley, 1946; 1950; Gray, 1953; cf. Buber, 1946; Meek, 1920-21; Binns, 1930). But it is generally agreed that they are depicted as a group of nomadic or semi-nomadic metalsmiths (see, e.g., Albright, 1957:257; 1963). This assertion is made on the basis of the observation that in biblical tradition the Kenites appear in various locations throughout Palestine in addition to the interpretation that their eponymous ancestor is Cain.[2] It has also been suggested that the

---

1 F. Charles Fensham (1964) has suggested that the relationship between the Kenites and the Israelites was based on a treaty between equals.
2 Jan Vansina (1985) has noted that traditional narratives tend to reflect ideal types to which the holders of particular roles or statuses are expected to conform. This often results in distortions of particular characters and/or the attribution of the characteristics of one idealized person to other prototypical characters, for example, the culture hero. Yet for the purposes of the historian the idealization itself may convey crucial cultural information. Viewed in ths light, whether or not the roles of the Kenites, Midianites, and Rechabites as portrayed in the Hebrew Bible are historically accurate,

Kenites functioned as priests and ritual specialists as well as smiths (e.g., Mazar, 1965:302-303; Aharoni, 1976:60).

The Kenites are listed in Gen. 15.19 as one of the peoples whose land is promised to Abraham's descendants. In Num. 24.21-22, where their dwellings ('nests') are described as being 'set in rock', it is foretold that they will perish, perhaps a reference to a loss of virtue resulting from the abandonment of their status as tent-dwellers to become city-dwellers (Leach, 1969:60). This is one of the rare instances in which they are viewed unfavorably.

The Rechabites
The relationship between the Kenites and the Rechabites is postulated on the basis of 1 Chron. 2.55 where a genealogical link is suggested. As is the case with the Kenites, the Rechabites are portrayed as fierce supporters of Yahwism (2 Kgs 10.15-28; Jer. 35). Also characteristic of the Rechabites is a strict avoidance of wine consumption and of agricultural and sedentary life.

> We will drink no wine, for Jonadab the son of Rechab, our father, commanded us, 'You shall not drink wine, neither you nor your sons forever; you shall not build a house; you shall not sow seed; you shall not plant or have a vineyard; but you shall live in tents all your days, that you may live many days in the land where you sojourn'. We have obeyed the voice of Jonadab the son of Rechab, our father, in all that he commanded us, to drink no wine in all our days, ourselves, our wives, our sons, or our daughters, and not to build houses to dwell in. We have no vineyard or field or seed; but we have lived in tents, and have obeyed and done all that Jonadab our father commanded us. (Jer. 35.6-10)

The proposal that the Rechabites shared the Kenites' vocation as metalworkers (Frick, 1971) seems sound given the genealogical link made in 1 Chronicles and their apparent marginal social position in Israel. The characteristics listed in Jeremiah 35 that contribute to their marginality are reminiscent of the typical position of metalsmiths in African societies and, as

> their roles in the narrative nevertheless convey significant cultural information about ancient Israel.

Max Weber has noted (1952:28), among the contemporary Bedouin. The marginal status of the related Kenites is further implied in Judges 4 where the house of the tent-dwelling Kenite Heber is referred to as having peaceful relations with Jabin the king of Hazor. In contrast, the actions of Jael, Heber's wife, on behalf of the Israelite tribes in killing Sisera suggest peaceful relations with the Israelites. This kind of marginal political status is also common among ironsmiths in East Africa, who often provide weapons for both parties engaged in warfare.

The Midianites
Also related to the Kenites in the biblical traditions are the Midianites. Moses' father-in-law is the key to this identification. In the Exodus stories he is called a Midianite, but in other passages a Kenite (Judg. 1.16; 4.11). In 1 Sam. 15.6, the Kenites are remembered as loyal supporters of Israel during the exodus, a role attributed to the Midianites in the Pentateuchal narratives. Whatever the explanation for this inconsistency (see, e.g., Parke-Taylor, 1975:23), it is clear that biblical tradition regarded the father-in-law of Moses as a Kenite. The problem of the identity of Moses' father-in-law is further complicated by the fact that in Exod. 3.1 he is called Jethro, in Exod. 2.18 he is called Reuel, and in Num. 10.29 Hobab. In Judg. 4.11 the descendants of Hobab are designated as Kenites, and in Judg. 1.16 Moses' father-in-law is called simply 'the Kenite'.[1] This traditional relatedness of the Midianites with the Kenites is a significant indicator of the role the Midianites play in Israel's sacred story.

In Exod. 2.15-3.15 and 18.1-27 are related the encounters of Moses and the Midianites before and following the exodus from Egypt. Moses is received by the Midianites after his flight from Egypt and marries the daughter of a Midianite priest. It is during Moses' residence in Midian that Yahweh reveals the Divine Self to Moses in the burning bush. There

---

1 W. F. Albright has attempted to come to terms with these inconsistencies by suggesting that Jethro was Moses' father-in-law, Hobab was his son-in-law, and they both belonged to the clan of Reuel (1963; 1983b).

follows an account of Moses' return to Egypt and of the exodus event. In ch. 18 Moses and the people again meet his father-in-law, who rejoices in the fact that Yahweh has delivered them from Egypt, offers up a sacrifice and presides over a covenantal meal attended by Aaron, and advises Moses in matters of governing the people (Exod. 18.1-27). Here again, we encounter some similarities with the ironsmiths of Africa. As a priest, Moses' father-in-law serves as a mediator between the divine and human realms. As an adviser to Moses on judicial affairs, he serves as a mediator in the human realm.[1]

One of the most enigmatic passages in the exodus traditions (Exod. 4.24-26) might be clarified somewhat by viewing it in relation to the African information on the role of ironsmiths.

> At a lodging place on the way the LORD met him [Moses] and sought to kill him. Then Zipporah took a flint and cut off her son's foreskin, and touched Moses' feet with it, and said, 'Surely you are a bridegroom of blood to me!' So he let him alone. Then it was that she said, 'You are a bridegroom of blood', because of the circumcision.

Brevard Childs' description of the interpretive problems inherent in this passage are revealing:

> Few texts contain more problems for the interpreter than these few verses which have continued to baffle throughout the centuries. The difficulties cover the entire spectrum of possible problems. First of all, the passage seems to have little connection with its larger context. Why should Yahweh suddenly seek to kill his messenger? No reason is given for the assault. Again, the reaction of Zipporah is without explanation. How did she know what to do? Furthermore, the lack of antecedents throughout the passage render it difficult to specify the agents involved. Whom did Yahweh seek to kill in v.24. Moses or his son? Again, in 25 the antecedents to the prepositions are uncertain: 'she touched his feet and said, "You are to me a blood-bridegroom."' Is the same person intended throughout the verse and who then is meant? Then again, what is the meaning of the term $h^a\underline{t}an$

---

1 This role may have been attributed to smiths in Assyria as well. Pleiner and Bjorkman (1974:304) note that metalworkers could be invited to be witnesses in various legal transactions.

dāmîm ('blood-bridegroom'?), and how does it relate to the circumcision of the child? (1974:95-96)

Clearly, the passage is fraught with difficulties, most of which cannot be solved here. However, it is relevant to suggest a possible, although admittedly partial, solution to Childs' questions concerning the role of Zipporah. Zipporah may take responsibility in this passage for carrying out the circumcision because she is a Midianite from a smithing clan. One of the primary ritual functions of smiths in both West and East Africa is that of circumcisor. Admittedly, this is as speculative as other interpretations that have been offered (see Childs, 1974:97-101), but the fact that Zipporah is a Midianite and the one who performs the circumcision offers at least minimal support to the interpretation that the Midianites were, or at least had some close relationship to, ancient metalworking clans. Furthermore, the insertion of the passage into its present context may have some structural significance in the narrative, since Moses is returning to Egypt and thus into another symbolic realm. This is an appropriate place in the overall structure of the exodus narratives to include a rite of passage (see the discussion of narrative structure below).

Apart from those traditions directly associated with the exodus from Egypt, the Midianites are not looked upon kindly in the biblical traditions and in fact are often portrayed as Israel's enemies in battle (see, e.g., Num. 31; Judg. 7–9; Ps. 83.9; Isa. 10.26). This shift in the perceived relationship between the two peoples is nowhere clarified, and it is not possible to determine whether there was any particular historical reason for it.

Numbers 25 stands out as a passage that may have some significance in support of the proposal that at least some of the Midianite clans were marginal smiths. According to many African traditions, intermarriage with individuals from smithing clans is dangerous and polluting. In Numbers 25, a plague is visited upon the people for the indiscretion of a man by the name of Zimri who 'brought a Midianite woman to his family' (v. 6). Both Zimri and the Midianite woman ('Cozbe the daughter of Zur, who was the head of the people of a father's house in Midian' [v. 15]) are slain by Phinehas the son

5. Biblical Symbols

of Eleazar, son of Aaron. Whether the apparent abhorrence of the interaction between Israelite and Midianite in this tradition has generally to do with the postexilic emphasis on maintaining the purity of the Jewish people[1] or has some other explanation is difficult to determine. In its present form, the emphasis in the passage is on the zeal of Phinehas in meting out the punishment and on the covenant established to guarantee the perpetual priesthood of Phinehas' descendants.[2] However, considered in light of the African material, it is possible that the gravity of the offense may have had more to do with the fact that it was committed with a polluting *Midianite* woman (i.e., a woman from a metalworking clan) than with entering into a relationship with just any 'non-Israelite' woman. This would explain the severity of the punishment and the effect the incident had (the plague) on the entire community—by entering into a relationship with a Midianite woman from a smithing clan, Zimri threatened the well-being and purity of the community.[3]

This tradition contrasts with the apparent acceptance of Moses' marriage to a Midianite woman. Since Moses himself is a mediator, and his role as mediator is related to his association with the Midianites, he seems to be exempt from the condemnation imposed on other Israelites in the biblical traditions.

Max Weber and the Social Status of the Israelite Smith

Max Weber's comments on smiths and artisans in ancient Israel are in accord with my proposal here that smiths are portrayed as marginal mediators in the Hebrew Bible. In his sociological study of ancient Israel, Weber includes artisans and merchants among the *gērîm* (sojourners) of Israelite cities. Weber compares the status of the *gērîm* to the social

---

1 The passage has been assigned to the Priestly tradition (see Snaith, 1969:184).
2 The Zadokites claim their descent from Eleazar through Phinehas (1 Chron. 24.3; see, e.g., Snaith, 1969:184).
3 Compare Ezra 2.61-63 and Neh. 7.63-65 where the descendants of Barzillai (from *barzel*, 'iron') are excluded by name from the priesthood as unclean, in spite of their ancestor's good relations with David (2 Sam. 17.27-29; 19.31-39).

position of artisans among the modern Bedouin for whom the smith, 'the single most important craftsman of the Bedouin', has a marginal status (1952:28). Among the Bedouin this guest artisan belongs to a 'caste' that is almost always viewed as ritually impure, is usually excluded from intermarriage and commensalism, and enjoys only traditional, usually religious, protection. Weber further notes that this same status is applied among the Bedouin to bards and musicians. In Weber's estimation, Cain not only is the eponymous ancestor of smiths and musicians, but of all typical guest tribes in ancient Israel, while at the same time he is the founder of cities. For Weber, then, the artisans descended from Cain were 'guest people' (*gērîm*) standing outside both the *gibbôrîm* (warriors and landowners) and the general Israelite population. Weber also points to the foreignness of the Phoenician artisans employed in building the Jerusalem Temple (1 Kgs 5–7; 1 Chron. 2–4).

On the basis of references in postexilic texts, Weber suggests (1952:29) that the social status of artisans in ancient Israel changed during the reconstitution of the postexilic Israelite community under Ezra and Nehemiah. According to his interpretation, during this period artisans were divested of their tribal foreignness, were organized into guilds, and were received into the Jewish confessional community organization. Associated with this shift in social status seems to be a shift in the degree to which the smith and his craft were feared. This hypothesis is in accord with Mary Douglas's proposal (1966:99; see Chapter 2) that the expression of attitudes toward those of marginal status in society varies according to the degree to which the power structure of the society is articulated and the degree to which marginal individuals have been integrated into society. If the power structure is well articulated, powers are vested more in those in authority and less in marginal individuals, whereas if the power structure is less well articulated, powers tend to be vested in marginal individuals who are perceived as potential sources of disorder. It is quite feasible that the ambivalence with which smiths were regarded in early Israel decreased over time as Israelite society became more centralized and craft organizations were institutionalized.

Alongside the artisans of guest status in early Israel were skilled artisans whom Weber defines as 'liberal charismatic artisans' (1952:28). This type of artisan is represented in the person of Bezaleel of the tribe of Judah, who is appointed and taught by Yahweh to construct the tabernacle and ark, and in order to carry out these tasks was 'filled with the spirit of God' (Exod. 31.1-11).

Egypt as an 'Iron Furnace'

Reference is made to Egypt as an 'iron furnace' (*kûr habbarzel*) in three biblical passages: Deut. 4.20; 1 Kgs 8.51; and Jer. 11.4. In each instance, Israel's sacred story and God's role in the sacred story are recounted. The reference in Deuteronomy occurs in the conclusion of Moses' first address. Moses refers to God's bringing the people out of the iron furnace as the basis of his appeal for faithful obedience to the covenant. In 1 Kings, the reference is included in Solomon's concluding prayer at the dedication of the Jerusalem Temple. Solomon links Israel as God's heritage with God's bringing the people out of the midst of the iron furnace. An appeal to the people to uphold the covenant is also made here. In the Jeremiah passage, God directs Jeremiah to proclaim the words of the covenant to the people of Judah, words that were commanded after God brought the people out of the iron furnace of Egypt (cf. Deutero-Isaiah's 'furnace of affliction' [Isa. 48.10]).

That these passages all link the furnace metaphor directly to claims about God's saving activity and to the covenant relationship between God and people is clear. Furthermore, because they are Deuteronomistic, it is likely that an implicit parallel is drawn in each case with the Babylonian exile. However, the significance and meaning of the metaphor are not stated directly. Two important questions are left unanswered: First, why is the metaphor of an 'iron furnace' used to encapsulate and express the relationships among God, people, and Egypt in the literary traditions? And second, why does Egypt play such a significant role in these traditions?

The traditional interpretation is that the metaphor conveys the meaning of oppression, oppression that was imposed on the people during their sojourn in Egypt. This interpretation is supported by those passages I have cited that use images associated with iron and metallurgy to symbolize Israel's oppression. However, as I have noted, oppression represents part of the process whereby a transformation is facilitated. The meaning operates on more levels and has much more depth and breadth than the simple association with oppression allows. This is in accord with Jan Vansina's assertion that the meanings of key words, symbols, metaphors, or stereotypes in traditional narratives that seem *apparent* to the interpreter are not necessarily the meanings that are *intended*.[1] Oppression is but one facet of the *transformative* quality of the Egypt/exodus traditions. It is this process of transforming that is conveyed most powerfully in the metaphor.

The iron furnace metaphor is an 'elaborating symbol' or 'root metaphor' of the type defined in Chapter 2 (see Ortner, 1973; cf. Turner, 1967:29-31; Fernandez, 1966:61-62). As was indicated there, this type of metaphor functions to order experience, that is, it is essentially analytical. It serves as a source of categories for conceptualizing the ordering of the world, as a means of orienting oneself in the world, and as a way of understanding and expressing the relationships of parts in a whole. The interrelationship among the parts of the root metaphor help to conceptualize and express in tacit form the interrelationship among the parts of the referent. As a root metaphor, 'Egypt as iron furnace' communicates in condensed and tacit form information about the development of Israel as a religious people.[2]

It is important to recognize that the meaning encapsulated in this metaphor is tacit rather than explicit. It has what Mary Douglas (1975) has defined as 'implicit meaning'. Condensed in the metaphor is information that is treated as self-evident truth by those for whom it has meaning, in this case a 'truth' associated with the transformative power of the iron-working process. Thus, it is not necessary to make its meaning explicit. It is too true to warrant elaboration. Douglas notes

---

1 On the problem of distinguishing between apparent and intended meaning see, e.g., Vansina, 1985.
2 The Egypt as iron furnace metaphor is very similar to the forge imagery of the Fang of West Africa which symbolizes on one level the relationship between past and present. See Chapter 2.

5. Biblical Symbols

that symbols with implicit meaning, since they are never made explicit, furnish the stable background on which more coherent meanings are based (1975:3-4). They provide necessary assumptions upon which ordinary explicit discourse is built. The implicit nature of the meanings conveyed also allows for flexibility in creating, revising, and reaffirming this implicit background without ever directing explicit attention upon it. When the background of assumptions (e.g., the Egypt as 'iron furnace' metaphor) upholds what is verbally explicit (e.g., the Pentateuchal narratives), meaning comes across 'loud and clear'.

The processual structure of rites of passage as defined by Victor Turner (e.g., 1969; see Chapter 2) serves as an appropriate analogy for revealing the implied structural relationships (whether made consciously or unconsciously) underlying the iron furnace metaphor and its referents. A similar approach to interpreting texts has been used by Edmund Leach (1983) and others (e.g., Flanagan, 1983; Niditch, 1985) in interpreting biblical traditions. According to Leach (1983: 100):

> if we consistently think of text in relation to ritual and *vice versa* instead of keeping the two modes of metaphorical expression in mutual isolation, then matters which might otherwise seem obscure may come into sharper or even quite different focus.

The analogy serves both as an analytical framework and as a heuristic device for defining the complex relationships among the domains of technology, history, and narrative tradition that are encapsulated in the iron furnace metaphor, and for identifying the nature of the transformation represented in each. It also offers a means for clarifying why it is that the technological process of ironworking serves as a mechanism for communicating and illuminating a crucial turning point in Israel's narrative tradition (see Table 20).

Table 20: *Egypt as an 'Iron Furnace'*

	death		rebirth
metaphor	previous 'state'	transition/transformative period	transformed 'state'
iron-working	soft metal/ore	furnace (smelting/forging)	strong/superior metal
historical periods	Late Bronze Age 1600–1200 BCE	Early Iron Age 1200–922 BCE	Iron Age 922–586 BCE
narrative perspective of 'history'	Ancestral period; Genesis	Egypt/Wilderness; Exodus–Deuteronomy	Israel in the Promised Land; Joshua–Kings

Implied in the iron furnace metaphor is an awareness of the transformation that iron ore undergoes when it is introduced into the furnace. Here, I emphasize again the analogy of the processual structure of rites of passage with the complex and mysterious technological process of iron production (see Chapter 2). Briefly, the correspondence in structure is as follows: In the preliminal phase the iron ore is a relatively soft material inferior to bronze. When the ore is introduced into the furnace, it is separated from its previous state and moves into the liminal or marginal phase during which it is transformed by the fire with the assistance of the smith. It is during this crucial phase that it is reoriented through carburization and forging and is prepared to move into a higher state as a strong metal superior to that which entered into the process. Once quenched, it is 'reborn'. It takes on a new set of characteristics that allow for its use in the form of tools and weapons.

Archaeological information illuminates this process of transforming in other spheres. Reflected in the metaphor of Egypt as iron furnace is the coincidence of sociopolitical and technological developments during the transition from the Bronze Age to the Iron Age (see Chapter 4). The Early Iron Age stands 'betwixt and between' the decline of the Late Bronze Age cultures of the Near East and the development or 'birth' of a new nation, Israel. It is a period of transition culturally, socially, and technologically. By the end of this transitional period, iron begins to surpass bronze as the preferred metal for manufacturing utilitarian objects. This technological shift corresponds roughly to the rise of the Israelite state—the emergence of Israel as a cohesive people. The Early Iron Age, then, is a time of rebuilding, a time of cultural and economic reorientation, a time of transformation that is directly linked to the introduction of iron.

Further insight into the transformative meaning underlying the iron furnace metaphor used in Deut. 4.20, 1 Kgs 8.51, and Jer. 11.4 is gained by considering other references in the Bible. Many of the symbols associated with iron in the Hebrew Bible refer to technological, military, or political superiority, or to strength, power, and oppression, meanings that are present in the Egypt as iron furnace metaphor as well. But in addition to its superiority and strength, the ancient Israelites were aware of the transformative power of the ironsmith's work. This awareness is apparent in those passages in which God is likened to a smith who transforms the people in a metaphorical furnace or smelting process (Ps. 12.7 [6]; Isa. 1.25; 31.9; 48.10; Ezek. 22.17-22; Zech. 13.9; Mal. 3.1-4). In Isaiah 48 and Ezekiel 22, the metaphor is used to symbolize the liminality of the Babylonian exile. The furnace metaphor was used in prophetic literature as early as the eighth century BCE (Isa. 31.9) and by at least the late seventh to early sixth centuries BCE it was specifically associated with the transformation of iron.

The most forceful testimony to the meaning of the iron furnace metaphor, however, is present in the structure of the Pentateuchal narratives about the development of God's relationship with Israel. It is clear that the editors who were responsible for the final form of the Pentateuch recognized a transitional period in Israel's national and religious development during which Israel was transformed from the disparate peoples represented in the ancestral stories in Genesis, to Israel as a national religious entity united under the guidance of Yahweh.

The structure underlying these narratives in their final form reveals diachronic and spatial literary relationships that are in themselves symbolic, and contribute to the potency of the Egypt as iron furnace metaphor. As Edmund Leach argues, these relationships have symbolic significance whether or not they happen to correspond to reality as normally understood (1987:581). The narrative structure is illuminated by again applying the phases in the processual structure of rites of passage. Israel's 'previous state' as a scattered people living in the geographical region of Canaan, with a promise yet to be fulfilled, is represented in the ancestral stories. Joseph's entrance into Egypt and the subsequent descent of his family represent a break from the past way of life and an entrance into the iron furnace Egypt (a kind of symbolic womb) in preparation for the fulfillment of the promise. In Egypt and the wilderness Israel experiences the topsy turvy realm that is so characteristic of the 'betwixt and between' (cf. Leach, 1987). The entrance into Egypt symbolizes a separation from Israel's previous state culturally, socially, spatially, and temporally. Cultural and social autonomy are lost to slavery and oppression, the land promised left behind, temporal reality between the times of Joseph and Moses passed over with a mere reference to the number of years spent in Egypt (Exod. 12.40).

In this light, the process of aggregation—the fulfillment of the promise, the forging of the people into the religious entity Israel—begins with the pivotal event in Israel's sacred story, the exodus from Egypt. It is at this point that the God Yahweh liberates the people from their bondage in the iron furnace, from the liminal 'betwixt and between' in which their status as an autonomous people is suspended and ambiguous. The motif of rebirth is clear from the creation imagery used in Exodus 15 (see Anderson, 1984). But this is only the first step toward the ultimate goal of achieving a new status as a people possessing a land of their own. Once they pass out of the furnace, symbolized by the crossing, or quenching, at the Reed Sea, they must be forged into a people with a common identity, sharing in further trials to cement their solidarity. The final steps toward transformation are taken in the wilderness. In the Hebrew Bible, wilderness symbolizes liminality or marginality *par excellence*. The wilderness is a place of chaos, of hunger and thirst, and of demons. But it is also a place of Divine revelation. In the wilderness Elijah experiences the 'small voice' that is God's (1 Kgs 19.12), Moses encounters the Divine, and Moses' followers experience both threats of death

5. Biblical Symbols

and hope for new life. The wilderness, in the words of Edmund Leach, is the 'Other World' in which everything happens in reverse—for example, heavenly bread falls from the sky and water emerges from a rock (Leach, 1987:587). 'Entering or leaving the Wilderness symbolizes a metaphysical movement from the here and now to the timelessness of the Other or vice versa' (Leach, 1987:586; cf. Turner, 1969:95). Following the forging in the wilderness, both through the gift of covenant law and through shared experience, the Israelites take the final step toward aggregation. Under the leadership of Joshua, the people pass over the Jordan River into the Promised Land. They are quenched and 'reborn'. They enter into the same land left behind by Joseph and his family, but they move back into this geographical realm as a transformed people, as 'Israel'. It is the same land, yet not the same land. Before, it was a land in which Abraham and his kin travelled and dwelt as sojourners. Now it is a land possessed, a land given as an inheritance by the graciousness of God. At one level in the narrative, then, Egypt as iron furnace is a transformative stage between Joseph's descent into Egypt and the ascent into the wilderness. But on another level, this whole complex—Joseph's descent into Egypt, the Egypt experience itself, and the wilderness experiences—is a transformative stage between the ancestral residence in the land and the final occupation of the Promised Land under the leadership of Joshua.

There are many rich symbols woven into this sacred tale of transformation: water as a symbol of rebirth, the wilderness as liminality, the image of the furnace as womb,[1] Pharaoh and the plagues as representatives of the chaos of liminality. But there is one important symbol whose meaning is not fully

---

[1] The symbol of the furnace as womb is always implicit rather than explicit in the Hebrew Bible. However, it is significant that in Mesopotamian literature this metaphor is sometime made explicit. Mircea Eliade (1978:71-78) makes reference to a number of texts outlining the correct ritual procedures for metallurgical operations which, in addition to emphasizing such things as the importance of sacrifice and maintaining ritual purity, use a number of sexual images to describe the process. Included among these sexual images are references to the furnace as a womb and, apparently, to the ore being transformed in the furnace as a fetus or embryo.

apparent unless viewed in relation to the iron furnace metaphor. This symbol, encapsulated in the literary roles of the Midianites and Moses, is the metalsmith as mediator (compare God as Divine Smith). It is the Midianites and Moses as Midianite who mediate the transitions in the narrative and the processual structure underlying it.

The structural role of the Midianites is clarified by social analogies used as a heuristic tool for identifying structural relationships. In African societies, the smith's role as mediator in the transformation of iron serves as a tacit cognitive or analytical model, as a metaphor, for mediating relationships. In African mythology, the first smith or iron god is often the culture hero. He serves as a facilitator of the formation of order out of chaos. As both a descendant of the gods and the first human ancestor, he mediates between the heavenly and earthly realms and transmits to humans crucial knowledge about social organization, agriculture, animal domestication, and technology. It is he who is able to maintain a balance between the divine and human spheres and who can resolve internal and external controversies.

The African smith is also a social and political mediator. By virtue of his ritual functions in the technological 'rite of passage', he is well-suited to serve in a similar capacity in social rituals. Thus his role is central in many initiation rites, and he occasionally attains the office of priest. For the same reason, he is recognized as a mediator in settling legal disputes and as upholder of social justice. All of these roles and offices are related to his role as craftsman in facilitating the 'death' and 'rebirth' of the material he transforms in the smelting and forging processes.

As an artisan, the smith is also set apart in African societies. Artisans are often considered to be socially and structurally inferior or 'marginal' (cf. Turner, 1969:96; 1974:231-33). Marginal peoples tend to play major roles in myths and popular tales as representatives or expressions of universal human values. They also tend to function *socially* as arbiters in disputes, as representatives of what Victor Turner calls 'communitas', as a kind of check on the normative system of bounded, structured, particularistic groups. The socially marginal position traditionally associated with the smith,

5. Biblical Symbols

then, is closely related to his social function as mediator, a role that he also plays in his craft.

The role of the Midianites/Kenites in the narrative structure of Israel's sacred story is clarified if viewed from this perspective. The Kenites are portrayed as a socially marginal group. Although they are fiercely devoted to Israel and to Yahwism, they are never fully incorporated into Israelite society. Cain, the eponymous ancestor of the Kenites, is a marginal and ambivalent figure, a mediator who represents the margins of oppositions.

In the Pentateuchal narratives, the Midianites are also mediators. Geographically, they are a marginal people in the Israelite world. They dwell in the margin between the Promised Land and the iron furnace Egypt. Again, Edmund Leach offers some insight into how the varied roles of the Midianites can be viewed as structurally consistent:

> ... if two biblical stories refer to individuals or places of the same name (or very similar names) in different contexts of time and place the *historian* will assume that two quite different 'real entities' are to be distinguished. For the *structuralist* on the other hand the fact that the same name crops up in two different places is of significance in itself in that it suggests a link between the two stories. He [sic!] is then immediately led to consider whether or not the two stories are associated in other ways also. (1969:34)

Of 'history' as 'myth', Leach suggests, it is quite sensible to ask: Why does this particular incident (rather than some other) occur in the story in this particular form (rather than some other)? The answer can be found in the patterned arrangement of stories.

In the Joseph stories (Gen. 37; 39–50), it is Midianite traders who are ultimately responsible for mediating the symbolic 'death' of Jacob's family by transporting Joseph to Egypt, into the betwixt and between where Israel's transformation as a people is to take place (Gen. 37.28, 36). Interpreters have suggested that the Joseph stories do not fit well into the narratives of the exodus traditions. Nevertheless, in the final canonical form of these narratives, the story has been recognized as serving an essential function that derives from its context. It serves as a bridge between the ancestral and exodus traditions (e.g., Noth, 1981:208-13; Coats, 1976). The Joseph story itself, then, can be interpreted as functioning to mediate the transition in the narrative traditions. In fact, Joseph, the central character in these stories, is a marginal mediator himself. His marginality is suggested by the fact that he moves back and forth between high- and low-status positions: from favored son to slave; from slave to a position of high rank in Potiphar's household; from high rank to prisoner; from prisoner to a position of high rank in Pharaoh's court.

The occurrence of the two references to the Midianites in the Joseph story has been viewed as problematic because it conflicts with the account of the sale of Joseph to the Ishmaelites (Gen. 37.25-28; cf. 39.1), it breaks the flow of the narrative, and it points to an element of disunity (Coats, 1976:17, 20). However, whether or not these two references are later glosses or secondary intrusions in the text, their *structural* significance in the final form of the narrative is clear if their role as symbolic mediators is recognized. From a structural point of view, the contradictions introduced into the story by the intrusion of the Midianites is a detail of little significance (cf. Leach, 1969:45).[1]

The Midianite role in mediating the subsequent rebirth of the people is more fully elaborated. It is the Midianites who give Moses refuge when he flees from Egypt. It is in the geographical boundary between Egypt and the Promised Land— Midian—where God reveals the Divine name to Moses and assigns him his mission (Exod. 3). Moses is commissioned to become the mediator of Divine liberation while in Midian. He becomes a Midianite himself by marrying into a Midianite family (Exod. 2.21). It might be argued that because of his marginal status, Moses is ultimately denied the opportunity to participate fully in the society to which he has helped give birth (cf. Num. 20.12; Deut. 32.48-52). He is not allowed by God to enter the Promised Land (Deut. 34).

Jethro (in Exod. 2.18 'Reuel' and in Num. 10.29 and Judg. 4.11 'Hobab'), Moses' father-in-law and priest of Midian,

---

1 Compare George W. Coats' suggestion (1976:17) that the glosses may have been introduced to alleviate the problem posed by the brothers selling one of their own into slavery.

plays an essential role in the narrative structure of the exodus and wilderness traditions. He is responsible for accepting Moses into Midianite society. Following the exodus, mediated by Moses, the marginal Israelite/Midianite, Jethro offers a sacrifice to God and presides over a sacred meal attended by Aaron (Exod. 18.10-12). He advises Moses in matters of governing the people and mediating disputes (Exod. 18.13-27). And in Num. 10.29-32, Moses requests that Hobab serve as the people's guide through the wilderness, as their eyes, because it is he who knows how to survive in this marginal realm.[1] Just as the Midianites are responsible in the narrative structure for facilitating the symbolic death represented by the descent of Joseph into Egypt, so a Midianite is given responsibility for guiding Israel through the final step in the process of rebirth—the passage through the liminality of wilderness toward the goal of the Promised Land.

The mediating roles of the Midianites in facilitating the transformation of Israel in the narratives are very similar to those of the smith in African societies. Jethro is a priest-smith who mediates between the realms of the Divine and the human. He mediates in the human realm as legal counselor, and, most importantly, he facilitates the completion of Israel's rite of passage into a new 'state' as a nation. He has a hand in assisting Yahweh, the Divine Smith, in 'forging' Israel into a united people.

The metaphor of Egypt as an iron furnace, then, serves in the Deuteronomistic traditions as a root metaphor for ordering Israel's religious development, as an implicit source of categories for conceptualizing and expressing the interrelationships of the events that led to the birth of a nation out of the iron furnace of Egypt. Encapsulated in the metaphor is an awareness of the structural congruence among the domains

---

[1] A similar role is played by Barzillai (2 Sam. 19.31-39; cf. 17.27-29) who escorts David across the Jordan River when he returns to Jerusalem following Absalom's revolt. Although Barzillai's occupation is not identified, his name is etymologically related to *barzel* ('iron'). It may be significant that Barzillai's descendants were excluded by name from the priesthood as unclean. Given the ambivalent attitude toward both iron and ironworkers, this exclusion is not surprising.

of iron technology, history, and narrative tradition and the transformations that are represented in each. Implied in the metaphor is the mystery of the Divine Smith's transforming power and the mystery and transforming power of the covenant relationship that forged Israel into a people united as well as the parallel transformation undergone during the Babylonian exile. Condensed in this powerful symbol is the *meaning* of Israel's relationship to God in the past, present, and future:

> ... as information is decreased, meaningfulness is increased; for similarities, substantive or structural, between that which we seek to understand and that which we already 'know,' are made explicit. Metaphors are constructed. The application of a rule, principle, or classificatory device to a wide range of phenomena ... invests the world with meaning, for everything is not only itself, but also an icon of other things. (Rappaport, 1979:156)

In ancient Israel, iron technology, as a defining technology, provided a rich reservoir of symbols upon which the Israelites drew to express meaning at multiple levels, particularly in the realm of relationships—the relationship between Israel and other nations, between the individual and God, between Israel and God, between past and present. These relationships are expressed in symbols of power, strength, durability, oppression, transformation, mediation, and so on. The 'multivocality' of iron technology as a key symbol made it susceptible to many meanings and allowed for each symbol associated with it to condense a number of references all at once.

Chapter 6

CONCLUSIONS

In the preceding chapters, I have considered ironworking in the ancient Near East and ancient Israel on the basis of two categories of information: archaeological and literary. For analytical purposes, each category is first considered separately and identified with the ancient domain of actions and notions respectively. When considered in isolation, each type of information conveys a 'blurred' picture of ancient perceptions of iron technology. Furthermore, when viewed in isolation from one another, the messages conveyed to the interpreter are incongruous. It is not until the ancient information is illuminated by the ethnographic information from contemporary societies that the relationship between the two domains is brought into clearer focus.

In considering each type of information I suggest that we not lose sight of the complexities associated with interpreting ancient societies and their cultural remains, whether material or textual. Nor should we obscure the complexities of the ancient social world by proposing simplistic answers to problems that arise from sparse or contradictory data. The interrelationship between the material and cultural realms of society needs to be considered, as does the fact that there are no easily discernible answers to the nature of this interrelationship, since the relationships themselves are always complex (see, e.g., Flanagan, 1988). Important examples with respect to interpreting material remains are Renfrew's distinction between the *invention* and *adoption* of new technologies (1984) and Hodder's conclusions regarding the complexities of the relationship between material culture and ethnicity (1982b). Also important is consideration of the complex interaction between technology and various cultural realms, that is, the economic, social, political, and religious. It is clear that the 'New Archaeology' (see, e.g., Dever, 1980) has made significant contributions to our understanding of ancient cultures, particularly with respect to economy, subsistence, settlement patterns, and so forth. But it is necessary to move beyond the orientation of the New Archaeology to consider historical factors, the relevance of values and beliefs in the patterning of material culture, and even the potential significance of the creativity and intentionality of individuals (see, e.g., Hodder, 1982a; Trigger, 1978; N. Davies, 1986).

The ethnographic information on iron technology in traditional African societies indicates that the relationship between the domains of actions and notions is especially problematic. On the one hand, the information from both ancient and contemporary societies indicates that iron is clearly accepted as a utilitarian metal valued for its contributions to the welfare of society. On the other hand, when perceptions and symbolic representations of ironworking are considered, there is clearly an ambivalent attitude toward the technology. This ambivalent attitude is directed toward both the metal iron and the process of ironworking, but also extends to the tools used in the process and, especially, to the individuals who are responsible for creating iron objects, that is, the ironsmiths. The basis for this ambiguity is not apparent until the relationship between the two domains is examined and the technological process itself considered. For example, iron tools and weapons are depended upon for survival. They are used to provide sustenance for the community and for protection from outside (or inside) threats to the society. However, iron, particularly in the form of weapons, is potentially responsible for death as well as life. This contributes in part to the ambivalent attitudes that surround the final products of the ironworking process. Also contributing to the apparent attitudes of ambivalence is the nature of the ironworking process. For those, including the ancient smith, who have no knowledge of the chemical changes that occur when iron is smelted, forged, and especially carburized, ironworking appears to be a somewhat mysterious and magical process, and thus is considered dangerous. This mystery is associated with the fact that when the procedures are carried out correctly there is a radical transforma-

6. Conclusions

tion in the substance that is manipulated by the smith. The end product, then, is also cloaked in mystery, as are the various elements that are crucial in facilitating the mysterious transformation. Thus the smith, the furnace, the smith's tools, and the smithy are both respected and feared at the same time because of the power they have in facilitating the transformation. Since iron is an economic and social necessity, yet is regarded with some amount of fear, the material and notional realms of culture come into conflict.

The apparent contradictions also affect the systems of meaning in the culture in which the conflict between actions and notions occurs. Since technology in many ways mediates between human beings and their world, it affects the ways in which they think and communicate meaning, and thus the means by which feelings, attitudes, and emotions are expressed. The material impact of iron technology, therefore, should not be confused with its impact on the ways societies apprehend and express meaning about the world. Nor should the material impact of technologies be considered in isolation from systems of meaning in interpreting culture change.

As was emphasized in Chapter 1, cultural meaning is often conveyed through symbols drawn from dominant or 'defining' technologies. Technologies are used as 'root metaphors' of the elaborating or structural type, which are primarily analytical. This type of symbol functions to sort out and express complex and undifferentiated feelings and ideas and make them comprehensible, communicable, and translatable into ordinary action (Ortner, 1973:1340). Because of their potential for conveying multiple levels of meaning (their 'multivocality'), such symbols can also express a wide variety of attitudes, feelings, emotions, social values, and beliefs. Thus, symbols drawn from iron technology can refer to power, prestige, strength, status, mediation, and transformation, or any combination of these referents, depending upon the intended meaning and the context in which the symbol functions. As is the case for other technologies, then, metaphors associated with iron technology serve as 'storage bins' of information for understanding, classifying, and communicating information about cosmologies, values, and cultural principles.

It is not possible to determine from the biblical texts what impact the introduction of iron technology had on Israel in the earliest period following its adoption. In interpreting iron's impact on Israel's symbol system, in most instances we can only interpret its significance in light of later periods when the texts were edited and eventually put in canonical form. It is in the arrangement and structure of the texts as we now have them that, for example, the mediating role of the Midianites/ Kenites is represented most forcefully. The antiquity of the application of the mediation metaphor to these peoples can only be conjectured, although it is quite possible that a group of people called the Kenites or Midianites had a relationship with pre-Israelite groups akin to that between smiths and traditional African societies.

The archaeological material from the Bronze and Early Iron Ages provides some information on the symbolic function of iron in early periods before its adoption. Iron seems to have been a metal of some value that was considered to be rare and precious and was possibly used ritually to represent status. In the form of meteorites, its clear association with the sky in some of the ancient texts suggests that it functioned as a symbol of mediation between the divine and earthly realms, a function that possibly reinforced its later role as a mediating symbol, which was associated primarily with the ancient interpretation of the metalworking process. In fact, it is possible that other symbolic representations (e.g., power, strength, status) began to develop fairly early because of these earlier symbolic representations. The emphasis on transformation may also have developed at this time since to some extent there was an association in earlier periods of mediation and transformation with artisans and their products in general (e.g., the mythical representations of the artisan god Enki).

Iron technology apparently was not adopted into general use in Palestine until the tenth century BCE (see Chapter 4). Although it is possible that the process of carburization began to be understood to some extent by some metalworkers as early as the twelfth century BCE, the actual adoption of the technological innovation seems to have taken about two centuries. Once iron technology was adopted in Israel, it was accepted in the domain of actions as the dominant means of

6. Conclusions

producing utilitarian tools and weapons. As such, it was highly valued, as is indicated in both the archaeological information and some biblical references. However, in the domain of notions, it continued for a number of centuries to be regarded with suspicion in spite of its value. This is evident, for example, in the taboo against using iron in constructing the Jerusalem temple and altars dedicated to Yahweh (Deut. 27.5; Josh. 8.31; 1 Kgs 6.7). The relationship between these domains was expressed in the symbols and metaphors constructed to convey beliefs and conceptions about history, social identity, social values, and so on. Thus iron was used to communicate meaning on a variety of levels. In particular, we find iron and iron technology used to convey meaning about relationships that establish Israel's social and religious identity. Where iron symbolizes strength, power, durability, status, or oppression, some kind of relationship is expressed: between God and Israel, between God and Israel's enemies, between a king and his subjects, or between Israel and an outside group. For example, God's sovereignty over Israel is expressed in the image of the Divine Smith (e.g., Isa. 48.10; Ezek. 22.17-22); the power of Yahweh over Israel's enemies is manifest in the use of an iron implement to mow them down (Isa. 10.34); the king's sovereignty over his subjects is represented in the symbol of iron horns (e.g., 1 Kgs 22.11); the Canaanite ascendency over Israel during the time of the settlement is represented in the image of 'chariots of iron' (Josh. 17.16, 18; Judg. 1.19; 4.3, 13).

Related to symbols derived from iron's qualities of strength and durability are symbols that convey meanings associated with significant transformations that contributed to Israel's social and religious identity in relation to past, present, and future. Typically related to these transformations was some form of oppression, a 'liminal' state often represented by an image associated with iron. Oppression is identified as a process of purification, just as iron is purified in the metalsmith's furnace. Thus, the two major transitions in Israel's history (from the perspective of the biblical writers), the exodus from Egypt and the Babylonian exile, are symbolized by reference to a furnace or to the metalworking process, whereby God is represented as the Divine Smith purifying and transforming the people in order to bring them into a new relationship with the

Divine. Perhaps contributing to the force of the iron furnace metaphor that represented the exodus experience was a tacit recognition of the coincidence of the formation of the Israelite state and the adoption of iron technology. The sociopolitical transformation was recognized as having been accompanied by a technological transformation.

Essential in the metaphors of transformation is the individual who is responsible for facilitating the transformation, that is, the ironsmith. The ironsmith is the mediator in the transformation of iron ore into a strong and durable metal. This image of mediator is transferred through the use of symbolic representations to other realms. It is also expressed in the marginal position of the smith in the social structure. This assertion seems to be in accord with the representations of smiths in the biblical texts, especially in portrayals of Cain the culture hero, the Kenites, the Midianites, and the Rechabites. The marginal character of all these groups as well as the eponymous ancestor Cain is clear, and an ambivalent attitude is clear at least in the portrayals of Cain and the Midianites. The role of mediator is most prominent in the structural role of the Kenites/Midianites in the Pentateuchal narratives and the image of God as Divine Smith. Both play essential roles in facilitating transformations of the people Israel. Although the Kenites, Midianites, and Rechabites are not identified as *iron*-smiths (or even explicitly as smiths for that matter), we can assume that by the time the narratives were edited in the exilic and postexilic periods the primary metalworker in ancient Israelite society was a worker of iron.

The 'history' recorded in the biblical narratives must be understood first and foremost as notions, beliefs, and myths constructed to serve some purpose in the social and historical contexts in which they were written, edited, or arranged in their present form. Biblical literature cannot be assigned status as historical 'fact' merely because it purports to be relating history. We must take into account the symbolic intentions of the texts as myths that convey some sort of essential truth about social and religious values, principles, and identity. The *meaning* conveyed in the biblical texts must be interpreted in relation to 'social dramas' that prompted their writing and editing. References to 'iron chariots', lack of access to smiths,

6. Conclusions

Egypt as an iron furnace, and so on have their primary meanings in the monarchic and later periods, not the premonarchic period. They do not record historical facts about Iron Age I. The history of the Late Bronze and Early Iron Ages is given meaning in relation to the present during the monarchic, exilic, and postexilic periods. The past only has meaning when it is considered in light of the present and perhaps an idealized future. As Victor Turner has noted:

> ... meaning always involves retrospection and reflexivity, a past, a history. Meaning is the only category which grasps the full relation of the part to the whole in life, for value, being dominantly affective, belongs essentially to an experience in a conscious present. (1981:152)

In crisis situations such as syncretism, political subordination, and exile, the biblical writers in various periods appealed to sacred history (myth) to legitimate claims about the present and to encourage others to accept these claims. Cultural metaphors associated with iron technology were used to convey essential cultural values and principles in support of the writer's claims. For example, in the Deuteronomistic traditions, the metaphor of Egypt as an iron furnace reminded the people of God's activity in transforming Israel in appeals to abandon syncretistic practices and return to the covenant relationship with God. Other furnace metaphors used to symbolize judgment and exile/restoration emphasized God's intention to effect transformation through crisis and oppression. Iron chariots, Goliath's spear, Og's bed, and similar symbols served as reminders to the people that God's transformation of Israel was possible even in the face of the strength and military superiority of Israel's enemies. Such symbols functioned in times of crisis to strengthen national identity and to emphasize the superiority of Israel's God. The past as remembered and recounted in light of a present crisis, and the symbols used in the recounting, would have functioned to reaffirm shared values or to reinterpret these values and legitimate them by reinterpreting the symbols.

BIBLIOGRAPHY

Ackroyd, Peter R.
    1979   'Note to *Parzon* "Iron" in the Song of Deborah'. *Journal of Semitic Studies* 24:19-20.

Adéníji, David A. A.
    1977   *Iron Mining and Smelting in Yorubaland*. Trans. and ed. R. G. Armstrong. Institute of African Studies Occasional Publications, 31. Ibadan: University of Ibadan.

Aharoni, Yohanan
    1971   'Khirbet Raddana and Its Inscriptions'. *Israel Exploration Journal* 21:130-35.
    1972   'The Stratification of Israelite Megiddo'. *Journal of Near Eastern Studies* 31:302-11.
    1976   'Nothing Early and Nothing Late: Rewriting Israel's Conquest'. *Biblical Archeologist* 39:55-76.
    1979   *The Land of the Bible: A Historical Geography*. Philadelphia: Westminster.

Albright, William Foxwell
    1932   *The Excavation of Tell Beit Mirsim I*. Annual of the American Schools of Oriental Research, 12. New Haven: American Schools of Oriental Research.
    1940   Review of *Megiddo I: Seasons of 1925-34, Strata I-V*, R. S. Lamon and G. M. Shipton and *Notes on the Megiddo Pottery of Strata VI-XX*, G. M. Shipton. *American Journal of Archaeology* 44:546-50.
    1943   *The Excavation of Tell Beit Mirsim III: The Iron Age*. Annual of the American Schools of Oriental Research, 21-22. New Haven: American Schools of Oriental Research.
    1957   *From the Stone Age to Christianity: Monotheism and the Historical Process*. Garden City: Doubleday.
    1963   'Jethro, Hobab and Reuel in Early Hebrew Tradition'. *Catholic Biblical Quarterly* 25:1-11.
    1976   'Moses in History and Theological Perspective'. Pp. 120-31 in *Magnalia Dei: The Mighty Acts of God*. Eds. Frank Moore Cross, Werner E. Lemke, and Patrick D. Miller. Garden City: Doubleday.
    1983a   'From the Patriarchs to Moses. I. From Abraham to Joseph'. Pp. 5-33 in *The Biblical Archaeologist Reader IV*. Eds. Edward F. Campbell, Jr. and David Noel Freedman. Sheffield: Almond.
    1983b   'From the Patriarchs to Moses. II. Moses out of Egypt'. Pp. 35-64 in *The Biblical Archaeologist Reader IV*. Eds. Edward F. Campbell, Jr. and David Noel Freedman. Sheffield: Almond.

Alt, Albrecht
    1968   *Essays on Old Testament History and Religion*. Trans. R. A. Wilson. Garden City: Doubleday. Reprinted Sheffield: JSOT, 1989.

Amitai, Janet, ed.
1985 *Biblical Archaeology Today*. Proceedings of the International Congress on Biblical Archaeology, Jerusalem, April 1984. Jerusalem: Israel Exploration Society.

Anderson, Bernhard W.
1984 'Mythopoeic and Theological Dimensions of Biblical Creation Faith'. Pp. 1-24 in *Creation in the Old Testament*. Ed. Bernhard W. Anderson. Philadelphia: Fortress.

Avi-Yonah, Michael, ed.
1975 *Encyclopedia of Archaeological Excavations in the Holy Land, I*. Englewood Cliffs, NJ: Prentice Hall.
1976 *Encyclopedia of Archaeological Excavations in the Holy Land, II*. Englewood Cliffs, NJ: Prentice Hall.

Avi-Yonah, Michael, and Ephraim Stern, eds.
1977 *Encyclopedia of Archaeological Excavations in the Holy Land, III*. Englewood Cliffs, NJ: Prentice Hall.
1978 *Encyclopedia of Archaeological Excavations in the Holy Land, IV*. Englewood Cliffs, NJ: Prentice Hall.

Awolalu, J. Omosade
1979 *Yoruba Beliefs and Sacrificial Rites*. London: Longmans.

Aycock, D. Alan
1983 'The Mark of Cain'. Pp. 120-27 in *Structuralist Interpretations of Biblical Myth*. Eds. Edmund Leach and D. Alan Aycock. Cambridge: Cambridge University Press.

Barnes, Sandra T.
1980 *Ogun: An Old God for a New Age*. ISHI Occasional Papers in Social Change, 3. Philadelphia: Institute for the Study of Human Issues.

Barnes, Sandra T., ed.
1989 *Africa's Ogun: Old World and New*. Bloomington: Indiana University Press.

Baumgartner, W., ed.
1976 *Hebräisches und Aramäisches Lexikon zum Alten Testament*. Leiden: Brill.

Beidelman, Thomas O.
1974 *W. Robertson Smith and the Sociological Study of Religion*. Chicago: University of Chicago Press.

Ben-Tor, A.
1975 'News and Notes'. *Israel Exploration Journal* 25:169.
1976 'News and Notes'. *Israel Exploration Journal* 26:200-201.

Bernard, H. Russell, and Pertti J. Pelto, eds.
1972 *Technology and Social Change*. New York: Macmillan.

Binns, L. Elliott
1930 'Midianite Elements in Hebrew Religion'. *Journal of Theological Studies* 31:337-54.

Bjorkman, Judith K.
1968 'A Sketch of Metals and Metalworkers in the Ancient Near East'. M.A. Thesis, University of Pennsylvania.
1973 'Meteors and Meteorites in the Ancient Near East'. *Meteorics* 8:91-130.

Bohannan, Paul
　1965　'The Tiv of Nigeria'. Pp. 513-46 in *Peoples of Africa*. Ed. James L. Gibbs, Jr. New York: Holt, Rinehart and Winston.
Bolter, J. David
　1984　*Turing's Man: Western Culture in the Computer Age*. Chapel Hill: University of North Carolina Press.
Booth, Newell S., Jr.
　1977　'God and the Gods in West Africa'. Pp. 159-81 in *African Religions: A Symposium*. Ed. Newell S. Booth, Jr. New York: NOK.
Bowman, John, ed.
　1977　*Samaritan Documents Relating to their History, Religion and Life*. Pittsburgh: Pickwick.
Brown, Jean
　1971　'Ironworking in Southern Mbeere'. *Mila* 2:37-50.
Buber, Martin
　1946　*Moses*. Oxford: East and West Library.
Budde, Karl
　1899　*The Religion of Israel to the Exile*. New York: G. P. Putnam's Sons.
Burckhardt, Titus
　1967　*Sacred Art in East and West*. Pates Manor: Perrenial.
　1971　*Alchemy: Science of the Cosmos, Science of the Soul*. Baltimore: Penguin.
Callaway, Joseph A.
　1976　'Excavating Ai (et-Tell): 1964-1972'. *Biblical Archeologist* 39:18-30.
Carmack, Robert M.
　1972　'Ethnohistory: A Review of Its Development, Definitions, Methods, and Aims'. *Annual Review of Anthropology* 1:227-46.
Charles, James A.
　1980　'The Coming of Copper and Copper-Base Alloys and Iron: A Metallurgical Sequence'. Pp. 151-81 in *The Coming of the Age of Iron*. Eds. Theodore A. Wertime and James D. Muhly. New Haven: Yale University Press.
Childs, Brevard S.
　1974　*The Book of Exodus: A Critical Theological Commentary*. Philadelphia: Westminster.
Cline, Walter
　1937　*Mining and Metallurgy in Negro Africa*. General Series in Anthropology, 5. Menasha, WI: George Banta.
Coats, George W.
　1976　*From Canaan to Egypt: Structural and Theological Context for the Joseph Story*. Catholic Biblical Quarterly Monograph Series, 4. Washington: Catholic Biblical Association.
Coghlan, H. H.
　1956　*Notes on Prehistoric and Early Iron in the Old World*. Occasional Papers on Technology, 8 (Pitt Rivers Museum). Oxford: Oxford University Press.
Cole, Herbert M.
　1982　*Mbari: Art and Life among the Owerri Igbo*. Bloomington: Indiana University Press.

Coy, Michael William, Jr.
1982 'The Social and Economic Relations of Blacksmiths among Kalenjin-Speaking Peoples of the Rift Valley, Kenya'. Ph.D. dissertation, University of Pittsburgh.

Culley, Robert C.
1985 'Exploring New Directions'. Pp. 167-200 in *The Hebrew Bible and its Modern Interpreters*. Eds. Douglas A. Knight and Gene M. Tucker. Philadelphia and Chico, CA: Fortress and Scholars Press.

Curtis, J. E., T. S. Wheeler, J. D. Muhly, and R. Maddin
1979 'Neo-Assyrian Ironworking Technology'. *Proceedings of the American Philosophical Society* 123:369-90.

Davies, Graham I.
1986 *Megiddo*. Cambridge: Lutterworth.

Davies, Nigel
1986 'The "New" Archaeology'. *The Intercollegiate Review* 22:27-32.

Davis, D., R. Maddin, J. D. Muhly, and T. Stech
1985 'A Steel Pick from Mt. Adir in Palestine'. *Journal of Near Eastern Studies* 44:41-51.

Dayton, J. E.
1971 'The Problem of Tin in the Ancient World'. *World Archaeology* 3:49-70.

Department of Antiquities
1968 'News and Notes: Tell 'Aitun'. *Israel Exploration Journal* 18:194-95.

Dever, William G.
1977 'Palestine in the Second Millennium BCE: The Archaeological Picture'. Pp. 70-120 in *Israelite and Judaean History*. Eds. John H. Hayes and J. Maxwell Miller. Philadelphia: Westminster.

Dever, William G., H. Darrell Lance, and G. Ernest Wright
1970 *Gezer I: Preliminary Report of the 1964-66 Seasons*. Annual of the Hebrew Union College Biblical and Archaeological School in Jerusalem, 1. Jerusalem: Hebrew Union College—Jewish Institute of Religion.
1980 'Archaeological Method in Israel: A Continuing Revolution'. *Biblical Archeologist* 43:41-48.

Dever, William G., H. Darrell Lance, Reuben G. Bullard, Dan P. Cole, and Joe D. Seger
1974 *Gezer II: Report of the 1967-70 Seasons in Fields I and II*. Annual of the Hebrew Union College/Nelson Glueck School of Biblical Archaeology, 2. Jerusalem: Hebrew Union College—Jewish Institute of Religion.

Dieterlen, Germaine
1960 *An Essay on the Religion of the Bambara*. Trans. Katia Wolf. New Haven: Human Relations Area Files.
1973 'A Contribution to the Study of Blacksmiths in West Africa'. Pp. 40-61 in *French Perspectives in African Studies*. Ed. Pierre Alexandre. London: Oxford University Press.

Dornemann, Rudolph Henry
1983 *The Archaeology of Transjordan in the Bronze and Iron Ages*. Milwaukee: Milwaukee Public Museum.

Dothan, Moshe
1955 'The Excavations at 'Afula'. *Atiqot* 1:19-52.

Bibliography 273

1971a   *Ashdod II-III*. 'Atiqot English Series, 9-10. Jerusalem.
1971b   'Ashdod of the Philistines'. Pp. 17-27 in *New Directions in Biblical Archaeology*. Eds. David Noel Freedman and Jonas C. Greenfield. Garden City: Doubleday.
1979   'Ashdod at the End of the Late Bronze Age and the Beginning of the Iron Age'. Pp. 125-34 in *Symposia*. Ed. Frank Moore Cross. Cambridge, MA: American Schools of Oriental Research.

Dothan, Trude
1957   'Archaeological Reflections on the Philistine Problem'. *Antiquity and Survival* 2:151-64.
1982   *The Philistines and their Material Culture*. New Haven: Yale University Press.
1989   'Iron Knives from Tel Miqne-Ekron'. *Eretz Israel* 20:154-63.

Dothan, Trude, and Seymour Gitin
1985   'News and Notes—Tel Miqne 1984'. *Israel Exploration Journal* 35:67-71.
1990   'Ekron of the Philistines'. *Biblical Archaeology Review* 16:20-36.

Douglas, Mary T.
1966   *Purity and Danger: An Analysis of Concepts of Pollution and Taboo*. New York: Praeger.
1970   *Natural Symbols: Explorations in Cosmology*. New York: Pantheon.
1975   *Implicit Meanings: Essays in Anthropology*. London: Routledge & Kegan Paul.

Doumbia, Paul-Emile-Namoussa
1936   'Etude du Clan des Forgerons'. *Bulletin du Comité d'Études historiques et scientifiques de l'Afrique Occidentale Française* 19:334-80.

Drennan, Robert D.
1976   'Religion and Social Evolution in Formative Mesoamerica'. Pp. 345-68 in *The Early Mesoamerican Village*. Ed. Kent V. Flannery. New York: Academic Press.

Drews, Robert
1989   'The "Chariots of Iron" of Joshua and Judges'. *Journal for the Study of the Old Testament* 45:15-23.

Dubos, R.
1965   *Man Adapting*. New Haven: Yale University Press.
1968   *So Human an Animal*. New York: Scribner.

Durkheim, Emil
1965   *The Elementary Forms of the Religious Life*. Trans. Joseph Ward Swain. New York: The Free Press.

East, Rupert
1939   *Akiga's Story: The Tiv Tribe as Seen by One of its Members*. London: Oxford University Press.

Eliade, Mircea
1968   'Notes on the Symbolism of the Arrow'. Pp. 463-76 in *Religions in Antiquity*. Ed. Jacob Neusner. Leiden: Brill.
1978   *The Forge and the Crucible: The Origins and Structures of Alchemy*. 2nd edn. Trans. Stephen Corrin. Chicago: University of Chicago Press.

Ellul, Jaques
1964   *The Technological Society*. New York: Random House.

Engberg, R. M.
    1941   'Megiddo—Guardian of the Carmel Pass'. *Biblical Archeologist* 13:28-46.

Evans-Pritchard, E. E.
    1973   'Social Anthropology: Past and Present'. Pp. 358-70 in *High Points in Anthropology*. Eds. Paul Bohannan and Mark Glazer. New York: Alfred A. Knopf.

Fagg, W.
    1952   'Ironworking with a Stone Hammer among the Tula of Nigeria'. *Man* 76.

Fensham, F. Charles
    1964   'Did a Treaty between the Israelites and the Kenites Exist?' *Bulletin of the American Schools of Oriental Research* 175:51-54.
    1969   'Iron in the Ugaritic Texts'. *Oriens Antiquus* 8:209-13.

Fernandez, James W.
    1965   'Symbolic Consensus in a Fang Reformative Cult'. *American Anthropologist* 67:902-29.
    1966   'Unbelievably Subtle Words: Representations and Integration in the Sermons of an African Reformative Cult'. *History of Religions* 6:43-69.
    1973   'The Exposition and Imposition of Order: Artistic Expression in Fang Culture'. Pp. 194-220 in *The Traditional Artist in African Societies*. Ed. Warren L. d'Azevedo. Bloomington: Indiana University Press.
    1974   'The Mission of Metaphor in Expressive Culture'. *Current Anthropology* 15:119-45.
    1977   'The Performance of Ritual Metaphors'. Pp. 100-31 in *The Social Use of Metaphor: Essays on the Anthropology of Rhetoric*. Eds. J. David Sapir and J. Christopher Crocker. Philadelphia: University of Pennsylvania Press.
    1982   *Bwiti: An Ethnography of the Religious Imagination in Africa*. Princeton: Princeton University Press.
    1986   *Persuasions and Performances: The Play of Tropes in Culture*. Bloomington: Indiana University Press.

Field, M. J.
    1937   *Religion and Medicine of the Gā People*. London: Oxford University Press.

Firth, Raymond
    1973   *Symbols: Public and Private*. Ithaca, NY: Cornell University Press.

Flanagan, James W.
    1981   'Chiefs in Israel'. *Journal for the Study of the Old Testament* 20:47-73.
    1983   'Social Transformation and Ritual in 2 Samuel 6'. Pp. 362-72 in *The Word of the Lord Shall Go Forth*. Eds. Carol Meyers and Michael P. O'Connor. Winona Lake, IN: Eisenbrauns.
    1985   'History as Hologram: Integrating Literary, Archaeological and Comparative Sociological Evidence'. Pp. 291-314 in *Society of Biblical Literature 1985 Seminar Papers*. Ed. Kent Harold Richards. Atlanta: Scholars Press.
    1988   *David's Social Drama: A Hologram of Israel's Early Iron Age*. Social World of Biblical Antiquity Series, 7. Sheffield: Almond.

Fleming, Stuart
   1986   'Mediaeval Metallurgy: The Monastic Influence'. *Archaeology* 39:74-75.
Forbes, R. J.
   1971   *Studies in Ancient Technology 8*. Leiden: Brill.
   1972   *Studies in Ancient Technology 9*. Leiden: Brill.
Foster, Mary LeCron
   1980   'The Growth of Symbolism in Culture'. Pp. 371-97 in *Symbol as Sense: New Approaches to the Analysis of Meaning*. Eds. Mary LeCron Foster and Stanley H. Brandes. New York: Academic Press.
Foster, Mary LeCron, and Stanley H. Brandes, eds.
   1980   *Symbol as Sense: New Approaches to the Analysis of Meaning*. New York: Academic Press.
Franken, H. J.
   1960   'The Excavations at Deir 'Alla in Jordan: 3rd Season'. *Vetus Testamentum* 10:378-82.
   1969   *Excavations at Deir 'Alla*. Leiden: Brill.
Frazer, James G.
   1981   *The Golden Bough: The Roots of Religion and Folklore*. New York: Avenel Books. Originally published in 1890 by Macmillan.
Frick, Frank S.
   1971   'The Rechabites Reconsidered'. *Journal of Biblical Literature* 90:279-87.
   1979   'Religion and Sociopolitical Structure in Early Israel: An Ethnoarchaeological Approach'. Pp. 233-53 in *Society of Biblical Literature 1979 Seminar Papers*. Ed. Paul J. Achtemeier. Missoula, MT: Scholars Press.
   1985   *The Formation of the State in Ancient Israel*. The Social World of Biblical Antiquity Series, 4. Sheffield: Almond.
Gamst, Frederick C.
   1984   *The Qemant: A Pagan Hebraic Peasantry of Ethiopia*. Prospect Heights, IL: Waveland.
Garbini, Giovanni
   1978   '*Parzon* "Iron" in the Song of Deborah?' *Journal of Semitic Studies* 23:23-24.
Gardi, René
   1969   *African Crafts and Craftsmen*. Trans. Sigrid MacRae. New York: Van Nostrand Reinhold.
Gaster, Theodor H.
   1950   *Thespis: Ritual, Myth and Drama in the Ancient Near East*. New York: Henry Schuman.
Geertz, Clifford
   1973   *The Interpretation of Cultures: Selected Essays*. New York: Basic Books.
   1980   'Blurred Genres: The Refiguration of Social Thought'. *American Scholar* 49:165-79.
Gennep, Arnold van
   1960   *The Rites of Passage*. Trans. Monika B. Vizedom and Gabrielli L. Caffe. Chicago: University of Chicago Press.
Gibson, J. C. L.
   1977   *Canaanite Myths and Legends*. Edinburgh: T. & T. Clark.

Glueck, Nelson
  1935 *Exploration in Eastern Palestine, II*. Annual of the American Schools of Oriental Research, 15. New Haven: American Schools of Oriental Research.
Goody, Jack
  1962 *Death, Property, and the Ancestors: A Study of the Mortuary Customs of the LoDagaa of West Africa*. Stanford: Stanford University Press.
  1971 *Technology, Tradition, and the State in Africa*. London: Oxford University Press.
Gordon, Robert L.
  1984 'Telul edh Dhahab Survey (Jordan) 1980 and 1982'. *Mitteilungen der Deutschen Orient-Gesellschaft* 116:131-37.
Gordon, Robert L., and Linda E. Villiers
  1983 'Telul edh Dhahab and Its Environs: Surveys of 1980 and 1982'. *Annual of the Department of Antiquities of Jordan* 27:275-89.
Gottwald, Norman K.
  1979 *The Tribes of Yahweh: A Sociology of the Religion of Liberated Israel, 1250-1050 B.C.E.* Maryknoll, NY: Orbis.
Grant, E.
  1929 *Beth Shemesh*. Haverford, PA.
Gray, John
  1953 'The God Yahweh in the Religion of Canaan'. *Journal of Near Eastern Studies* 12:278-85.
Greenberg, Raphael
  1987 'New Light on the Early Iron Age at Tell Beit Mirsim'. *Bulletin of the American Schools of Oriental Research* 265:55-80.
Gressmann, Hugo
  1913 *Mose und seine Zeit*. Göttingen: Vandenhoeck & Ruprecht.
Griaule, Marcel
  1960 'The Idea of Person among the Dogon'. Pp. 365-71 in *Cultures and Societies of Africa*. Eds. Simon and Phoebe Ottenberg. New York: Random House.
  1965 *Conversations with Ogotemmêli: An Introduction to Dogon Religious Ideas*. Oxford: Oxford University Press.
Griaule, Marcel, and Germaine Dieterlen
  1954 'The Dogon'. Pp. 83-110 in *African Worlds: Studies in the Cosmological Ideas and Social Values of African Peoples*. Ed. Daryll Forde. London: Oxford University Press.
Guggenheim, H.
  1961 'Smiths of the Sudan'. *Natural History* 70:8-19.
Haaland, Randi, and Peter Shinnie, eds.
  1985 *African Ironworking: Ancient and Traditional*. London: Norwegian University Press.
Hahn, Herbert F.
  1966 *The Old Testament in Modern Research*. Philadelphia: Fortress.
Hallpike, C. R.
  1968 'The Status of Craftsmen among the Konso of South-West Ethiopia'. *Africa* 38:258-69.
Hamilton, R. W.
  1935 *Excavations at Tell Abu Huwam*. Quarterly of the Department of Antiquities in Palestine, 4. London: Oxford University Press.

Hammond, Peter B.
  1966   *Yatenga: Technology and Culture of a West African Kingdom.* New York: Collier-Macmillan.
Har-El, Menashe
  1977   'The Valley of the Craftsmen (Ge' Haḥarašim)'. *Palestine Exploration Quarterly* 109:75-86.
Harding, G. L.
  1955   'An Early Iron Age Tomb at Madeba'. *Palestine Exploration Fund Annual* 6:27-33.
Harris, Marvin
  1968   *The Rise of Anthropological Thought.* New York: Thomas Y. Crowell.
Harrod, James B.
  1981   'The Bow: A Techno-Mythic Hermeneutic—Ancient Greece and Mesopotamia'. *Journal of the American Academy of Religion* 49:425-46.
Henderson, Richard N.
  1972   *The King in Every Man: Evolutionary Trends in Onitsha Ibo Society and Culture.* New Haven: Yale University Press.
Herskovits, Melville J.
  1938   *Dahomey: An Ancient West African Kingdom.* New York: J. J. Augustin.
Herskovits, Melville J. and Frances S.
  1933   *An Outline of Dahomean Religious Belief.* Memoirs of the American Anthropological Association, 41. Menasha, WI: The American Anthropological Association.
Heskel, Dennis, and Carl Clifford Lamberg-Karlovsky
  1980   'An Alternative Sequence for the Development of Metallurgy: Tepe Yahya, Iran'. Pp. 229-65 in *The Coming of the Age of Iron.* Eds. Theodore A. Wertime and James D. Muhly. New Haven: Yale University Press.
Hodder, Ian
  1982a *Symbols in Action: Ethnoarchaeological Studies of Material Culture.* Cambridge: Cambridge University Press.
  1982b *Symbolic and Structural Archaeology.* Cambridge: Cambridge University Press.
Hollis, A. C.
  1905   The *Masai.* Oxford: Oxford University Press.
  1909   *The Nandi: Their Language and Folk-lore.* Oxford: Clarendon.
Hooke, S. H.
  1933   *Myth and Ritual: Essays on the Myth and Ritual of the Hebrews in Relation to the Culture Pattern of the Ancient East.* London: Oxford University Press.
  1935   *The Labyrinth: Further Studies in the Relation between Myth and Ritual in the Ancient World.* New York: Macmillan.
  1953   *Babylonian and Assyrian Religion.* London: Hutchinson's University Library.
  1958   *Myth, Ritual, and Kingship: Essays on the Theory and Practice of Kingship in the Ancient Near East and Israel.* Oxford: Clarendon.

Hopkins, David C.
1985 *The Highlands of Canaan: Agricultural Life in the Early Iron Age*. The Social World of Biblical Antiquity Series, 3. Sheffield: Almond.
Huntingford, G. W. B.
1931 'Free Hunters, Serf-tribes and Submerged Classes in East Africa'. *Man* 31:262-66.
1953 *The Nandi of Kenya: Tribal Control in a Pastoral Society*. London: Routledge & Kegan Paul.
1955 *The Galla of Ethiopia: The Kingdoms of Kafa and Janjero*. London: International African Institute.
Ibrahim, Moawiyah
1978 'The Collared Rim Jar of the Early Iron Age'. Pp. 116-25 in *Archaeology in the Levant: Essays for Kathleen Kenyon*. Eds. Roger Moorey and Peter Parr. Warminster: Aris & Phillips.
Idowu, E. Bolaji
1962 *Olódùmarè: God in Yoruba Belief*. London: Longmans.
Jacobsen, Thorkild
1976 *The Treasures of Darkness: A History of Mesopotamian Religion*. New Haven: Yale University Press.
Jaggar, P. J.
1973 'Kano City Blacksmiths: Precolonial Distribution, Structure and Organisation'. *Savanna* 2:11-25.
James, Frances
1966 *The Iron Age at Beth Shan*. Museum Monographs. Philadelphia: University Museum.
1978 'Chariot Fittings from Late Bronze Age Beth Shan'. Pp. 103-15 in *Archaeology in the Levant: Essays for Kathleen Kenyon*. Eds. Roger Moorey and Peter Parr. Warminster: Aris & Phillips.
Jeffreys, M. D. W.
1952 'Some Notes on the Bikom Blacksmiths'. *Man* 52: 49-51.
Karageorghis, V.
1973 'Contribution to the Religion of Cyprus in the 13th and 12th Centuries BCE'. Pp. 105-109 in *Acts of the International Archaeological Symposium: 'The Mycenaeans in the Eastern Mediterranean'*. Nicosia: Department of Antiquities.
Kelso, James L.
1968 *The Excavation of Bethel (1934-1960)*. Annual of the American Schools of Oriental Research, 39. Cambridge, MA: American Schools of Oriental Research.
Kempinski, A.
1974 'Tell el-'Ajjul—Beth Aglayim or Sharuḥen?' *Israel Exploration Journal* 24:145-52.
Kense, Francois J.
1983 *Traditional African Iron Working*. African Occasional Papers, 1. Calgary: University of Calgary.
Kenyon, Kathleen M.
1979 *Archaeology in the Holy Land*. 4th edn. London: Ernest Benn.
Kesby, John D.
1977 *The Cultural Regions of East Africa*. New York: Academic Press.

Knierim, Rolf
1985 'Criticism of Literary Features, Form, Tradition, and Redaction'. Pp. 123-65 in *The Hebrew Bible and Its Modern Interpreters*. Eds. Douglas A. Knight and Gene M. Tucker. Philadelphia and Chico, CA: Fortress and Scholars Press.

Knight, Douglas A., and Gene M. Tucker, eds.
1985 *The Hebrew Bible and Its Modern Interpreters*. Philadelphia and Chico, CA: Fortress and Scholars Press.

Kochavi, Moshe
1985 'The Israelite Settlement in Canaan in Light of Archaeological Surveys'. Pp. 54-60 in *Biblical Archaeology Today*. Proceedings of the International Congress on Biblical Archaeology, Jerusalem, April 1984. Ed. Janet Amitai. Jerusalem: Israel Exploration Society.

Košak, Silvin
1986 'The Gospel of Iron'. Pp. 125-35 in *Kaniššuwar: A Tribute to Hans G. Güterbock on His Seventy-Fifth Birthday*. Assyriological Studies, 23. Eds. Harry H. Hoffner, Jr. and Gary M. Beckman. Chicago: University of Chicago Press.

Kramer, Samuel Noah
1956 *From the Tablets of Sumer*. Indian Hills, CO: The Falcon's Wing Press.
1963 *The Sumerians: Their History, Culture, and Character*. Chicago: University of Chicago Press.

Laessøe, J.
1955 *Studies on the Assyrian Ritual and Series bît rimki*. Copenhagen.

Lancy, David F.
1980 'Becoming a Blacksmith in Gbarngasuakwelle'. *Anthropology and Education Quarterly* 11:266-74.

Lang, Bernhard, ed.
1985 *Anthropological Approaches to the Old Testament*. Issues in Religion and Theology, 8. Philadelphia: Fortress.

Lapp, Nancy L., ed.
1975 *The Tale of the Tell*. Pittsburgh: Pickwick.

Lapp, Paul W.
1964 'The 1963 Excavation at Ta'annek'. *Bulletin of the American Schools of Oriental Research* 173:4-44.
1969 'The 1968 Excavations at Tell Ta'annek'. *Bulletin of the American Schools of Oriental Research* 195:2-49.

Laughlin, Charles D., Jr., and Christopher D. Stephens
1980 'Symbolism, Canalization, and P-Structure'. Pp. 323-63 in *Symbol as Sense: New Approaches to the Analysis of Meaning*. Eds. Mary LeCron Foster and Stanley H. Brandes. New York: Academic Press.

Lawson, E. Thomas
1984 *Religions of Africa: Traditions in Transformation*. San Francisco: Harper & Row.

Leach, Edmund
1969 *Genesis as Myth and Other Essays*. London: Jonathan Cape.
1976 *Culture and Communication: The Logic by which Symbols are Connected*. Cambridge: Cambridge University Press.

1982 'Anthropological Approaches to the Study of the Bible during the Twentieth Century'. Pp. 73-94 in *Humanizing America's Iconic Book*. Eds. Gene M. Tucker and Douglas A. Knight. Chico, CA: Scholars Press.
1983 'Against Genres: Are Parables Lights Set in Candlesticks or Put under a Bushel?' Pp. 89-112 in *Structuralist Interpretations of Biblical Myth*. Eds. Edmund Leach and D. Alan Aycock. Cambridge: Cambridge University Press.
1987 'Fishing for Men on the Edge of the Wilderness'. Pp. 579-99 in *The Literary Guide to the Bible*. Eds. Robert Alter and Frank Kermode. Cambridge, MA: Belknap of Harvard University.

Leslau, Wolf
1979 *Falasha Anthology*. New Haven: Yale University Press.

Levenson, Jon D.
1985 *Sinai and Zion: An Entry into the Jewish Bible*. Minneapolis: Winston.

Lévi-Strauss, Claude
1963 *Structural Anthropology*. Trans. Claire Jacobson and Brooke Grundfest Schoepf. New York: Basic Books.

Lewis, Herbert S.
1965 *A Galla Monarchy: Jimma Aba Jifar, Ethiopia 1830-1932*. Madison: The University of Wisconsin Press.
1970 'Wealth, Influence, and Prestige among the Shoa Galla'. Pp. 163-86 in *Social Stratification in Africa*. Eds. Arthur Tuden and Leonard Plotnicov. New York: Free Press.

Lewis, I. M.
1955 *Peoples of the Horn of Africa: Somali, Afar, and Saho*. London: International African Institute.
1961 *A Pastoral Democracy: A Study of Pastoralism and Politics among the Northern Somali of the Horn of Africa*. London: Oxford University Press.

Liebowitz, Harold
1981 'Excavations at Tell Yinam: The 1976 and 1977 Seasons'. *Bulletin of the American Schools of Oriental Research* 243:79-94.
1983 'Reply to Beno Rothenberg'. *Bulletin of the American Schools of Oriental Research* 252:71-72.

Lloyd, Peter C.
1953 'Craft Organization in Yoruba Towns'. *Africa* 23:30-44.
1965 'The Yoruba of Nigeria'. Pp. 547-82 in *Peoples of Africa*. Ed. James L. Gibbs, Jr. New York: Holt, Rinehart and Winston.

Loud, Gordon, ed.
1948 *Megiddo II: Seasons of 1935-1939*. Chicago: University of Chicago Press.

Lucas, J. Olumide
1948 *The Religion of the Yorubas*. Lagos, Nigeria: C. M. S. Bookshop.

MacAlister, R. A. Stewart
1912 *The Excavation of Gezer, I*. London: John Murray.

MacKenzie, Duncan
1912-13 *Excavations at Ain Shems*. Jerusalem: Palestine Exploration Fund.

Maddin, Robert, and Tamara Stech-Wheeler
  1976 'Metallurgical Study of Seven Bar Ingots'. *Israel Exploration Journal* 26:170-73.
Maddin, Robert, James D. Muhly, and Tamara S. Wheeler
  1977 'How the Iron Age Began'. *Scientific American* 237:122-31.
Maisler [Mazar], B.
  1951 'The Stratification of Tell Abu Huwam on the Bay of Acre'. *Bulletin of the American Schools of Oriental Research* 124:21-25.
Maret, Pierre de
  1985 'The Smith's Myth and the Origin of Leadership in Central Africa'. Pp. 73-87 in *African Iron Working: Ancient and Traditional*. Eds. Randi Haaland and Peter Shinnie. London: Norwegian University Press.
Margarido, Alfredo, and Françoise Germaix Wasserman
  1972 'On the Myth and Practice of the Blacksmith in Africa'. *Diogenes* 78:87-122.
Margetts, Edward L.
  1965 'Traditional Yoruba Healers in Nigeria'. *Man* 65:115-18.
Marx, Leo
  1964 *The Machine in the Garden: Technology and the Pastoral Ideal in America*. New York: Oxford University Press.
  1965 'The Impact of the Railroad on the American Imagination as a Possible Comparison for the Space Impact'. Pp. 202-16 in *The Railroad and the Space Program*. Ed. Bruce Maclish. Cambridge, MA: MIT.
Maxwell-Hyslop, K. R., Tamara Stech-Wheeler, Robert Maddin, and James D. Muhly
  1978 'An Iron Dagger from Tomb 240 at Tell Fara South'. *Levant* 10:112-15.
Maxwell-Hyslop, Rachel
  1972 'The Metals amūtu and aši'u in the Kültepe Texts'. *Anatolian Studies* 22:159-62.
Mayr, Otto
  1986 *Authority, Liberty, and Automatic Machinery in Early Modern Europe*. Baltimore: Johns Hopkins Press.
Mazar, Amihai
  1975 'Excavations at Tell Qasile, 1973-74'. *Israel Exploration Journal* 25:77-88.
  1980 *Excavations at Tell Qasile. Part I. The Philistine Sanctuary: Architecture and Cult Objects*. Qedem, 12. Jerusalem: Hebrew University.
  1985a 'The Emergence of the Philistine Material Culture'. *Israel Exploration Journal* 35:95-107.
  1985b *Excavations at Tell Qasile Part II*. Qedem, 20. Jerusalem: Hebrew University.
  1985c 'The Israelite Settlement in Canaan in Light of Archaeological Excavations'. Pp. 61-71 in *Biblical Archaeology Today*. Proceedings of the International Congress on Biblical Archaeology, Jerusalem, April 1984. Ed. Janet Amitai. Jerusalem: Israel Exploration Society.

Mazar, B.
1965 'The Sanctuary of Arad and the Family of Hobab the Kenite'. *Journal of Near Eastern Studies* 24:297-303.

McCarter, P. Kyle, Jr.
1980 *I Samuel*. Garden City: Doubleday.
1984 *II Samuel*. Garden City: Doubleday.

McClellan, Thomas L.
1979 'Chronology of the "Philistine" Burials at Tell el-Farah (South)'. *Journal of Field Archaeology* 6:57-73.

McCown, Chester Charlton
1947 *Tell en-Nasbeh I*. Berkeley and New Haven: The Palestine Institute of Pacific School of Religion and the American Schools of Oriental Research.

McGovern, Patrick E.
1981 'Baq'ah Valley Project 1980'. *Biblical Archaeologist* 44:126-28.
1982a 'Baq'ah Valley Project 1981'. *Biblical Archaeologist* 45:122-24.
1982b 'Exploring the Burial Caves of the Baq'ah Valley in Jordan'. *Biblical Archaeology Review* September/October:46-53.

McNaughton, Patrick Ronle
1977 'The Bamana Blacksmiths: A Study of Sculptors and Their Art'. Ph.D. dissertation, Yale University.

McNutt, Paula M.
1983 'An Inquiry into the Significance of Iron Technology in Early Iron Age Palestine'. Master's thesis, University of Montana.

Meek, C. K.
1970 *Law and Authority in a Nigerian Tribe: A Study in Indirect Rule*. New York: Barnes & Noble.

Meek, T. J.
1920-21 'Some Religious Origins of the Hebrews'. *The American Journal of Semitic Languages and Literatures* 37:101-31.

Mendenhall, George E.
1973 *The Tenth Generation: The Origins of the Biblical Tradition*. Baltimore: Johns Hopkins University Press.

Mercier, P.
1954 'The Fon of Dahomey'. Pp. 210-34 in *African Worlds: Studies in the Cosmological Ideas and Social Values of African Peoples*. Ed. Daryll Forde. London: Oxford University Press.

Merwe, Nikolaas J. van der
1980 'The Advent of Iron in Africa'. Pp. 463-506 in *The Coming of the Age of Iron*. Eds. Theodore A. Wertime and James D. Muhly. New Haven: Yale University Press.

Merwe, Nikolaas van der, and Donald H. Avery
1987 'Science and Magic in African Technology: Traditional Iron Smelting in Malawi'. *Africa* 57:143-72.

Miller, J. Maxwell
1977 'Archaeology and the Israelite Conquest of Canaan: Some Methodological Observations'. *Palestine Exploration Quarterly* 109:87-93.

Morgenstern, Julian
1920-21 'The Elohist Narrative in Exodus 3:1-15'. *The American Journal of Semitic Languages and Literatures* 37:242-62.

Morton-Williams, Peter
1964 'An Outline of the Cosmology and Cult Organization of the Oyo Yoruba'. *Africa* 34:243-61.
Muhly, James D.
1973 *Copper and Tin*. Transactions of the Connecticut Academy of Arts and Sciences, 43. Hamden: Archon.
1976 *Supplement to Copper and Tin*. Transactions of the Connecticut Academy of Arts and Sciences, 46. Hamden: Archon.
1980 'The Bronze Age Setting'. Pp. 25-69 in *The Coming of the Age of Iron*. Eds. Theodore A. Wertime and James D. Muhly. New Haven: Yale University Press.
1982 'How Iron Technology Changed the Ancient World'. *Biblical Archaeology Review* November/December: 42-54.
Muhly, J. D., R. Maddin, T. Stech, and E. Özgen
1985 'Iron in Anatolia and the Nature of the Hittite Iron Industry'. *Anatolian Studies* 35:67-84.
Mumford, Lewis
1967 *The Myth of the Machine: Technics and Human Development*. New York: Harcourt, Brace, & World.
Nadel, S. F.
1942 *A Black Byzantium: The Kingdom of Nupe in Nigeria*. London: Oxford University Press.
Nasr, Sayyed Hossein
1981 *Knowledge and the Sacred*. New York: Crossroad.
Neaher, Nancy C.
1979 'Awka Who Travel: Itinerant Metalsmiths of Southern Nigeria'. *Africa* 49:352-66.
Needham, Joseph
1980 'The Evolution of Iron and Steel Technology in East and Southeast Asia'. Pp. 507-41 in *The Coming of the Age of Iron*. Eds. Theodore A. Wertime and James D. Muhly. New Haven: Yale University Press.
Newall, Venetia
1970 'Smith'. Pp. 2616-20 in *Man, Myth, and Magic*, 19. New York: Marshall Cavendish.
Niditch, Susan
1985 *Chaos to Cosmos: Studies in Biblical Patterns of Creation*. Scholars Press Studies in the Humanities, 6. Chico, CA: Scholars Press.
Noth, Martin
1981 *A History of Pentateuchal Traditions*. Chico, CA: Scholars Press. German original, 1948.
Ohata, Kiyoshi, ed.
1967 *Tell Zeror II*. Tokyo: The Society for Near Eastern Studies in Japan.
Ohata, Kiyoshi
1970 *Tell Zeror III*. Tokyo: The Society for Near Eastern Studies in Japan.
Oren, E. D.
1978 'Esh-Shari'a Tell (Tel Sera')'. Pp. 1059-68 in *Encyclopedia of Archaeological Excavations in the Holy Land, IV*. Eds. Michael Avi-Yonah and Ephraim Stern. Englewood Cliffs, NJ: Prentice Hall.

Ortner, Sherry B.
  1973   'On Key Symbols'. *American Anthropologist* 75:1338-46.
Parke-Taylor, G. H.
  1975   *Yahweh: The Divine Name in the Bible*. Waterloo, Ontario: Wilfred Laurier University.
Parr, Peter
  1978   'Pottery, People, and Politics'. Pp. 202-209 in *Archaeology in the Levant: Essays for Kathleen Kenyon*. Eds. Roger Moorey and Peter Parr. Warminster: Aris & Phillips.
Parrinder, Geoffrey
  1961   *West African Religion: A Study of the Beliefs and Practices of Akan, Ewe, Yoruba, Ibo, and Kindred Peoples*. London: The Epworth Press.
  1969   *Religion in Africa*. London: Pall Mall.
Paulme, Denise
  1973   'Blood Pacts, Age Classes and Castes in Black Africa'. Pp. 73-95 in *French Perspectives in African Studies*. Ed. Pierre Alexandre. London: Oxford University Press.
Pedersen, Johannes
  1926-40 *Israel: Its Life and Culture*. 4 vols. London: Oxford University Press.
Pelton, Robert D.
  1980   *The Trickster in West Africa: A Study of Mythic Irony and Sacred Delight*. Berkeley: University of California Press.
Petrie, W. M. F.
  1928   *Gerar*. London.
  1930   *Beth-Pelet I*. British School of Archaeology in Egypt, 48. London.
  1937   *Anthedon Sinai*. London.
Pigott, V. C., McGovern, P. E., and Notis, M. R.
  1982   'The Earliest Steel from Transjordan'. *Museum of Applied Science Center for Archaeology Journal* 2:35-39.
Pleiner, Radomír
  1980   'Early Iron Metallurgy in Europe'. Pp. 375-415 in *The Coming of the Age of Iron*. Eds. Theodore A. Wertime and James D. Muhly. New Haven: Yale University Press.
Pleiner, Radomír, and Judith K. Bjorkman
  1974   'The Assyrian Iron Age: The History of Iron in the Assyrian Civilization'. *Proceedings of the American Philosophical Society* 118:283-313.
Porteous, Norman W.
  1965   *Daniel*. Philadelphia: Westminster.
Prausnitz, M.
  1975   'Achzib (Ez-Zib)'. Pp. 26-30 in *Encyclopedia of Archaeological Excavations in the Holy Land, I*. Ed. Michael Avi-Yonah. Englewood Cliffs, NJ: Prentice Hall.
Pritchard, James B.
  1980   *The Cemetery at Tell es-Saʻidiyeh, Jordan*. University Museum Monograph, 41. Philadelphia: University of Pennsylvania Press.
  1985   *Tell es-Saʻidiyeh*. Philadelphia: University of Pennsylvania Press.
Pritchard, James B., ed.
  1955   *Ancient Near Eastern Texts Relating to the Old Testament*. 2nd edn. Princeton: Princeton University Press.

Quirin, James Arthur
  1977 'The Beta Israel (Felasha) in Ethiopian History: Caste Formation and Culture Change'. Ph.D. dissertation, University of Minnesota.
Ramsey, George W.
  1981 *The Quest for the Historical Israel*. Atlanta: John Knox.
Rappaport, Roy A.
  1979 *Ecology, Meaning, and Religion*. Richmond, CA: North Atlantic Books.
Rast, Walter E.
  1978 *Taanach I: Studies in the Iron Age Pottery*. Cambridge, MA: American Schools of Oriental Research.
Reminick, Ronald A.
  1974 'The Evil Eye Belief among the Amhara of Ethiopia'. *Ethnology* 13:279-91.
Rendsburg, Gary A.
  1982 'Semitic *PRZL/BRZL/BRḎL*, "Iron"'. *Scripta Mediterranea* 3:54-71.
Renfrew, Collin
  1984 'The Anatomy of Innovation'. Pp. 390-418 in *Approaches to Social Archaeology*. Edinburgh: Edinburgh University Press.
Richardson, H. C.
  1943 'A Mitannian Battle Axe from Ras Shamra'. *Berytus* 8:72.
Richter, Dolores
  1980 'Further Considerations of Caste in West Africa'. *Africa* 50:37-54.
Rickard, T. A.
  1941 'The Use of Meteoric Iron'. *Journal, Royal Anthropological Institute of Great Britain and Ireland* 71:55-65.
Robins, Frederick William
  1953 *The Smith; The Traditions and Lore of an Ancient Craft*. New York: Rider.
Rothenberg, Beno
  1972 *Timna; Valley of the Biblical Copper Mines*. London: Thames and Hudson.
  1975 'Metals and Metallurgy'. Pp. 72-83 in *Investigations at Lachish: The Sanctuary and the Residency (Lachish V)*. By Yohanan Aharoni. Tel Aviv: Tel Aviv University Institute of Archaeology (Gateway).
  1983 'Corrections on Timna and Tel Yinam in the *Bulletin*'. *Bulletin of the American Schools of Oriental Research* 252:69-70.
Rothenberg, Beno, and Jonathan Glass
  1983 'The Midianite Pottery'. Pp. 65-124 in *Midian, Moab and Edom: The History and Archaeology of Late Bronze and Iron Age Jordan and North-West Arabia*. Journal for the Study of the Old Testament Supplement Series, 24. Eds. John F. A. Sawyer and David J. A. Clines. Sheffield: JSOT.
Rowlands, M. J.
  1971 'The Archaeological Interpretation of Prehistoric Metalworking'. *World Archaeology* 3:210-24.
Rowley, H. H.
  1946 *The Re-discovery of the Old Testament*. Philadelphia: Westminster.

1950   *From Joseph to Joshua: Biblical Traditions in the Light of Archaeology*. The Schweich Lectures of the British Academy 1948. London: Oxford University Press.

Sanders, Nancy K.
1978   *The Sea Peoples*. London: Thames and Hudson.

Sapir, J. David
1977   'The Anatomy of Metaphor'. Pp. 3-32 in *The Social Use of Metaphor: Essays on the Anthropology of Rhetoric*. Eds. J. David Sapir and J. Christopher Crocker. Philadelphia: University of Pennsylvania Press.

Sapir, J. David, and J. Christopher Crocker, eds.
1977   *The Social Use of Metaphor: Essays on the Anthropology of Rhetoric*. Philadelphia: University of Pennsylvania Press.

Sasoon, Hamo
1964   'Iron Smelting in the Hill Village of Sukur, North-Eastern Nigeria'. *Man* 64:174-78.

Sauer, James A.
1985   'Ammon, Moab and Edom'. Pp. 206-14 in *Biblical Archaeology Today*. Proceedings of the International Congress on Biblical Archaeology, Jerusalem, April 1984. Ed. Janet Amitai. Jerusalem: Israel Exploration Society.

Sawyer, John F. A.
1983   'The Meaning of *Barzel* in the Biblical Expressions "Chariots of Iron", "Yoke of Iron", etc.' Pp. 129-34 in *Midian, Moab and Edom: The History and Archaeology of Late Bronze and Iron Age Jordan and North-West Arabia*. Journal for the Study of the Old Testament Supplement Series, 24. Eds. J. F. A. Sawyer and D. J. A. Clines. Sheffield: JSOT.

Schapera, Isaac
1985   'The Sin of Cain'. Pp. 26-42 in *Anthropological Approaches to the Old Testament*. Issues in Religion and Theology, 8. Ed. Bernhard Lang. Philadelphia: Fortress.

Seligman, C. G. and B. Z.
1928   'The Bari'. *Journal of the Royal Anthropological Institute of Great Britain and Ireland* 58:409-79.

Sellers, O. R., R. W. Funk, J. L. McKenzie, and N. and P. Lapp
1968   *The 1957 Excavation at Beth-Zur*. Annual of the American Schools of Oriental Research, 38. Cambridge, MA: American Schools of Oriental Research.

Shack, William A.
1964   'Notes on Occupational Castes among the Gurage of Southwest Ethiopia'. *Man* 54:50-52.

1966   *The Gurage: A People of the Ensete Culture*. London: Oxford University Press.

1974   'Falasha'. In *Amhara, Tigrena, and Related Peoples*. London: International African Institute.

Shiloh, Yigal
1970   'The Four-Room House: Its Situation and Function in the Israelite City'. *Israel Exploration Journal* 20:180-90.

Shorter, Aylward
1974   *East African Societies*. London: Routledge & Kegan Paul.

Sinclair, Lawrence A.
- 1960 'An Archaeological Study of Gibeah (Tell el-Fûl)'. Pp. 1-52 in *Annual of the American Schools of Oriental Research, 34-35*. New Haven: American Schools of Oriental Research.
- 1964 'An Archaeological Study of Gibeah'. *Biblical Archeologist* 27:52-64.

Singer, K. H.
- 1980 *Die Metalle Gold, Silber, Bronze, Kupfer und Eisen im Alten Testament und ihre Symbolik*. Forschung zur Bibel, 43. Würzburg: Echter Verlag.

Smith, Cyril S.
- 1968 'Matter versus Materials: A Historical View'. *Science* 162:637-44.
- 1970 'Art, Technology, and Science: Notes on Their Historical Interaction'. *Technology and Culture* 11:493-549.
- 1977 *Metallurgy as a Human Experience: An Essay on Man's Relationship to His Materials in Science and Practice Throughout History*. New York: American Society for Metals and the Metallurgical Society of AIME.

Smith, William Robertson
- 1894 *Lectures on the Religion of the Semites*. London: A. and C. Black.

Snaith, N. H.
- 1969 *Leviticus and Numbers*. Greenwood, SC: Attic.

Snodgrass, Anthony
- 1980 'Iron and Early Metallurgy in the Mediterranean'. Pp. 335-74 in *The Coming of the Age of Iron*. Eds. Theodore A. Wertime and James D. Muhly. New Haven: Yale University Press.

Southall, Aidan
- 1972 'Twinship and Symbolic Structure'. Pp. 73-114 in *The Interpretation of Ritual*. Ed. Jean S. LaFontaine. London: Tavistock.

Sperber, Dan
- 1974 *Rethinking Symbolism*. Cambridge: Cambridge University Press.

Spores, Ronald M.
- 1973 'Research in Mexican Ethnohistory'. Pp. 25-48 in *Research in Mexican History*. Eds. Richard E. Greenleaf and Michael C. Meyer. Lincoln: University of Nebraska Press.
- 1980 'New World Ethnohistory and Archaeology, 1970-1980'. *Annual Review of Anthropology* 9:575-603.

Stager, Lawrence E.
- 1985 'Respondent'. Pp. 83-87 in *Biblical Archaeology Today*. Proceedings of the International Congress on Biblical Archaeology, Jerusalem, April 1984. Ed. Janet Amitai. Jerusalem: Israel Exploration Society.

Starkey, J. L., and G. L. Harding
- 1932 *Beth Pelet II*. London: British School of Archaeology in Egypt.

Stech-Wheeler, T., J. D. Muhly, K. R. Maxwell-Hyslop, and R. Maddin
- 1981 'Iron at Taanach and Early Iron Metallurgy in the Eastern Mediterranean'. *American Journal of Archaeology* 85:245-68.

Stewart, David
- 1981 'Religion, Technology, and Change'. *Listening*: 110-21.

Temple, Robert
1986 *The Genius of China: 3,000 Years of Science, Discovery, and Invention.* New York: Simon and Schuster.
Tessman, Günter
1959 *The Fang Peoples, an Ethnographic Monograph on a West African Negro Group.* Vol. I, Second Part. Trans. Richard Neuse. Human Relations Area Files.
Thompson, R. Campbell
1908 *Semitic Magic: Its Origin and Development.* London: Luzac.
Todd, D. M.
1977 'Caste in Africa?' *Africa* 47:398-412.
Trigger, Bruce
1969 'The Myth of Meroe and the African Iron Age'. *African Historical Studies* 2:23-50.
1978 *Time and Traditions: Essays in Archaeological Interpretation.* New York: Columbia University Press.
Tuden, Arthur, and Leonard Plotnicov, eds.
1970 *Social Stratification in Africa.* New York: Free Press.
Tufnell, Olga
1953 *Lachish III, The Iron Age.* London: Oxford University Press.
Turner, Victor
1967 *The Forest of Symbols.* Ithaca, NY: Cornell University Press.
1969 *The Ritual Process: Structure and Anti-Structure.* Ithaca, NY: Cornell University Press.
1973 'Symbols in African Ritual'. *Science* 179:1100-1105.
1974 *Dramas, Fields, and Metaphors: Symbolic Action in Human Society.* Ithaca, NY: Cornell University Press.
1977 'Process, System, and Symbol: A New Anthropological Synthesis'. *Daedalus* 1:61-80.
1979 'Betwixt and Between: The Liminal Period in *Rites de Passage*'. Pp. 234-43 in *Reader in Comparative Religion.* 4th edn. Eds. William A. Lessa and Evon Z. Vogt. New York: Harper & Row.
1981 'Social Dramas and Stories about Them'. Pp. 137-64 in *On Narrative.* Ed. W. J. T. Mitchell. Chicago: University of Chicago Press.
Tylecote, Ronald F.
1965 'Iron Smelting in Pre-industrial Communities'. *Journal of the Iron and Steel Institute* 203:340-48.
1980 'Furnaces, Crucibles, and Slags'. Pp. 183-228 in *The Coming of the Age of Iron.* Eds. Theodore A. Wertime and James D. Muhly. New Haven: Yale University Press.
Ussishkin, David
1978 *Excavations at Tel Lachish 1973-1977. Preliminary Report.* Tel Aviv: Institute of Archaeology, Tel Aviv University.
1987 'Lachish: Key to the Israelite Conquest of Canaan?' *Biblical Archaeology Review* 13:18-39.
Vansina, Jan
1985 *Oral Traditions as History.* Madison: University of Wisconsin Press.

Vaughan, James A., Jr.
 1970 'Caste Systems in the Western Sudan'. Pp. 59-92 in *Social Stratification in Africa*. Eds. Arthur Tuden and Leonard Plotnicov. New York: Free Press.
 1973 'Enkyagu as Artists in Marghi Society'. Pp. 162-93 in *The Traditional Artist in African Societies*. Ed. Warren L. d'Azevedo. Bloomington: Indiana University Press.

Vaux, Roland de
 1961 *Ancient Israel: Its Life and Institutions*. New York: McGraw-Hill.
 1976 'El-Far'ah, Tell'. Pp. 395-404 in *Encyclopedia of Archaeological Excavations in the Holy Land, II*. Ed. Michael Avi-Yonah. Englewood Cliffs, NJ: Prentice Hall.

Verdon, Michel
 1983 *The Abutia of West Africa: A Chiefdom that Never Was*. New York: Mouton.

Wainwright, G. A.
 1936 'The Coming of Iron'. *Antiquity* 10:5-24.

Waldbaum, Jane C.
 1966 'Philistine Tombs at Tell Fara and Their Aegean Prototypes'. *American Journal of Archaeology* 70:331-40.
 1978 *From Bronze to Iron: The Transition from the Bronze Age to the Iron Age in the Eastern Mediterranean*. Göteborg: Paul Åströms Förlag.
 1980 'The First Archaeological Appearance of Iron and the Transition to the Iron Age'. Pp. 69-98 in *The Coming of the Age of Iron*. Eds. Theodore A. Wertime and James D. Muhly. New Haven: Yale University Press.

Weber, Max
 1952 *Ancient Judaism*. Trans. Hans H. Gerth and Don Martindale. New York: The Free Press.

Weippert, Manfred
 1971 *The Settlement of the Israelite Tribes in Palestine: A Critical Survey of Recent Scholarly Debate*. Studies in Biblical Theology, 21. Napierville, IL: Alec R. Allenson.

Wertime, Theodore A.
 1964 'Man's First Encounters with Metallurgy'. *Science* 146:1257-67.
 1973 'The Beginnings of Metallurgy: A New Look'. *Science* 182:875-87.
 1980 'The Pyrotechnologic Background'. Pp. 1-24 in *The Coming of the Age of Iron*. Eds. Theodore A. Wertime and James D. Muhly. New Haven: Yale University Press.

Wertime, Theodore A., and James D. Muhly, eds.
 1980 *The Coming of the Age of Iron*. New Haven: Yale University Press.

Wheeler, Tamara S., and Robert Maddin
 1980 'Metallurgy and Ancient Man'. Pp. 99-126 in *The Coming of the Age of Iron*. Eds. Theodore A. Wertime and James D. Muhly. New Haven: Yale University Press.

Wilson, Robert R.
 1984 *Sociological Approaches to the Old Testament*. Philadelphia: Fortress.

Wise, R.
 1958 'Some Rituals of Iron-Making in Ufipa'. *Tanganyika Notes and Records* 51:232-38.

Wright, G. Ernest
- 1938 'Iron in Israel'. *Biblical Archeologist* 1:5-12.
- 1939 'Iron: The Date of Its Introduction into Common Use in Palestine'. *American Journal of Archaeology* 43:458-63.
- 1943 'I Sam. 13:19-20'. *Biblical Archeologist* 6:34.
- 1978 'A Characteristic North Israelite House'. Pp. 149-54 in *Archaeology in the Levant: Essays for Kathleen Kenyon*. Eds. Roger Moorey and Peter Parr. Warminster: Aris & Phillips.

Yadin, Yigal
- 1963 *The Art of Warfare in Biblical Lands in the Light of Archaeological Study*. 2 vols. New York: McGraw-Hill.
- 1972 *Hazor*. The Schweich Lectures, 1970. London: Oxford University Press.
- 1977 'Megiddo'. Pp. 830-56 in *Encyclopedia of Archaeological Excavations in the Holy Land, III*. Eds. Michael Avi-Yonah and Ephraim Stern. Englewood Cliffs, NJ: Prentice Hall.

Zahan, Dominique
- 1979 *The Religion, Spirituality, and Thought of Traditional Africa*. Trans. Kate Ezra Martin and Lawrence M. Martin. Chicago: University of Chicago Press.

Zuesse, Evan M.
- 1979 *Ritual Cosmos: The Sanctification of Life in African Religions*. Athens, OH: Ohio University Press.

INDEXES

INDEX OF BIBLICAL REFERENCES

Genesis
1.26   213
4.1-16   213
4.12-13   240
4.15   214, 240
4.16   240
4.17-22   213, 240
4.17   240
4.20   240
4.22   236, 240
6-9   214
9.20-27   214
11.1-9   214
15.9   243
25.3   236
37   257
37.25-28 258
37.28   257
37.36   257
39-50   257
39.1   258

Exodus
2.15–
 3.15   244
2.18   244, 258
2.21   258
3   258
3.1   244
4.24-26   245
12.40   254
15   254
18.1-27   244, 245
18.10-12 259
18.13-27 259
20.25   219

31.1-11   249
31.1-5   231, 237

Leviticus
26.19   225

Numbers
10.29-32 259
10.29   244, 258
20.12   258
21.30   174
24.21-22 243
25   246
26.33   182
31   246
31.22   216
31.23   239
36.10-11 182

Deuteronomy
3.2   223
3.11   223
4.20   237, 249, 253
8.9   115, 116, 216
27.1-8   217
27.5   217, 265
27.15   235, 238
28.23   225
28.48   226
32.48-52 258
33.13-17 220
33.24-25 220
34   258

Joshua
6.19   216
6.24   216
8.1-29   163
8.30-35   217
8.31   217, 265
10.15   173
10.26   173
10.33   169
11.10-13 172
11.22   164
12.12   169
12.21   175
13.3   164
15.31   185
15.39   173
15.58   169
16.3   169
16.10   169
17.3   182
17.11-13 175
17.11   166
17.16   214, 224, 265
17.18   214, 224, 265
19.6   183
19.29   163
19.41   168
21.16   168
21.21   169
22.8   216
32-33   173

Judges
1.16   244

1.19	214, 224, 265	8.3-4	214	22.8	219
		10	174	22.14	218
1.27-28	175	12.31	225, 226	22.15-16	218
1.27	166, 177, 193	17.27-29	247, 259	24.3	247
		19.31-39	247, 259	28.3	219
1.29	169	23.7	222	29	218
1.31	163	23.29	171	29.2	218
4	244			29.5	235
4.3	214, 224, 265	*1 Kings*			
		1.50-53	219	*2 Chronicles*	
4.11	244, 258	2.28-31	219	2.7	218
4.13	214, 224, 265	4.9	168	2.13-14	231, 238
		4.12	175	2.13	218
4.17-22	242	5–7	248	2.14	218
5.7	215	6.7	217, 265	11.17	169
5.11	215	7.13-14	231, 238	13.2	171
5.19	175, 177	7.45-46	106	18.10	221
5.24-27	242	8.51	237, 249, 253	24.12	218, 235
7–9	246				
14	171	9.15-17	169	*Ezra*	
19–20	171	9.15	172, 175	2.61-63	247
20.1ff.	184	9.16	170		
		15.17-22	184	*Nehemiah*	
1 Samuel		19.12	254	7.63-65	247
5	164	22.11	221, 265	11.35	235
6.9ff.	168				
7.16-17	184	*2 Kings*		*Job*	
8.4-22	214	6.1-7	217	19.23-24	220
10.26	171	10.15-28	214, 243	19.25-29	220
11.4	171	24.14	235, 236	20.24	222
13.19-23	144, 158, 205	24.16	235, 236	40.15-18	223
				41.27	223
13.19-22	238	*1 Chronicles*			
13.19	19, 235, 238	2–4	248	*Psalms*	
		2.45	169	2.7-9	221
15.6	242, 244	2.55	243	2.9	221
15.34ff.	171	4.14	235	8.4-8	213
17.4	223	4.30	185	12.7[6]	239, 253
17.5-6	223	6.67	169	83.9	246
17.7	223	7.28	169	105.18	225
27.6-7	185	7.29	175	107.10	225
27.6	185	11.31	171	107.16	225
30	185	12.3	171	149.5-8	226
30.29	242	14.16	169, 170		
31.12	166	19	174	*Proverbs*	
		20.3	225	17.3	239
2 Samuel		20.4	169, 170		
5.25	169, 170	22.3	218		

Index of Biblical References

Isaiah	
1.25	239, 253
10.26	246
10.34	222, 265
31.9	239, 253
40.19	235, 238
41.7	235, 236, 238
44.12	235, 238
44.13	235
45.2	226
48.10	239, 249, 253, 265
54.16	235, 238
60.15-18	217

Jeremiah	
1	221
1.18-19	222
10.9	235, 238
11.4	237, 249, 253
15.12	223
17.1	220
24.1	235, 236
28.13-14	226
29.2	235, 236
35	214, 243
35.6-10	243

Ezekiel	
22.17-22	239, 253, 265
27	217
27.12	106, 217
27.19	217

Daniel	
2.31-45	15, 226
2.36-38	227
2.39	227
2.40-41	227
2.42	227
2.44	227
7-8	220
7.7	226
7.19	226

Hosea	
8.6	235, 238
13.2	235, 238

Amos	
1.3	223

Micah	
4.13	221

Zechariah	
2.1-4 [1.18-21]	220
13.9	239, 253

Malachi	
3.1-4	239, 253

Sirach	
38	231, 237
38.24-34	236
38.28	236, 237

INDEX OF AUTHORS

Ackroyd, P. R. 215
Adéníji, D. A. A. 87
Aharoni, Y. 173, 176, 243
Albright, W. F. 27, 143, 162, 176, 181, 182, 231, 233, 242, 244
Alt, A. 27, 144
Amitai, J. 192
Anderson, B.W. 254
Avi-Yonah, M. 160
Avi-Yonah, M. & E. Stern 160
Awolalu, J. O. 60, 61, 62
Aycock, D. A. 240

Barnes, S. T. 60
Baumgartner, W. 216
Beidelman, T. O. 24
Ben-Tor, A. 189
Bernard, H. R. & P. J. Petro 13
Binns, L. E. 242
Bjorkman, J. K. 129-32, 134-37, 228
Bohannan, P. 65
Bolter, J. D. 14, 16, 18
Booth, N. S. Jr. 59, 60
Bowman, J. 217
Brown, J. 87
Buber, M. 242
Budde, K. 242
Burckhardt, T. 44, 87

Callaway, J. A. 163
Carmack, R. M. 22
Causse, A. 27
Charles, J. A. 111, 112
Childs, B.S. 245, 246
Cline, W. 47, 54, 64, 65, 72-74, 87
Coats, G. W. 258
Coghlan, H. H. 109, 110, 113, 114-16, 118, 121-24, 127, 139, 140, 148, 152
Cole, H. M. 66
Coy, M. W. Jr. 40, 74-76, 84
Culley, R. C. 23

Curtis, J. E. et al. 147

Davies, G. I. 176
Davies, N. 262
Davis, D. et al. 123, 150
Dayton, J. E. 106
Dever, W. G. 146, 262
Dever, W. G. et al. 170
Dieterlen, G. 49, 50, 52-54, 57, 58
Dornemann, R. H. 160, 191, 208
Dothan, M. 164
Dothan, T. 19, 153, 160, 161, 164, 165, 167-70, 175, 176, 180-90, 196
Dothan, T. & S. Gitin 160, 189, 209
Douglas, M. T. 25, 91-93, 248, 250
Drennan, R. D. 206, 207
Drews, R. 224
Dubos, R. 13
Durkheim, E. 25, 92

East, R. 65
Edelstein, G. 181
Eliade, M. 16, 17, 44-46, 62, 87, 93, 255
Ellul, J. 13
Engberg, R. M. 176
Eusebius 234
Evans-Pritchard, E. E. 22

Fagg, W. 87
Fensham, F. C. 134, 242
Fernandez, J. W. 16, 65-69, 84-87, 94, 250
Field, M. J. 60
Firth, R. 86, 94
Flanagan, J. W. 19, 23, 31-34, 36, 39, 101, 162, 192, 210, 213, 251, 261
Fleming, S. 44
Forbes, R. J. 44-47, 97, 100, 104, 108, 109, 114, 115, 118, 121, 122,

124, 126-28, 132-36, 138, 139, 148, 152
Foster, M. LeC. 84
Franken, H. J. 208
Frankfort 120
Frazer, J. G. 25, 91
Freud, S. 25
Frick, F. S. 19, 23, 31, 210, 243

Gamst, F. C. 80
Garbini, G. 215
Gardi, R. 87
Gaster, T. H. 233, 234
Geertz, C. 16, 23, 35
Gennep, A. van 83
Gibson, J. C. L. 233, 234
Glueck, N. 115
Goetze, A. 140
Goody, J. 63, 64
Gordon, R. L. 207
Gordon, R. L. & L. E. Villiers 207
Gottwald, N. K. 19, 23, 30, 144, 210
Grant, E. A. 168
Gray, J. 242
Greenberg, R. 181, 182
Gressmann, H. 242
Griaule, M. 49-51, 53, 56
Griaule, M. & G. Dieterlen 49, 51
Guggenheim, H. 43
Gunkel, H. 27

Hahn, H. F. 24, 27
Hallpike, C. R. 78
Hamilton, R. W. 180
Hammond, P. B. 64
Harding, C. L. 174
Har-El, M. 115, 235
Harris, M. 25, 27
Harrod, J. B. 16
Henderson, R. N. 65
Herskovits, M. J. 59
Hesiod 15, 227
Heskel, D. & C. C. Lamberg-Karlovski 98, 104, 156, 157
Hocart, A. M. 28
Hodder, I. 195, 196, 206, 261, 262
Hollis, A. C. 72, 73
Homer 150

Hooke, S. H. 23, 28, 233
Hopkins, D. C. 19, 210
Huntingford, G. W. B. 72, 73, 77

Ibrahim, M. 162, 185, 193
Idowu, E. B. 60, 61

Jacobsen, T. 228, 230-33
Jaggar, P. J. 65
James, F. 167, 214
Jeffreys, M. D. W. 87

Karageorghis, V. 208
Kelso, J. L. 166
Kempinski, A. 181
Kense, F. J. 87
Kesby, J. D. 70-72, 74, 77
Knierim, R. 23, 27
Knight, D. A. & G. M. Tucker 23
Košak, S. 129
Kramer, S. N. 229, 230

Laessoe, J. 232
Lang, B. 23
Lapp, N. L. 160
Lapp, P. 160, 179
Laughlin, C. D. & C. D. Stephens 85
Lawson, E. T. 60-62
Leach, E. 24, 36, 56, 85, 88-91, 240, 243, 251, 253-55, 257, 258
Leslau, W. 80, 81
Levenson, J. D. 219
Lévi-Strauss, C. 88
Lewis, H. S. 76-78
Lewis, I. M. 77
Liebowitz, H. 207
Lloyd, P. C. 62
Lods, A. 27
Loud, G. 176
Lucas, J. O. 41, 60

MacAlister, R. A. S. 123, 169, 170
MacKenzie, D. 168
Maddin, R. & T. Stech-Wheeler 111
Maddin, R. et al. 107, 112, 148, 150, 154

Maisler [Mazar], B. 180
Margarido, A. & F.G .
    Wasserman 40, 49, 53, 71-74, 84
Margetts, E. L. 62
Marx, K. 26, 30
Marx, L. 18
Maxwell-Hyslop, K. R. *et al.* 160
Maxwell-Hyslop, R. 130-32
Mayr, O. 17, 18
Mazar, A. 161, 171, 178, 188, 189, 193, 194
Mazar, B. 176, 243
McCarter, P. K. Jr. 222, 223
McClellan, T. L. 183
McCown, C. C. 185
McGovern, P. E. 165
McNaughton, P. R. 53-58
McNutt, P. M. 160
Meek, C. K. 65
Meek, T. J. 242
Mendenhall, G. E. 30, 144, 193, 197
Mercier, P. 58, 59
Merwe, N. J. van der 43, 44, 148
Merwe, N. J. van der & D. H.
    Avery 87
Miller, J. M. 144
Morgenstern, J. 242
Muhly, J. D. 97, 102-106, 115,116, 126, 130, 132, 134, 139, 146, 150, 150-54
Muhly, J. D. *et al.* 102, 108, 121, 124, 129, 140, 142, 153
Mumford, L. 13

Nadel, S. F. 65
Nasr, S. H. 82
Neaher, N. C. 65
Needham, J. 108
Newall, V. 44
Niditch, S. 251
Noth, M. 27, 29, 258

Ohata, K. 190
Oren, E. D. 186
Ortner, S. B. 14, 84-86, 94, 250, 263
Ovid 15, 227

Parke-Taylor, G. H. 244

Parr, P. 193, 194
Parrinder, G. 47, 60, 62, 65
Paulme, D. 55, 56
Pedersen, J. 27
Pelton, R. D. 49, 59, 61
Petrie, W. M. F. 183, 186, 187
Pigott, V. C. et al. 155, 160, 165, 185
Pleiner, R. 108
Pleiner, R. & J. K. Bjorkman 147, 222, 225, 228, 245
Pliny 100, 102
Porteous, N. W. 226, 227
Prausnitz, M. 163
Pritchard, J. B. 137, 185, 230-32

Quirin, J. A. 40, 77, 80, 81

Ramsey, G. W. 144
Rappaport, R. A. 33, 260
Rast, W. E. 175, 178-80
Read 113
Reminick, R. A. 81, 82
Rendsburg, G.A. 216
Renfrew, C. 156, 261
Richardson, H. C. 127
Richter, D. 55, 58
Rickard, T. A. 108
Robins, F. W. 44
Rothenberg, B. 191, 192, 207
Rowley, H. H. 242

Sapir, J. D. 85
Sasoon, H. 87
Sawyer, J. F. A. 19, 216, 217, 220, 223, 237
Schapera, I. 240
Seligman, C. G. & B. Z. 66
Sellers, O. R. et al. 169
Shack, W. A. 78-81
Shiloh, Y. 162
Shorter, A. 71, 72
Sinclair, L. A. 171
Singer, K. H. 19
Smith, C. S. 16, 111
Smith, W. R. 23-25, 91
Snaith, N. H. 247

Snodgrass, A. 99, 101, 102, 110, 116, 135, 140, 142, 147, 148, 153-55
Southall, A. 49
Sperber, D. 86
Spores, R. M. 22
Stager, L. E. 154, 194
Starkey, J. L. & G. L. Harding 183
Stech-Wheeler, T. et al. 19, 100, 115, 135, 139, 140, 142, 146, 151, 153, 155, 156, 164, 177-79, 189, 203, 207, 209, 224, 238

Temple, R. 108
Tessman, G. 67
Thompson, R. C. 233
Todd, D. M. 79
Trigger, B. 41, 43, 262
Tuden, A. & L. Plotnicov 55, 70
Tufnell, O. 174
Turner, V. 22, 28, 33, 35, 36, 83, 86, 88-90, 93, 94, 250, 251, 255, 256, 267
Tylecote, R. F. 87, 107, 148

Ussishkin, D. 173, 174

Vansina, J. 22, 242, 250
Vaughan, J. A. Jr. 55, 58, 84
Vaux, R. de 27, 183, 219
Verdon, M. 58

Wainwright, G. A. 118, 128
Waldbaum, J. C. 19, 99-102, 110, 116, 118, 120-24, 127, 129, 132-35, 140-42, 145-48, 151, 152, 160, 163, 179, 181, 183, 184, 186, 198, 199, 201-203, 207, 235, 238
Weber, M. 26, 218, 238, 244, 247-49
Weippert, M. 144
Wertime, T. A. 99, 102-106, 108, 111, 114, 118, 130, 153, 156
Wertime, T. A. & J. D. Muhly 19
Wheeler, T. S. & R. Maddin 97, 148, 150
Wilson, R. R. 24
Wise, R. 87
Wright, G. E. 139, 153, 162

Yadin, Y. 172, 176

Zahan, D. 54, 55, 92
Zuesse, E. M. 47, 49, 50, 60

INDEX OF SUBJECTS

Abydos
  iron artifacts from 120, 126
Achzib
  iron artifacts from 163, 202
Actions and notions
  cultural domains of 32, 33, 35, 36, 39, 75, 213-15, 261-65
African iron gods
  Gu 59-60
  Ogun 60-62
African peoples, East and African Horn 70-82
  Amhara 79-82
  Beta Israel (Falasha) 79-82
  Chaga 74
  Dime 79
  Galla 77-78
  Gurage 78-79
  Kalenjin 74-76
  Masai 71-73, 74
  Nandi 73, 74
  Somali 76-77
  Tigre 79-82
African peoples, West 47-69
  Bambara 53-58, 59, 241
  Dogon 47, 49-53, 54, 59, 93, 241
  Ewe (Fon) 58-60
  Fang 66-69, 94
  Ibo (Igbo) 65-66, 93
  LoDagaa 62-63
  Mande 53, 55, 56
  Mossi 63-64
  Tiv 64-65
  Yatenga (Mossi) 63-64
  Yoruba 58, 60-62
'Ai (et-Tell)
  iron artifacts from 163-64, 201
Ajlun hills
  as source of iron ore 115

Alaca Hüyük
  iron artifacts from 119, 121, 125
Alalakh
  iron artifacts from 124
Alalakh texts
  references to iron in 129, 134
Alexandria, Syria
  source of iron near 115
Alishar Hüyük
  iron artifacts from 122, 123
Alloys 103, 105
  in casting copper 105
Amarna letters
  references to iron in 135
Amūtu
  Akkadian term for iron 130-32
AN.BAR GE nepišiš
  Hittite term for iron 132, 135
Anatolia
  and the origins of iron technology 139-42, 144, 147, 152-53
  iron artifacts from 119, 121, 122, 123, 125, 128
Ancient Near Eastern artisan gods
  Enki (Ea) 228-33, 264
  Kothar wa-Hasis 233-34
Anitta texts
  references to iron in 129
Annealing 103
Anthropoid clay coffins
  as indicators of ethnicity 161
Anthropology 22-24, 35
Archaeological information
  problems in interpreting 99-101, 144, 261-62
Armant
  iron artifacts from 118

Armenia
  as a source of iron ore 114
Artifacts
  as cultural symbols 195-96, 205-209, 262
Artifactual information
  for the development or iron technology 116-29, 163-92
Artisans (see also: Smiths)
  as castes 55-56
  as manipulators of supernatural power 54-57, 82
  as marginal mediators 89-90
  social separation of 53, 54-55, 77-78, 79-82, 247-48
Artisans in the Hebrew Bible
  Bezalel 237-38, 249
  Hiram of Tyre 106, 238
  Huramabi 218, 238
  skill and wisdom of 218, 236-38
  social status of 247-49
Ashdod
  iron artifacts from 164, 202
Aši'u
  Akkadian term for iron 130-32
Atrahasis 231
Azor
  iron artifacts from 164-65, 199
Baq'ah Valley
  iron artifacts from 165, 199
Barzel
  Hebrew term for iron 20, 216, 237
Beth Shean
  iron artifacts from 166-67, 199, 202
Beth Shemesh
  iron artifacts from 168, 201, 202
Beth Zur
  iron artifacts from 168-69, 201
Bethel
  iron artifacts from 165-66, 202
Bia' n pet
  Egyptian term for iron 132, 135, 136
Bloom, iron 112-14, 130, 131
Bogazköy
  iron artifacts from 125
  textual references to iron from 133-34, 138, 139-40
Bronze technology
  development of 102-107
Buhen
  iron artifacts from 122
Cain
  as a culture hero 240, 266
  as a marginal mediator 240-41, 257, 266
  as an ambivalent figure 213-14, 240, 248, 257
  mark of 214, 240-41
Canaanites
  as symbols of the dangers of civilization and technology 214
Carburization 113-14, 138, 144, 146, 148-51, 155, 203, 207, 210, 264
Carchemish
  sources of iron ore near 115
Cast iron 112
Castes
  artisans as 55-56
Caucasia
  as a source of iron ore 114
Celestial omens
  references to meteorites in 136-37
Chagar Bazar
  iron artifacts from 119
Chariots
  as symbols of superior technology 214, 265
Chariots of iron 215, 224, 265, 266, 267
Chieftaincy
  in early Israel 31-32, 34, 209-11
Civilization
  ambivalent attitudes toward, in Israel 213-14, 219
Collared-rim jar
  as an indicator of ethnicity 161-62, 193, 194
Comparative sociology 24
Copper technology

Index of Subjects 301

development of 104-105
Creation myths
  ironworking symbols in 67-69, 94
  role of divine smiths in 47, 49-54, 59-60, 88, 229-31
Cultural dominance
  problems of identifying from material culture 192-98, 206
David
  as a chief 31, 34
Defining technologies 14
  iron technology as 38, 40, 260, 263
Deir 'Alla
  association of metalworking with cultic material 208, 209
Deir el-Bahari
  iron artifacts from 120
Diffusionist theory 28, 41, 43, 104, 109, 138-42, 144, 156-58
Dorak
  iron artifacts from 120, 121
Early Bronze Age
  and the development of iron technology 118-22, 123
Egypt
  and the development of iron technology 148
  iron artifacts from 118, 120, 121, 122, 123, 126, 127-28
Egypt as an 'iron furnace' 249-60, 265-67
Egyptian Book of the Dead
  references to iron in 136
El-Gerzeh
  iron artifacts from 118
Elburz mountains
  sources of iron ore near 115
Enki (Ea) 228-33
  as culture hero 229-31
  as mediator 230-33, 234, 264
Enkidu
  mediating role of 137
Enuma Anu Enlil
  references to meteorites in 136
Ethnicity

  problems of identifying from material culture 192-98, 261
Ethnoarchaeology 22, 29, 195
Ethnographies
  as heuristic aids for interpreting ancient information 36, 39-42, 261-63
Ethnohistory 21-22
Evil-eye
  smiths as bearers of 78, 81-82
Exodus from Egypt 254-60, 266
Fluxes
  in bronze-smelting 107, 111
  in iron-smelting 114
Forge imagery
  in Fang Bwiti rituals 68-69, 94
  in the Hebrew Bible (see: Egypt as an 'iron furnace')
Furnace
  as a symbol of mediation and transformation 68-69
  as a symbol of oppression 249-50, 265-66
  as a symbol of purification and transformation 239, 250-60, 265-66
  as a symbolic womb 255
Furnaces
  for smelting and casting bronze 107
Galilee
  as a source of iron ore 115
Germanicia
  sources of iron ore near 115
Gezer
  iron artifacts from 169-71, 200, 202
Gibeah (Tell el-Fûl)
  iron artifacts from 171, 201
Gilgamesh Epic
  references to meteorites in 137
Giza
  iron artifacts from 120
God as Divine Smith 238-39, 253, 256, 260, 265, 266
Goliath 223, 267
Greece

and the origins of iron
    technology 144, 146-47, 153
Har Adir
    iron artifacts from 171-72, 199
Ḥārāš
    Hebrew term for smith 235
Hathor Temple (Timna')
    association with
        metalworking 191-92, 208
Hazor
    iron artifacts from 172, 202
Hematite 107, 108, 111, 112
Hittite inventory texts
    references to iron in 134
Hittite 'monopoly' on
    ironworking 127, 128, 132,
        134, 139-42
Hittite ritual texts
    references to iron in 134
Holography
    as an interpretive model 32-33
Homer's *Odyssey*
    reference to quenching in 150
Invention (see also: Technological
        innovations)
    vs innovation and adoption 156-
        58, 210-11, 261-62
Iran
    iron artifacts from 118
Iron
    ambivalent attitudes
        toward 46, 216-27, 262
    as a mediating symbol 64, 65-
        66, 92, 93, 263, 264
    as a precious material 110, 121,
        131-33, 138, 216, 217, 264
    as a symbol of Divine
        power 222, 265
    as a symbol of military and
        technological
        superiority 223-25,
        265
    as a symbol of oppression 225-
        27, 265
    as a symbol of power and
        prestige 64-65, 206-209
    as a symbol of royal power 220-
        22, 265
    as a symbol of strength, power,
        and durability 219-24, 225,
        253, 265
    medicinal power of 74
    oaths sworn on 62, 64
    ornamental or ceremonial use
        of 108, 109, 118, 121, 123,
        134, 147
    practical utility of 20, 116, 128,
        146, 202, 210, 211
    protective power of 64, 74
    symbolism of 46, 50, 206-209,
        211, 216-28, 261-267
    taboos against use of, in the
        Hebrew Bible 217-19, 265
Iron Age I
    as a transitional period 143-48,
        209-11, 252-53
Iron gods
    as mediators 61, 89
    as mediators of justice 62
Iron ore
    sources of 114-16
Iron oxide
    as a flux in bronze- and copper-
        smelting 107, 111
Iron smelting
    early processes of 112-14
    origins of 109-12, 122, 129
Iron technology
    adoption of, in Palestine 151-58,
        209-11, 261-67
    ambivalent attitudes toward, in
        ancient Israel 216-27, 262,
        263, 265
    and the rise of the Israelite
        state 209-11, 253, 266-67
    as a defining technology 38, 40,
        260, 263
    development of 19, 20-21, 97-142
    development of, in Africa 43
    developments in Iron Age I
        143-211
    in traditional African
        societies 39-95
    origins of 108-12, 138-42

Index of Subjects   303

symbolic significance of 19-20,
  38, 82-95, 138, 206-209, 213-60,
  261-67
Ironsmiths (see: Smiths)
Ironworking
  as a symbol of mediation and
    transformation 68-69, 82-95,
    263, 265-66
  biblical symbols 213-60
  rituals associated with 45-46,
    47, 87
'Israelite' four-room house
  as an indicator of ethnicity 162,
    194, 197
Jethro 244
  as mediator 245, 258-59
  as ritual specialist 245, 258-59
Joseph
  as marginal mediator 258
Jubal 240
Kenites
  as mediators 264, 266
  as ritual specialists 243
  as smiths 239-40, 242-43, 244
  marginal social status of 245,
    257, 266
  possible association with
    metalworking at Timna' 192
Khafajah
  iron artifacts from 119
Khirbet Raddana
  iron artifacts from 173, 201
Kish
  iron artifacts from 119
Kition, Cyprus
  association of metalworking
    with cultic material 208-209
Kothar wa-Hasis 233-34
  as mediator 234
Kültepe
  textual references to iron
    from 129, 130-32
Kurdistan
  sources of iron ore near 115
Kusura
  iron artifacts from 122
Lachish
  iron artifacts from 173-74, 202

Late Bronze Age
  and the development of iron
    technology 123-29
  social disruptions 143, 145-46,
    151-52, 154
  textual references to iron 133-
    36
Late Bronze Age-Iron Age
  transition 145-48, 252-53, 267
Liminality 66, 68, 253, 254, 259,
  265
  and marginal social groups 90
  in rites of passage 83, 252
Literary information
  problems in interpreting 101
Lōṭēš
  Hebrew term for smith 236
Madeba
  iron artifacts from 174, 199
Magnetite 108, 112
Makhtesh
  as source of iron ore 115
Mari
  iron artifacts from 119
Mari texts
  references to iron in 129, 133
Masgēr
  Hebrew term for smith 235
Megiddo
  iron artifacts from 125, 174-77,
    199, 201, 202
Mesopotamia
  and the development of iron
    technology 147-48
  iron artifacts from 118, 119,
    121, 123, 124
Metal technology
  and the evolution of
    civilization 97-99
  development of, diffusion vs
    local origins 104
Metallurgy
  and symbols 205-209
  development of 102-104
Meteoric iron
  and the origins of iron
    technology 108-109, 122, 128-
    29

textual references to 135-38
Meteorites
    as mediation symbols 138, 264
Middle Bronze Age
    and the development of iron
        technology 122-23
    textual references to iron 129-33
Midian
    marginality of 257, 258
Midianites
    as mediators 256-60, 264, 266
    as smiths 240, 244, 256
    marginality of 257, 266
    possible association with
        metalworking at
        Timna' 191-92, 208
    restrictions on intermarriage
        with 246-47
Minet el-Beida
    iron artifacts from 124
Monarchy
    transition to, in ancient
        Israel 31-32, 34, 209-11, 267
Moses
    as mediator 247, 256, 258
    relationship to Midianites 244-46, 247
Myth and Ritual School 28-29
Nabataean pottery
    as an indicator of ethnicity 193-94
Nahal-Mishmar
    hoard of copper objects
        from 104-105
Namburû texts
    references to meteorites in 136
Nehushtan 192
Nineveh
    sources of iron ore near 115
Nubia
    iron artifacts from 122, 123
Nuzi
    iron artifacts from 124
Nuzi texts
    references to iron in 134
Og's iron bed 223, 267
Palestine

iron artifacts from 123, 125, 128, 163-92
    sources of iron ore in 115
Peasant revolt hypothesis 30-31
Pentateuch
    narrative structure of 246, 253-60, 264, 266-67
Persepolis
    sources of iron ore near 115
Philistine 'monopoly' on
    ironworking 153, 158, 197-198, 200, 238
Philistine pottery
    as an indicator of ethnicity 160-61, 196
Philistines
    and the introduction of iron
        technology 19, 142, 144, 153
    as mediators 34
Qatna
    textual references to iron
        from 134
Quenching 149-51
Ras Shamra (see: Ugarit)
Rechabites 214
    as smiths 240, 242, 243-44
    marginal social status of 243-44, 266
Religion
    and culture 25
Rites of passage, processual
    structure of 82-83
    as a model for interpreting
        texts 251-60
    as analogy for ironworking
        process 82-84, 86-87, 251-52
Ritual (see also: Rites of
    passage) 25, 28-29, 34
Samara
    iron artifacts from 118
Saul
    as a chief 31
'Settlement' of Israelite tribes 29-31, 143-44
Smiths (see also: Artisans)
    ambivalent attitudes
        toward 45, 46, 55-56, 74, 89,

Index of Subjects

91-92, 219, 237-38, 248, 262, 263, 266
as a 'despised' social group 71-72, 76, 90-92
as bearers of the evil-eye 78, 81-82
as counselors and advisors 45, 58, 74, 75, 245
as culture heroes 44-45, 47, 49-53, 54, 58-60, 65, 88, 256
as diviners 57, 65, 74
as healers 45, 53, 57, 62, 65
as manipulators of supernatural power 54-57, 58, 74, 78, 82, 241
as mediators 45, 53, 87-90, 256, 266
as mediators of justice 58, 65, 89, 90, 256
as ritual specialists 45, 47, 51, 52-53, 57-58, 62-64, 65, 78-79, 87-90, 243, 256
as sculptors 57
as social caste 70
as sorcerers and magicians 46, 62, 78
as targets of taboos 91-92
association with Earth shrines 62-64
avoidance of 72, 81, 91-92
circumcision performed by 51, 52-53, 57, 78, 90, 245-46
danger of 72
excision performed by 51, 57, 90
exclusion from agricultural work 53
exclusion from social activities 75, 77
exempt from threats in warfare 75
guild organization of 45, 46, 47, 62, 65
impurity of 51, 72, 73, 78, 79, 91-92, 219, 241, 246-47
in ancient Israel 235-49, 266
power of curse 73, 74, 75

restrictions on intermarriage with 52, 73, 74, 76, 77, 78, 81, 246-47
restrictions on land ownership 78, 79, 80
restrictions on ownership of cattle 73, 75, 79
restrictions on participation in warfare 73, 74
restrictions on social activities 79
skill and wisdom of, in the Hebrew Bible 236-38
social marginality of (see also: Smiths, social separation of; Smiths, social status of) 45, 46-47, 70, 75-76, 89-92, 243-44, 245, 256, 257, 266
social separation of 45, 46-47, 51-53, 54-58, 63, 70, 72-73, 76-77, 78, 79-82, 256
social status of 44-45, 46-47, 51-53, 54-58, 65, 70, 73, 74, 84, 89-92
agricultural vs pastoral societies 45, 46, 70-71, 74, 92
in ancient Israel 236-37, 239, 243-44, 247-49, 256-57, 266
Smithy
as a ritual center 46, 62-63, 92-93, 191, 206-209
as a social gathering place 46, 54, 62, 64, 74, 92-93
symbolism of 51, 92-93
Social scientific interpretations of the Hebrew Bible 23-36
Steel
production of (see also: Carburization) 148-52
Susa texts
references to iron in 129, 133
Symbolic anthropology 22-23, 35
Symbols
and technology 14-19, 35, 263
condensation 86
dominant 86
elaborating 84-87, 250-251, 263
key 14, 69, 84-86, 94, 260

referential 86
root metaphors 14, 85-86, 94,
    250-51, 259, 263
summarizing 84
Syria
    iron artifacts from 123, 124,
        126-27, 128, 147
Ta'anach
    association of metalworking
        with cultic material 178-79,
        209
    iron artifacts from 177-79, 201,
        202
Tarsus
    iron artifacts from 120
Taurus mountains
    sources of iron ore near 115
Technological innovations
    acceptance of 98, 156-58, 261-62
    in the development of metal
        technology 104, 156-58
Technology
    ambivalent attitudes toward, in
        Israel 213-14
    and culture 13-19, 213-15, 261-63
    and culture change
        in Africa 40-41
        the Fang Bwiti cult 66-69
    and symbols 14-19, 35, 213-15,
        261-67
Tel Miqne
    association of metalworking
        with cultic material 209
Tell Abu Huwam
    iron artifacts from 179-80, 202
Tell 'Aitun
    iron artifacts from 180-81, 199
Tell Amal
    iron artifacts from 181, 202
Tell Asmar (see: Ur)
Tell Beit Mirsim
    iron artifacts from 181-82, 202
Tell el-'Ajjul
    iron artifacts from 181, 202
Tell el-Amarna
    iron artifacts from 126
Tell el-Far'ah North
    iron artifacts from 182-83, 202
Tell el-Far'ah South
    iron artifacts from 183-84, 199,
        201
Tell en-Nasbeh
    iron artifacts from 184-85, 202
Tell es-Sa'idiyeh
    iron artifacts from 185, 199
Tell esh-Shari'a
    iron artifacts from 185, 201
Tell es-Zuweyid
    iron artifacts from 125, 186,
        199, 201, 202
Tell Jemmeh
    iron artifacts from 186-87, 201,
        202
Tell Qasile
    iron artifacts from 187-89, 199,
        201, 202
Tell Qiri (Ha-Zore'a)
    iron artifacts from 189, 199
Tell Zeror
    iron artifacts from 189-90, 201
Telluric iron
    and the origins of iron
        technology 108-109
Temperatures
    importance of in
        ironworking 112-13, 149
Tempering 149, 151
Tepe Sialk
    iron artifacts from 118
Textual information
    for the development of iron
        technology 129-38
Thebes
    iron artifacts from 126
Timna'
    association of metalworking
        with cultic material 191-92,
        208, 209
    iron artifacts from 190-92, 199
Timna' Valley
    as a source of copper 190
Tin
    as an alloy in bronze
        casting 105-106

Index of Subjects 307

as evidence of long-distance
   trade 105-106
problem of sources 105-106
shortage of, as explanation for
   increased use of iron 153-54
Tools, ironworking
   as symbolic mediators of
      justice 93
   as symbols of mediation 92-94,
      263
   protective power of 64, 74, 93
   sexual symbols associated
      with 46, 47, 50-51, 54, 69, 93
Transcaucasia
   as a source of iron ore 114
Troy
   iron artifacts from 119, 121
Tubal-cain 236, 240
Tutankhamen's tomb
   iron objects from 109, 126, 127-28

Ugarit (Ras Shamra)
   iron artifacts from 124, 126-27
Ur (Tell Asmar)
   iron artifacts from 119, 121
Uruk-Warka
   iron artifacts from 119
Wadi es-Sabrah
   as source of iron ore 115
Wadi Arabah
   as a source of copper 190
   as a source of iron ore 115
Wilderness
   as liminality 254-55, 259
Wrought iron
   and the development of iron
      technology 112-14, 122, 123,
      148
Zipporah
   circumcision performed
      by 245-46

JOURNAL FOR THE STUDY OF THE OLD TESTAMENT

Supplement Series

25 THE DAMASCUS COVENANT:
    AN INTERPRETATION OF THE 'DAMASCUS DOCUMENT'
    P.R. Davies
26 CLASSICAL HEBREW POETRY:
    A GUIDE TO ITS TECHNIQUES
    W.G.E. Watson
27 PSALMODY AND PROPHECY
    W.H. Bellinger
28 HOSEA: AN ISRAELITE PROPHET IN JUDEAN PERSPECTIVE
    G.I. Emmerson
29 EXEGESIS AT QUMRAN
    4QFOLRILEGIUM IN ITS JEWISH CONTEXT
    G.J. Brooke
30 THE ESTHER SCROLL: THE STORY OF THE STORY
    D.J.A. Clines
31 IN THE SHELTER OF ELYON:
    ESSAYS IN HONOR OF G.W. AHLSTRÖM
    Edited by W.B. Barrick & J.R. Spencer
32 THE PROPHETIC PERSONA:
    JEREMIAH AND THE LANGUAGE OF THE SELF
    T. Polk
33 LAW AND THEOLOGY IN DEUTERONOMY
    J.G. McConville
34 THE TEMPLE SCROLL:
    AN INTRODUCTION, TRANSLATION AND COMMENTARY
    J. Maier
35 SAGA, LEGEND, TALE, NOVELLA, FABLE:
    NARRATIVE FORMS IN OLD TESTAMENT LITERATURE
    Edited by G.W. Coats
36 THE SONG OF FOURTEEN SONGS
    M.D. Goulder
37 UNDERSTANDING THE WORD:
    ESSAYS IN HONOR OF BERNHARD W. ANDERSON
    Edited by J.T. Butler, E.W. Conrad & B.C. Ollenburger

38 SLEEP, DIVINE AND HUMAN, IN THE OLD TESTAMENT
   T.H. McAlpine
39 THE SENSE OF BIBLICAL NARRATIVE II:
   STRUCTURAL ANALYSES IN THE HEBREW BIBLE
   D. Jobling
40 DIRECTIONS IN BIBLICAL HEBREW POETRY
   Edited by E.R. Follis
41 ZION, THE CITY OF THE GREAT KING:
   A THEOLOGICAL SYMBOL OF THE JERUSALEM CULT
   B.C. Ollenburger
42 A WORD IN SEASON: ESSAYS IN HONOUR OF WILLIAM MCKANE
   Edited by J.D. Martin & P.R. Davies
43 THE CULT OF MOLEK:
   A REASSESSMENT
   G.C. Heider
44 THE IDENTITY OF THE INDIVIDUAL IN THE PSALMS
   S.J.L. Croft
45 THE CONFESSIONS OF JEREMIAH IN CONTEXT:
   SCENES OF PROPHETIC DRAMA
   A.R. Diamond
46 THE BOOK OF JUDGES: AN INTEGRATED READING
   W.G. Webb
47 THE GREEK TEXT OF JEREMIAH:
   A REVISED HYPOTHESIS
   S. Soderlund
48 TEXT AND CONTEXT:
   OLD TESTAMENT AND SEMEITIC STUDIES FOR F.C. FENSHAM
   Edited by W. Claassen
49 THEOPHORIC PERSONAL NAMES IN ANCIENT HEBREW
   J.D. Fowler
50 THE CHRONICLER'S HISTORY
   M. Noth
51 DIVINE INITIATIVE AND HUMAN RESPONSE IN EZEKIEL
   P. Joyce
52 THE CONFLICT OF FAITH AND EXPERIENCE IN THE PSALMS:
   A FORM-CRITICAL AND THEOLOGICAL STUDY
   C.C. Broyles
53 THE MAKING OF THE PENTATEUCH:
   A METHODOLOGICAL STUDY
   R.N. Whybray
54 FROM REPENTANCE TO REDEMPTION:
   JEREMIAH'S THOUGHT IN TRANSITION
   J. Unterman

55 THE ORIGIN TRADITION OF ANCIENT ISRAEL:
   THE LITERARY FORMATION OF GENESIS AND EXODUS 1–23
   T.L. Thompson
56 THE PURIFICATION OFFERING IN THE PRIESTLY LITERATURE:
   ITS MEANING AND FUNCTION
   N. Kiuchi
57 MOSES: HEROIC MAN, MAN OF GOD
   G.W. Coats
58 THE LISTENING HEART: ESSAYS IN WISDOM AND THE PSALMS
   IN HONOR OF ROLAND E. MURPHY, O. CARM.
   Edited by K.G. Hoglund
59 CREATIVE BIBLICAL EXEGESIS:
   CHRISTIAN AND JEWISH HERMENEUTICS THROUGH THE CENTURIES
   B. Uffenheimer & H.G. Reventlow
60 HER PRICE IS BEYOND RUBIES:
   THE JEWISH WOMAN IN GRAECO-ROMAN PALESTINE
   L.J. Archer
61 FROM CHAOS TO RESTORATION:
   AN INTEGRATIVE READING OF ISAIAH 24–27
   D.G. Johnson
62 THE OLD TESTAMENT AND FOLKLORE STUDY
   P.G. Kirkpatrick
63 SHILOH: A BIBLICAL CITY IN TRADITION AND HISTORY
   D.G. Schley
64 TO SEE AND NOT PERCEIVE:
   ISAIAH 6.9–10 IN EARLY JEWISH AND CHRISTIAN INTERPRETATION
   C.A. Evans
65 THERE IS HOPE FOR A TREE:
   THE TREE AS METAPHOR IN ISAIAH
   K. Nielsen
66 SECRETS OF THE TIMES:
   MYTH AND HISTORY IN BIBLICAL CHRONOLOGY
   J. Hughes
67 ASCRIBE TO THE LORD:
   BIBLICAL AND OTHER ESSAYS IN MEMORY OF PETER C. CRAIGIE
   Edited by L. Eslinger & G. Taylor
68 THE TRIUMPH OF IRONY IN THE BOOK OF JUDGES
   L.R. Klein
69 ZEPHANIAH, A PROPHETIC DRAMA
   P.R. HOUSE
70 NARRATIVE ART IN THE BIBLE
   S. Bar-Efrat
71 QOHELET AND HIS CONTRADICTIONS
   M.V. Fox

72 CIRCLE OF SOVEREIGNTY:
    A STORY OF STORIES IN DANIEL 1–6
    D.N. Fewell
73 DAVID'S SOCIAL DRAMA:
    A HOLOGRAM OF THE EARLY IRON AGE
    J.W. Flanagan
74 THE STRUCTURAL ANALYSIS OF BIBLICAL AND CANAANITE POETRY
    Edited by W. v.d. Meer & J.C. de Moor
75 DAVID IN LOVE AND WAR:
    THE PURSUIT OF POWER IN 2 SAMUEL 10–12
    R.C. Bailey
76 GOD IS KING:
    UNDERSTANDING AN ISRAELITE METAPHOR
    M. Brettler
77 EDOM AND THE EDOMITES
    J.R. Bartlett
78 SWALLOWING THE SCROLL:
    TEXTUALITY AND THE DYNAMICS OF DISCOURSE IN EZEKIEL'S PROPHECY
    E.F. Davies
79 GIBEAH:
    THE SEARCH FOR A BIBLICAL CITY
    P.M. Arnold
80 THE NATHAN NARRATIVES
    G.H. Jones
81 ANTI-COVENANT:
    COUNTER-READING WOMEN'S LIVES IN THE HEBREW BIBLE
    M. Bal
82 RHETORIC AND BIBLICAL INTERPRETATION
    D. Patrick & A. Scult
83 THE EARTH AND THE WATERS IN GENESIS 1 AND 2
    D.T. Tsumura
84 INTO THE HANDS OF THE LIVING GOD
    L. Eslinger
85 FROM CARMEL TO HOREB:
    ELIJAH IN CRISIS
    A.J. Hauser & R. Gregory
86 THE SYNTAX OF THE VERB IN CLASSICAL HEBREW PROSE
    A. Niccacci
87 THE BIBLE IN THREE DIMENSIONS
    Edited by D.J.A. Clines, S.E. Fowl & S.E. Porter
88 THE PERSUASIVE APPEAL OF THE CHRONICLER:
    A RHETORICAL ANALYSIS
    R.K. Duke

89 THE PROBLEM OF THE PROCESS OF TRANSMISSION
IN THE PENTATEUCH
R. Rendtorff
90 BIBLICAL HEBREW IN TRANSITION:
THE LANGUAGE OF THE BOOK OF EZEKIEL
M.F. Rooker
91 THE IDEOLOGY OF RITUAL:
SPACE, TIME, AND STATUS IN THE PRIESTLY THEOLOGY
F.H. Gorman
92 ON HUMOUR AND THE COMIC IN THE HEBREW BIBLE
Edited by Y.T. Radday & A. Brenner
93 JOSHUA 24 AS POETIC NARRATIVE
W.T. Koopmans
94 WHAT DOES EVE DO TO HELP? AND OTHER READERLY QUESTIONS
TO THE OLD TESTAMENT
D.J.A. Clines
95 GOD SAVES: LESSONS FROM THE ELISHA STORIES
R.D. Moore
96 ANNOUNCEMENTS OF PLOT IN GENESIS
L.A. Turner
97 THE UNITY OF THE TWELVE
P.R. House
98 ANCIENT CONQUEST ACCOUNTS: A STUDY IN ANCIENT NEAR
EASTERN AND BIBLICAL HISTORY WRITING
K. Lawson Younger, Jr
99 WEALTH AND POVERTY IN THE BOOK OF PROVERBS
R.N. Whybray
100 A TRIBUTE TO GEZA VERMES: ESSAYS ON JEWISH AND CHRISTIAN
LITERATURE AND HISTORY
Edited by P.R. Davies & R.T. White
101 THE CHRONICLER IN HIS AGE
P.R. Ackroyd
102 THE PRAYERS OF DAVID (Psalms 51–72)
M.D. Goulder
103 THE SOCIOLOGY OF POTTERY IN ANCIENT PALESTINE:
THE CERAMIC INDUSTRY AND THE DIFFUSION OF CERAMIC STYLE
IN THE BRONZE AND IRON AGES
Bryant G. Wood
104 PSALM-STRUCTURES:
A STUDY OF PSALMS WITH REFRAINS
Paul R. Raabe
105 TEMPLUM AMICITIAE:
ESSAYS ON THE SECOND TEMPLE PRESENTED TO ERNST BAMMEL
Edited by W. Horbury